A
CONSPIRACY
OF
INDIFFERENCE

5171-GERS

A

CONSPIRACY

OF

INDIFFERENCE

The Raoul Wallenberg Story

Alan Gersten

To order additional copies of this book, contact:
Xlibris Corporation
1-888-7-XLIBRIS
www.Xlibris.com
Orders@Xlibris.com

CONTENTS

To Marjorie

While about 1,000 dignitaries flowed into the Rotunda of the U.S. Capitol on November 2, 1995, English, Swedish, Hungarian and Hebrew flowed around the great hall. The stirring music of the U.S. Army Band reverberated throughout the Rotunda, the center of Western democracy. Periodically, the morning sun broke free of its cloud cover and shined through the windows just below the dome, 180 feet above the floor.

Like arrows, everyone's eyes shot to the cloth-draped structure at the right of the podium and in front of a white statue of Lincoln that, in turn, was framed by two giant paintings of George Washington in war and peace. Just behind the bust were two flags, one showing a man's picture superimposed over the Swedish flag and another simply bore the initials "MIA/POW." Beneath the yellow cloth stood a bust that had drawn everybody—including Congressional leaders, a Supreme Court Justice and Parliamentary speakers from four countries—to Washington for that day's ceremony. Each guest knew this bust depicted a hero of the Holocaust, a Swedish diplomat named Raoul Wallenberg.

They had come to praise this unique man, who became first a hero, then a prisoner. Though these statesmen remained separated by geography and lineage, all became united in their commendations of Wallenberg. Even American Democrats and Republicans, who lash each other daily, unified under Wallenberg's spell.

A remarkable man, Wallenberg saved 100,000 Hungarian Jews while serving as a Swedish diplomat during World War II. At the moment of Wallenberg's greatest triumph, however, the Russians arrested him—50 years before the Rotunda ceremony—at Debrecen, Hungary, and swept him into the Gulag Archipelago, the desolate and endless Russian prison system. Many ex-prisoners said they saw Wallenberg or met people who said they saw Wallenberg in the 1950s, '60s, '70s, '80s, telling tales that included how he took ersatz saunas in Russian snowbanks, but no one in the free world has seen Wallenberg in more than half a century.

Tom Lantos, a California congressman and the driving force behind placing the bust in the Capitol, told the audience at the ceremony he and his wife, Annette, had succeeded in their first goal for Wallenberg, and then his voice dropped to a mournful pitch, "but we collectively failed in the other."

Tom and Annette Lantos, both Hungarian refugees whom Wallenberg helped save, had made Wallenberg internationally known, but they failed to free him. Today, most experts think Wallenberg is dead, but a flicker of hope remains. Nina Lagergren, Wallenberg's half-sister, who attended the unveiling, has spent much of the last 56 years trying to free Wallenberg, who, if alive, would have been 83 at the time of the Rotunda ceremony. Mrs. Lagergren, along with her brother, Guy von Dardel, Wallenberg's half-brother, who didn't come to Washington, refuse to stop searching for Wallenberg until the Russians release him or provide definitive proof that he is, in fact, dead. Others, like Annette Lantos, feel Wallenberg died years ago, and it is more important to build statues or busts to his memory.

Whether Wallenberg is alive or dead, many questions still remain about his mission and motivation. In 1994, the Central Intelligence Agency released 1,500 documents about Wallenberg, which detail for the first time Wallenberg's exact involvement with the U.S. government, explanations for his initial incarceration, various attempts to free him and why three governments abandoned him. On January 12, 2001, a joint Russian Swedish commission that had worked for more than nine years to try to solve the mystery of Raoul Wallenberg issued two reports—206 pages from the Swedes and 37 pages from the Russians. The Swedish report was inconclusive, discussing and discarding many theories. The

Russians were blunter—saying Wallenberg died or was killed in 1947, probably executed. All cliches are true. In this instance, that's the Russian's story and they're sticking to it.

This abundance of material has put light into some dark corners. Until now, a compelling question had remained unanswered: Did Wallenberg spy for the United States? Wallenberg did work for an American spy, Iver C. Olsen, but Wallenberg was not a spy himself, merely a man interested in saving humanity.

Tragically, however, the Russians arrested Wallenberg, convinced he was a spy because of his links to Olsen, who they knew worked for the Office of Strategic Services, predecessor of the Central Intelligence Agency. During Wallenberg's mission in Budapest, Olsen gave him free access to 260,000 Swedish kronor, including 10,000 from President Franklin D. Roosevelt's "secret fund," money Wallenberg used to bribe German and Hungarian fascists in a successful attempt to save Hungarian Jews while he unintentionally created a special status for himself.

Raoul Wallenberg is a hero, living in that orbit occupied by the unusual. A restive scion of a famous Swedish family, Wallenberg at 31 was looking for some achievement to justify his illustrious lineage. That task became saving the remnants of European Jewry. By July 1944, a focal point in history, the Nazis had already exterminated millions of Jews, and now the Americans recruited and sent this Swedish Gentile into Nazi-occupied Budapest.

When he arrived, Wallenberg confronted his main adversary, Adolf Eichmann. Each had a plan for the Hungarian Jews. One advocated genocide, the other humanitarianism.

Armed only with his wits, Wallenberg outmaneuvered and outsmarted Eichmann, who worked to complete Adolf Hitler's "Final Solution" for European Jewry by killing them in the gas chambers. In fact, Eichmann managed to murder several thousand more Hungarian Jews, but he lost the climatic battle to Wallenberg.

Wallenberg, from July through December 1944, created thousands of Swedish passports for Hungarian Jews, preventing the

Nazis from deporting them to death. He took incredible personal risks, constantly showing his heroism during his six months in Budapest.

Once, Wallenberg literally ran across the top of a sealed Nazi freight train yelling, "Are there any Swedish-protected Jews in there who've lost their passes?" Condemned Jews shoved their hands through the air vents, and Wallenberg thrust blank Swedish passes into each hand, saving hundreds of lives.

Fearless, Wallenberg moved all over Budapest, using brains and chutzpah in his relentless quest to save Jews. Aided by an unyielding Russian advance from the east, Wallenberg stopped a final mass execution of 70,000 Jews, which the Nazis planned as they evacuated Budapest in January 1945.

Wallenberg achieved the unachievable and personally saved more than 100,000 Jews. But his liberators became his captors. The Soviets kidnapped Wallenberg and incarcerated him in the Soviet gulag, where he still may exist after more than 50 years. In late 2000, the Russians publicly acknowledged they arrested Wallenberg, adding that he died in a Soviet prison two years later. But the Russians can't or won't supply specific details about the circumstances of Wallenberg's death, so the questions remain unanswered.

Wallenberg defeated the Germans, but lost to the Russians. He bested the Nazis, but fell victim to the Communists.

The Russians failed to believe Wallenberg was a secular savior driven by a humanitarian impulse. They thought he was a spy, asking why had a wealthy Swede come to rescue poor Jews?

In the last 50-plus years, many have tried and all have failed to free Wallenberg. His mother, Maj von Dardel, who led a tireless quest—halted only by her death—to free her first born son, sent impassioned letters to Eleanor Roosevelt and later to Henry Kissinger. Guy von Dardel, Maj's other son, wrote President Harry Truman, Secretary of State Dean Acheson and Michigan Senator Arthur Vandenberg, also to try to free Wallenberg. Five times the State Department ignored the appeals.

Others had more physical ideas about freeing Wallenberg. Once, a self-styled soldier of fortune, who had worked in a Finnish boiler room, suggested a commando raid to free Wallenberg from his Latvian prison. All attempts to free Wallenberg, perpetually bungled, included proposed spy swaps and a legal effort that initially won, but ultimately lost an unusual lawsuit against the Soviet Union.

With all rescue efforts turning into failures, many people—like Sonja Sonnenfeld, who runs the Raoul Wallenberg Committee in Sweden—have concluded that the hero of Budapest has perished. During a telephone conversation from her home in Stockholm, Sonnenfeld said her "special sources," whom she declined to identify, had until the early 1990s told her Wallenberg was alive. In May 1994, she said, "I haven't heard from them in three years."

Nevertheless, Sonnenfeld thinks Wallenberg could be alive. "The Russians cannot come up with anything which proves that he is not alive. We have not found one single statement."

Then Sonnenfeld said if Wallenberg is alive, he may be a different person, someone with a new name, a new identity. "He could be anywhere; there are so many hidden places in Russia, camps of silence."

Guy von Dardel also refuses to stop hoping. In his calm, measured Scandinavian voice, von Dardel explains over the telephone from his summer home in Switzerland, "As long as there is no compelling reason to say he's dead, he is still alive."

When asked why he persists in his quest for his half-brother, von Dardel—a retired nuclear research physicist—responds, "Partly curiosity. I would like to know what happened and put it right. The scientist view if you want. Partly, I do not want the Russians to get away with what they have done to him."

Then von Dardel told a caller he would soon leave for another trip to Russia in his continuing effort to determine what happened to his half-brother. When in Russia, von Dardel worked with a soulmate—a University of Chicago professor who became a prisoner in the Soviet gulag during the 1960s, where he was two cells away from one of Wallenberg's cellmates. The professor, Marvin W. Makinen, has become a ceaseless source of energy to try to discover the truth about Wallenberg. Since 1990, Makinen has made 15 trips to Russia and his efforts have unearthed startling information from Wallenberg's cellmates, one of his interrogators, a German who met the imprisoned Wallenberg, five Polish prisoners in a labor camp near the Mongolian border who saw Wallenberg and a Russian cleaning woman who remembers a complaining prisoner, whose photograph she identified. All these people met Wallenberg long after his supposed death. Until 2001, the official Soviet version of Wallenberg's death, disputed by most in the West, had said he died of a heart attack in 1947 while incarcerated in Lubyanka prison.

In 1983, a retired Swedish judge linked to the Wallenbergs heard another version of how Wallenberg died from a mysterious Norwegian arms dealer with ties to the KGB, the Russian intelligence service.

At some point in his imprisonment, Wallenberg was definitely alive, so why didn't Sweden or the United States save him? Both countries, including the CIA, displayed minimal subsurface interest for various reasons, ranging from jealousy to fear.

The Swedish government expended only rhetoric in trying to free their own diplomat, who had risked his life countless times to save Hungarian Jews. Only citizen protests, agitation from the press and Wallenberg committees forced the Swedish government to start "toothless protests" to the Soviets about Wallenberg. Through the 1990s, Wallenberg remained an embarrassment to Sweden because the country of his birth abandoned him for more than 50 years. Though Lantos wanted the King of Sweden, Carl XVI Gustaf, at the Wallenberg bust ceremony, he did not attend, but neither did then President Bill Clinton nor Vice President Albert Gore, all of whom Lantos' staff was assiduously trying to get for the dedication.

Russia imprisoned Wallenberg while the Swedish and American

governments basically ignored him. The latter two countries acknowledged his bravery but avoided his rescue, mostly out of disinterest. Wallenberg's heroism lasted six months, but his betrayal by others, including the Swedish and U.S. governments, still continues.

Through the prism of contemporary interviews along with the recently declassified CIA documents as well as examination of 500 State Department documents at the National Archives in Washington and another 500 at the Franklin D. Roosevelt Library in Hyde Park, New York, as well as the Swedish and Russian reports, one sees new details and insights into a basic conflict:

Raoul Wallenberg's immediate family and friends have waged a relentless 56-year fight to free him, but two Western and one Communist government stymied their efforts and let Raoul Wallenberg remain in the gulag. The hero of Hungarian Jewry fell to a conspiracy of indifference.

CHAPTER 1

Fourteen blocks west of the U.S. Capitol in Washington stands the United States Holocaust Memorial Museum, which opened April 22, 1993. About seven years earlier—December 19, 1985—Congress renamed 15th Street, which forms the museum's western boundary, as Raoul Wallenberg Place. A plaque at the corner of Independence Avenue and Wallenberg Place said Wallenberg's "mission of mercy on behalf of the United States behind enemy lines during World War II is unprecedented in the history of mankind. He is responsible for saving tens of thousands of lives during the Holocaust. A shining light in a dark and depraved world, he proved that one person who has the courage to care can make a difference."

Inside, the museum traces the Nazis' murderous reign, showing through films, displays and actual recordings of survivors' stories the horrifying killing machine the Nazis created. In 1933, more than nine million Jews lived in Continental Europe. By 1945, six million had died.

This bloody trail led back most prominently to one man, Adolf Eichmann. But in 1944, Adolf Eichmann was discontented. He didn't have enough Jews to kill.

Eichmann, an overachiever who had risen through the ranks of the Nazi's SS to reach lieutenant colonel, was in March 1944 overseeing the building of a hostel for Gestapo officers 50 miles from Berlin. His department handled Jewish Affairs and Deportation, which really meant the gathering, deporting and murdering of Jews in Nazi-held Europe as well as those of the Nazis' allies and satellites. With consummate skill, Eichmann had exterminated hundreds of thousands of Jews in Germany, Austria,

Holland, Belgium, France and the other countries Germany had conquered. But now, near his perverted moment of triumph, Eichmann had been refused permission to get at the greatest masses of Jews under the Nazi yoke—Poland and the parts of the Soviet Union the Nazis' controlled. Instead, he had the mundane task of construction about which he knew little.

However, one Jewish enclave, Hungary, remained within Germany and Eichmann's grasp. More than 750,000 Jews still lived there in safety, for the regent, Miklós Horthy, who did not particularly like Jews, still would not let "his" Jews suffer extermination by Hitler, particularly since he felt his Nazi brethren would lose the war.

Suddenly everything changed. Eichmann's superiors ordered him to go to Hungary quickly, for the Germans planned to take over that country from Horthy and make him obey Hitler's plan for the elimination of European Jewry.

An overjoyed Eichmann knew this was a major task to solidify his credentials among the Nazi elite as a first class killer of Jews. Initially, in the 1930s, Eichmann practiced massive deportation of Jews, but after the outbreak of World War II with Hitler's invasion of Poland, he turned his skills to murder, which failed to dilute his zeal.

The Germans estimated there were 11 million Jews in Europe, including those of Britain and neutral Ireland, Sweden, Switzerland, Spain, Turkey and the Soviet Union. All were to be exterminated, with Eichmann playing a crucial role. By conquering Poland, Germany and Eichmann acquired 2.5 million Jews, whom he planned to eliminate. Politics kept Eichmann from exterminating these Polish Jews, but other Nazis handled the job. Still, the Germans overran most of Europe and soon had 3.5 million Jews under their control. By March 1944, Germany had liquidated five million Jews, but Eichmann had "only" eliminated about 750,000, far below the planned estimates. Though this ghastly number was unspeakably high, he had fallen short of his quotas.

Eichmann had no enthusiasm for the actual killing. Instead,

he was a master of organization, administration and logistics. Initially, the Nazis used mass shootings to kill Jews, but even the toughened Nazi troopers couldn't tolerate such massacres. Many drank and some even shot their officers.

Even worse to the Germans, this method of killing was wasteful and public. Eichmann was summoned to create greater efficiencies of death. After some experimentation, Eichmann knew he needed an effective gas. In November 1941, the Germans discovered Zyklon B, or prussic gas, which was quick working and could be stored in a dry, solid form in cans. When exposed to air, the chalky pellets turned to gas, the solution for the Final Solution. Soon, the Germans began producing Zyklon B in mass amounts.

To complete their murderous work, the Nazis in 1940 established Auschwitz, the largest German concentration camp, which was in occupied Poland. More than a million Jews perished at Auschwitz. They died from executions—gassing, shooting or hanging—as well as disease, torture, starvation and hard labor.

Josef Mengele, who earned the name "Angel of Death," greeted each arrival at Auschwitz in polished boots. While whistling Wagner, he would decide who went to a labor camp and who went to the bunkers, made to disrobe and taken to the chamber of death.

Outside the underground gas chambers of the crematorium, it said in seven languages, "baths." The victims were given a small square object that resembled a piece of soap and herded into the gas chambers, where guards bolted shut an airtight metal door. SS men, wearing gas masks, climbed on the roof, opened the traps and dropped the pellets. The victims, told they would receive a shower, instead received pellets that fell to the floor, releasing the deadly gas. The victims lost their ability to absorb oxygen and died from asphyxiation. Most died in a few minutes; in twenty minutes the ventilators eliminated the poisonous air. At Auschwitz, SS guards could view the death process through a small glass peephole.

After the gassing, the women's hair was cut and gold teeth

extracted. Eichmann told Rudolph Hoess, commandant of Auschwitz, that the jewelry and currency taken from the Jewish victims were sold in Switzerland and these sales dominated the Swiss market.

Those who volunteered to help with the operation in the gas chambers, apparently hoping this could save them, were themselves killed after weeks of a wretched life. No one was spared; everyone died.

As Dr. Miklós Nyiszli, a doctor at Auschwitz, later recalled in gripping detail:

The ventilators, patented "Exhator" system, quickly evacuated the gas from the room, but in the crannies between the dead and the cracks of the doors small pockets of it always remained. Even two hours later it caused a suffocating cough. For that reason the Sonderkommando group which first moved into the room was equipped with gas masks. Once again the room was powerfully lighted, revealing a horrible spectacle.

The bodies were not lying here and there throughout the room, but piled in a mass to the ceiling. The reason for this was that the gas first inundated the lower lays of air and rose but slowly towards the ceiling. This forced the victims to trample one another in a frantic effort to escape the gas. Yet a few feet higher up the gas reached them. What a struggle for life there must have been! Nevertheless it was merely a matter of two or three minutes' respite. If they had been able to think about what they were doing, they would have realized they were trampling their own children, their wives, their relatives. But they couldn't think. Their gestures were no more than the reflexes of the instinct of self-preservation. I noticed that the bodies of the women, the children, and the aged were at the bottom of the pile; at the top, the strongest. Their bodies, which were covered with scratches and bruises from the struggle which had set them against each other, were often interlaced. Blood oozed from their noses and mouths; their faces, bloated and blue, were so deformed as to be almost unrecognizable. Nevertheless, some of the Sonderkommando often did recognize their kin. The encounter was not easy, and I dreaded it for myself. I had no reason to be here, and yet I had come down among the dead. I felt it my duty to my people and the entire world to be able to give an accurate account of what I had seen if ever, by some miraculous whim of fate, I should escape.[1]

Eichmann wanted to treat every Jew the same way—with death. He once told a friend, "I will jump into my grave laughing because the fact that I have the deaths of five million Jews on my conscience gives me extraordinary satisfaction." Now, with Hungary, Eichmann had his chance to annihilate another 750,000 Jews. But blocking his path was a blueblood Swede named Raoul Wallenberg.

When Raoul Gustav Wallenberg was born August 4, 1912, his father had died three months before, which was only eight months after his marriage to Maj Wising. Suddenly stricken with cancer, Wallenberg's father suffered before dying. Maj, 21, named her first born after her late husband, who was 23 and had been an officer in the Swedish Navy.

In Sweden, the Wallenberg name was and is like the Rockefeller name in America. The family's financial success started with Andre Wallenberg, the son of a bishop of the Lutheran Church at Linkoping in the 19th Century. He began the Stockholm Enskilda Bank in 1856 following a visit to the United States. There he had witnessed the aftermath of the United States banking crisis in 1837. The surging growth of the Enskilda Bank created comparisons between the Wallenberg and Rothschild families and later the Rockefellers. Propelled by the bank's financial power, the family accumulated $50 million in assets. Other Wallenbergs were and are diplomats, bankers, bishops of the Lutheran church, confidant to kings and other members of the elite. Maj, a beauty and daughter of Sweden's first professor of neurology, Per Wising, suffered another tragedy in November 1912 when her father died. That left two widows and one baby boy.

The two women put all their love into this child, who Nina Lagergren, Wallenberg's half-sister, said, "gave and received so much love that he grew up to be an unusually generous loving, and compassionate person."[2]

In 1918, six years after her husband died, Maj Wallenberg married Fredrik von Dardel, a young civil servant in the Health Ministry who ultimately became head of Sweden's biggest hospital, the Karolinska. They had two children, Guy, who became one of Sweden's best nuclear physicists, and Nina, who married Gunnar Lagergren, a Swedish international lawyer. Much later, Nina Lagergren said, "We never thought of Raoul as being of a different father. He was completely of us and we of him, and my father adored him as much as the two of us."[3]

But Raoul remained a Wallenberg and fell under the influence of his paternal grandfather, Gustav Wallenberg, a Swedish ambassador. Raoul graduated from high school and finished his mandatory military service, an overall three-year commitment. Then his grandfather sent him to France for a year to make him as skilled in French as he was in English and German. Next, young Wallenberg went to the United States to study architecture at the University of Michigan, though his grandfather wanted him to go into banking, a family legacy.

Wallenberg entered Michigan in 1931 and excelled there. An oft-told story explains Wallenberg's appetite for danger. In 1933, Wallenberg spent his summer working at the Chicago World's Fair, in the Swedish pavilion, of course, where he made three dollars daily. Rashly, he decided to hitchhike back to Ann Arbor.

In a letter to his mother, Wallenberg said, "a gentleman in a fine car" gave him a ride. "We were going along at about 70 miles an hour, when all of a sudden we saw a train crossing the highway about 150 yards ahead." After the driver slammed on his brakes, the car skidded and wound up damaged, though he and Wallenberg survived unhurt. A tow truck took away the car and driver, leaving Wallenberg with two suitcases and no ride.

He waited for a long time before a car carrying four men stopped. "They didn't look at all nice, but by this time I was desperate so I got in with them," Wallenberg wrote to his mother.

"They began asking me about money and how much would it be worth to take me all the way to Ann Arbor. I told them I didn't have any."

Then came further danger. The car exited the main road onto a secondary road and into the woods.

"I was told to get out of the car. One of them had a revolver, so I obeyed. They asked for money and I gave them what I had," Wallenberg said.

His money in their pockets, the robbers threw Wallenberg into a ditch with his suitcases atop him. He feared a bullet as a parting present, but that didn't happen. After freeing himself from the ditch, Wallenberg walked to a railway track and ultimately had a suburban train stop.

Despite what happened, Wallenberg wrote his mother, "I will not give up hitchhiking because of this experience. Instead, I will take less money with me and be more cautious."

After college, Wallenberg returned to Sweden, where ambassador Wallenberg made him keep his promise to study banking. He worked in Cape Town, South Africa, for Ardener, Scott, Thesen, and Co., a business closely linked to his grandfather. Wallenberg traveled throughout South Africa, selling chemicals, timber and building materials. His grandfather then became Swedish ambassador to Istanbul in 1936 and there met Erwin Freund, who suggested the ambassador's grandson work for his Holland bank branch in Haifa, and Wallenberg obediently moved to what was then Palestine.

While in Palestine, Wallenberg met some young Jews who had fled from Nazi Germany and disembarked at Haifa, Palestine's central port. Wallenberg saw the frightened and terrified Jewish refugees, an image he always remembered. Wallenberg took a room at a "kosher" boarding house in Haifa and his first contact with refugees from Hitler continued to affect him, probably because of his humanitarianism and the fact that he was one-sixteenth Jewish.

His maternal great-great-grandfather was named Benedicks, a Jew who had come to Sweden near the close of the 18th Century.

One of the first Jews to live in Sweden, Benedicks became a Lutheran, married a Christian woman, did well and in 12 months became jeweler to the court of King Gustav IV Adolf. Later, he became financial adviser to a subsequent king, Charles XIV John, while Benedicks' son was a founder of Sweden's steel industry. Raoul Wallenberg proudly told others about his Jewish roots. He left Haifa in the fall of 1936, still lacking purpose.

Ironically, Eichmann, who became Wallenberg's main adversary in Budapest, came to Palestine just after Wallenberg had left.[4] As a young SS recruit, Eichmann worked in the Jewish Department and became an officer in 1937. Soon afterward, Eichmann was sent to the Middle East to investigate the situation in that region with special emphasis on Palestine. Eichmann's report to his superiors, jointly written with Herbert Hagen, another member of the mission, was extremely anti-Jewish and anti-Zionist. In the report, Palestine was presented as "an economic chaos" in which Jews cheated one another because they had no Gentiles to deceive. Upon his return from Palestine, Eichmann was climbing the Nazi ladder, every rung another body.

Upon his return from Haifa, Wallenberg, now 23, was annoyed by his grandfather's attempt to run his life. That problem ended in early 1937 when the old man died, leaving Wallenberg adrift. After some false starts, Wallenberg—through his family connections—met Kálmán Lauer, who ran an import-export business, handling specialty foodstuffs. Lauer, a Hungarian Jew, living in Sweden needed a good Gentile employee who could move freely through Europe, including the Nazi-held countries. Helped by his language skills, enthusiasm and personality, Wallenberg became a junior partner and director of the firm, the Central European Trading Company, while becoming friends with Lauer.

While traveling on business, Wallenberg learned how to deal with the Nazi bureaucracy—when to threaten, when to flatter, when to bribe and when to tie up the Nazis with their love of paperwork, all crucial skills for later. When back in Stockholm,

Wallenberg had a comfortable bachelor life, dating such beautiful women as Viveca Lindfors, who became a famous actress.[5]

One night after they had been out dancing, Wallenberg—a man of medium height who had curly brown (thinning) hair, an aristocratic nose, full lips and passionate brown eyes—took Lindfors back to his office, where as she said in a Canadian documentary film she thought he would try to seduce her. "I was a hot young girl, and it would have been easy to remember him as a hot young man, but we never got to that point. I did have a feeling he might have wanted to get to that point." Rather, she learned, "He was incredibly intense; instead of dealing with me as a young girl he might have been interested in . . . He talked about the Jews and what happened to them in Germany. I remember my own reaction, which I am certainly not proud of. My own reaction was, 'That's not true.'"

To Lindfors, that is a very Swedish thing: when things become too intense, Swedes cast them aside. "When I think about Raoul nowadays, I sometimes have this fantasy that we're dancing together and I confess to him how stupid I was that night."[6]

Soon afterward, President Franklin Delano Roosevelt established the mechanism to permit Wallenberg's heroics. At the urging of Treasury Secretary Henry Morgenthau Jr., FDR agreed on January 22, 1944, to establish the War Refugee Board, which was designed to save Jews and other possible victims of the Nazis. The War Refugee Board worked with Jewish organizations to evacuate Jews from German-controlled territory.

The U.S. State Department had long fought the effort to rescue European Jews. Morgenthau, a Jew, found out in December 1943 the State Department had for more than six months blocked a plan to rescue 70,000 Romanian Jews in exchange for 170,000 in Romanian currency. Next, Morgenthau learned the State Department had hidden from him a cable from the U.S. legation in Switzerland, which confirmed Hitler had a plan to exterminate the Jewish people.

In late December 1943, Morgenthau confronted Breckinridge

Long,[7] the assistant secretary at the State Department who was in charge of European Affairs and asked him if he were anti-Semitic. Long said no.

The next month, Morgenthau wrote a nasty critique of the State Department, called "Report to the Secretary on the Acquiescence of This Government in the Murder of the Jews." The report contended the State Department was "guilty not only of gross procrastination and willful failure to act, but even of willful attempts to prevent action from being taken to rescue Jews from Hitler."

Roosevelt received the report and a few days later agreed to establish the War Refugee Board. The President wanted Henry Stimson, Secretary of the War Department, Cordell Hull, Secretary of State, and Morgenthau to supervise the WRB, but Stimson delegated this responsibility to John J. McCloy, his assistant secretary.[8] McCloy, a powerful Wall Street lawyer who became an adviser to eight presidents, including FDR, was Henry Stimson's top man at the War Department.

John Pehle was named executive director of the War Refugee Board. He said the board had issued licenses to the World Jewish Congress to let that group transfer funds overseas to finance the evacuation of refugees from France and Romania into Spain, Switzerland and North Africa.

Though Hitler's plan for the Final Solution had been confirmed in 1942, millions of European Jews had died as the State Department halted all efforts to ransom Jews or encourage them to seek refuge in the United States, Palestine, Turkey, Switzerland or other possible safe areas. The only European Jews left were in Hungary.

The Joint Chiefs of Staff rejected rescue operations, a precedent that had been established in November 1943. Then the World Jewish Congress asked the War Department to help about 4,000 refugees stranded on Rab,[9] an Adriatic island. Yugoslav partisans had freed these refugees from Nazi concentration camps in Yugoslavia, and they were sent to Rab.

But the Nazis were posed to capture Rab, so the Yugoslav embassy in Washington requested military transportation to take the refugees to Allied-controlled Italy. The allied area commander decided "the military situation did not permit the rendition of direct assistance to these refugees, the majority of whom were Jews."

If any refugees had made it to Italy, the commander would have taken care of them. At the same time, the army was taking thousands of non-Jewish refugees from Italy to Egypt and there was plenty of shipping available to transport the refugees. The Joint Chiefs of Staff feared the rescue of the refugees on Rab "might create a precedent which would lead to other demands and an influx of additional refugees."

Pehle suggested sending a cable to all theater commanders, ordering them to undertake whatever refugee rescue operations they thought proper with the war effort. McCloy wrote on it, "I am very chary of getting the Army involved in this while the war is on."

McCloy never challenged the War Department's rejection of this idea to rescue refugees, though as Stimson's liaison to the War Refugee Board, McCloy could initiate consideration of military operations to save Jews. A World War I veteran, McCloy loathed "Prussian militarism,"[10] but he also distrusted atrocity stories then floating around Washington. Plus, he and others thought the reports from Europe were too dreadful to be believed. The sources of these reports were mainly Jewish and, some detractors felt, self-serving.

Felix Frankfurter, the Supreme Court Justice, and Walter Lippmann, the famous newspaper columnist, both Jews, didn't believe the Holocaust stories. These men were friends of McCloy, who because his two Jewish friends didn't believe the Holocaust stories had trouble believing them himself.

An upperclass, 20th Century American like McCloy couldn't believe such atrocities occurred. Although not an anti-Semite, McCloy held some of the prejudices of his generation and lofty social standing. The Ivy League schools then had quotas limiting the number of Jewish students. On Wall Street, the legal profession was segregated. A Jew, even if he had gone to Yale or Harvard, could not get a partnership at most of the elite, or "downtown," firms.

The Jewish leaders were divided while the leading U.S. newspapers did not provide adequate coverage of the Holocaust, making it hard for McCloy to help the Jews in Europe. To McCloy, this problem was inferior to having General Dwight D. Eisenhower make contact with the French resistance.

In the middle of the Twentieth Century, anti-Semitism and racial prejudice remained within many Americans and was difficult to uproot.[11] McCloy thought many American soldiers believed Jewish capitalists may have started the war, so he felt it prudent to do nothing that could suggest to the soldiers or American public that the war was fought for the Jews.

McCloy's indifference became important during the summer of 1944. In June, an official of the Agudath Israel World Organization, a group that represented ultra-orthodox American Jews, wrote letters to several high-ranking Washington officials, asking them to stop the deportation of Hungary's Jews. The letters were forwarded to Pehle along with a request to bomb the rail junctions for Auschwitz.

This information had been available for a few months. In April, United Press reported 300,000 Hungarian Jews had been forced into assembly camps. On May 10, 1944, the New York Times reported the Budapest government "is now preparing for the annihilation of Hungarian Jews." A week later the Times printed a story saying the first group of Jews had left the Hungarian countryside for "murder camps in Poland." In fact, the Times was very close, for the trains had left three days before.

Two Jews escaped from Auschwitz on April 10 and provided information that convinced Jewish leaders to ask for the bombing of Auschwitz. The pair, Rudolf Vrba and Alfred Wetzler, fled by foot at night and slept during the day, reaching Slovakia April 21 and found the Jewish underground. Then they wrote a 30-page report to specify what they had seen at Auschwitz. The two had worked, mostly as registrars, for two years at Auschwitz, where they saw millions of Jews processed throughout the camp. They wanted to tell the Hungarian Jews what awaited them. Vrba had seen the Nazis build a new railroad ramp in January right up to one of the gas chambers in the Birkenau section of Auschwitz for the Hungarian Jews. The two escapees' report for the first time gave the main death camp the name Auschwitz and described the gas chambers.

This report went to Budapest and the leaders of the Hungarian Jews in early May 1944. By June, the report went to Roswell McClelland, the War Refugee Board's representative in Geneva. On June 24, he sent a three-page cable to Pehle in Washington. The same day Pehle and McCloy discussed the bombing proposal. Pehle asked McCloy to investigate the matter.

As early as May 1944, the United States could have bombed Auschwitz. In July 1944, U.S. bombers flew above railway lines through Hungary. On August 20, 1944, Allied bombers struck Buna, a synthetic-rubber works using slave labor, which was less than five miles east of Auschwitz. The camp was untouched.

If Allied bombers had destroyed the gas chambers at Auschwitz, that would have forced the Germans to rebuild them or build elsewhere. True, many Jews would have died in the bombing, but many more did die because the gas chambers were not bombed. If the Allies had bombed the Auschwitz gas chambers, 100,000 Hungarian Jews would have escaped death by gassing.

The Holocaust Museum displays letters from McCloy, which argued against bombing Auschwitz. In McCloy's letter dated August 14, 1944, to the World Jewish Congress, he wrote that such a bombing would necessitate a diversion of "considerable air forces." McCloy's letter added the bombing would be "of such doubtful efficacy that it would not warrant the use of our resources."

Finally, McCloy wrote the bombing "might provoke even more vindictive action by the Germans."

One can only ask: How more vindictive could the Nazis have become?

McCloy's inaction left Auschwitz, which became a synonym for death, still functioning. Hoess, the Auschwitz commandant, bragged that no one ever survived the gas chambers. One girl did, for a while.

Dr. Nyiszli, the Auschwitz doctor, explained how he had found a sixteen-year old girl naked and gasping for breath.[12]

The chief of the gas chamber kommando almost tore the hinges off the door to my room as he arrived out of breath, his eyes wide with fear or surprise.

"Doctor," he said, "come quickly. We just found a girl alive at the bottom of the pile of corpses."

I grabbed my instrument case, which was always ready, and dashed to the gas chamber. Against the wall, near the entrance of the immense room, half covered with other bodies, I saw a girl in the throes of a death-rattle, her body seized with convulsions. The gas kommando men around me were in a state of panic. Nothing like this had ever happened in the course of their horrible career.

We removed the still living body from the corpses pressing against it. I gathered the tiny adolescent body into my arms and carried it back into the room adjoining the gas chamber, where normally the gas kommando men change clothes for work. I laid the body on a bench. A frail young girl, almost a child, she could have been no more than fifteen. I took out my syringe, and, taking her arm—she had not yet recovered consciousness and was breathing with difficulty—I administered three intravenous injections. My companions covered her body which was as cold as ice with a heavy overcoat. One ran to the kitchen to fetch some tea and warm broth. Everybody wanted to help, as if she were his own child.

The reaction was swift. The child was seized by a fit of coughing, which brought up a thick globule of phlegm from her lungs. She opened her eyes and looked fixedly at the ceiling. I kept a close watch for every sign of life. Her breathing became deeper and more and more regular. Her lungs, tortured by the gas, inhaled the fresh air avidly. Her pulse became perceptible, the result of the injections. I waited impatiently. The injections had not yet been completely absorbed, but I saw that within a few minutes she was going to regain consciousness; her circulation began to bring color back into her cheeks, and her delicate face became human again.

She looked around her with astonishment, and glanced at us. She still did not realize what was happening to her, and was still incapable of distinguishing the present, of knowing whether she was dreaming or really awake. A veil of mist clouded her consciousness. Perhaps she vaguely remembered a train, a long line of box cars which had brought her here. Then she had lined up for selection and, before she knew what was happening, been swept along by the current of the mass into a large, brilliantly lighted underground room. Everything had happened so quickly. Perhaps she remembered that everyone had had to undress. The impression had been disagreeable, but everybody had yielded resignedly to the order. And so, naked, she had been swept along into another room. Mute anguish had seized them all. The second room had also been lighted by powerful lamps. Completely bewildered, she had let her gaze wander over the mass huddled there, but found none of her family. Pressed close against the wall, she had waited, her heart frozen, for what was going to happen. All of a sudden, the light had gone out, leaving her enveloped in total darkness. Something had stung her eyes, seized her throat, suffocated her. She had fainted. There her memories ceased.

Her movements were becoming more and more animated; she tried to move her hands, her feet, to turn her head left and right. Her face was seized by a fit of convulsions. Suddenly she grasped my coat collar and gripped it convulsively, trying with all her might to raise herself. I laid her back down again several times, but she continued to repeat the same gesture. Little by little, however, she grew calm and remained stretched out, completely exhausted. Large tears shone in her eyes and rolled down her cheeks. She was not crying. I received the first reply to my questions. Not wanting to tire her, I asked only a few. I learned that she was sixteen years old, and that she had come with her parents in a convoy from Transylvania.

The kommando gave her a bowl of hot broth, which she drank voraciously. They kept bringing her all sorts of dishes, but I could not allow them to give her anything. I covered her to her head and told her that she should try and get some sleep.

My thoughts moved at a dizzy pace. I turned towards my companions in the hope of finding a solution. We racked our brains, for we were now face to face with the most difficult problem: what to do with the girl now that she has been restored to life? We knew that she could not remain here for very long.

What could one do with a young girl in the crematorium's Sonderkommando? I knew the past history of the place: no one had ever come out of here alive, either from the convoys or from the Sonderkommando.

Little time remained for reflection. Oberschaaführer Mussfeld arrived to supervise the work, as was his wont. Passing by the open door, he saw us gathered in a group. He came in and asked what was going on. Even before we told him he had seen the girl stretched out on the bench.

I made a sign for my companions to withdraw. I was going to attempt something I knew without saying was doomed to failure. Three months in the same camp and in the same milieu had created, in spite of everything, a certain intimacy between us. Besides, the Germans generally appreciate capable people, and, as long as they need them, respect them to a certain extent, even in the (camp). Such was the case for cobblers, tailors, joiners and locksmiths. From our numerous contacts, I had been able to ascertain that Mussfeld had a high esteem for the medical expert's professional qualities. He knew that my superior was Dr. Mengele, the (camp's) most dreaded figure, who, goaded by racial pride, took himself to be one of the most important representatives of German medical science. He considered the dispatch of hundreds of thousands of Jews to the gas chambers as a patriotic duty. The work carried on in the dissection room was for the furtherance of

German medical science. As Dr. Mengele's pathological expert, I also had a hand in this progress, and therein lay the explanation for a certain form of respect that Mussfeld paid me. He often came to see me in the dissecting room, and we conversed on politics, the military situation and various other subjects. It appeared that his respect also arose from the fact that he considered the dissection of bodies and his bloody job of killing to be allied activities. He was the commandant and ace shot of number one crematorium. Three other SS acted as his lieutenants. Together they carried out the "liquidation" by a bullet in the back of the neck. This type of death was reserved for those who had been chosen in camp, or else sent from another on their way to a so-called "rest camp." When there were merely 500 or less, they were killed by a bullet in the back of the neck, for the large factory of gas chambers was reserved for the annihilation of more important numbers. As much gas was needed to kill 500 as to kill 3,000. Nor was it worthwhile to call out the Red Cross truck to bring the canisters and gas butchers for such a trifling number of victims. Nor was it worth the trouble of having a truck come to collect the clothes, which were scarcely more than rags anyway. Such were the factors which determined whether a group would die by gas or by a bullet in the back of the neck.

And this was the man I had to deal with, the man I had to talk into allowing a single life to be spared. I calmly related the terrible case we found ourselves confronted with. I described for his benefit what pains the child must have suffered in the undressing room, and the horrible scenes that preceded death in the gas chamber. When the room had been plunged into darkness, she had breathed in a few lungfuls of [Zyklon] gas. Only a few, though, for her frail body had given way under the pushing and shoving of the mass as they fought against death. By chance she had fallen with her face against the wet concrete floor. That bit of humidity had kept her from being asphyxiated, for [Zyklon] gas does not react under humid conditions.

These were my arguments, and I asked him to do something for the child. He listened to me attentively, then asked me exactly what I proposed doing. I saw by his expression that I had put him face to face with a practically impossible problem. It was obvious that the child could not remain in the crematorium. One solution would have been to put her in front of the crematorium gate. A kommando of women always worked here. She could have slipped in among them and accompanied them back to the camp barracks after they had finished work. She would never relate what had happened to her. The presence of one new face among many thousands would never be detected, for no one in the camp knew all the other inmates.

If she had been three or four years older that might have worked. A girl of twenty would have been able to understand clearly the miraculous circumstances of her survival, and have enough foresight not to tell anyone about them. She would wait for better times, like so many other thousands were waiting, to recount what she had lived through. But Mussfeld thought a young girl of sixteen would in all naïveté tell the first person she met where she had just come from, what she had seen and what she had lived through. The news would spread like wildfire, and we would all be forced to pay for it with our lives.

"There's no way of getting around it," he said, "the child will have to die."

Half an hour later the young girl was led, or rather carried into the furnace room hallway, and there Mussfeld sent another in his place to do the job. A bullet in the back of the neck.

With Auschwitz intact, the War Refugee Board needed other maneuvers to save European Jews. When the Germans occupied Hungary March 19, that country became the board's biggest priority. Cordell Hull sent a cable from Washington to Herschel V. Johnson, the U.S. ambassador in Stockholm, asking the Swedes to increase their delegation in Hungary to prevent the extermination of Jews there.[13] "The lives of 800,000 human beings in Hungary may well depend on the restraint that may result from the presence in that country of the largest possible number of foreign observers," Hull said in the cable.

Though the Americans also asked Switzerland, Spain, Portugal and Turkey to expand their diplomatic and consular staffs in Hungary, only Sweden responded. This was the same Sweden that had uncomfortably cooperated with the Germans. At the start of the war in 1939, Sweden declared its neutrality. When the Soviet Union invaded Finland, both Sweden and Norway refused to let the Allies march through Sweden to intervene. After Germany occupied Norway and Denmark in 1940, German military power forced the Swedes to grant the Nazi troops transit rights through Sweden to Norway. Following Germany's invasion of the Soviet Union in June 1941, the Nazis again demanded transit for a division of German troops from Norway to Finland. Under threat of Nazi military action, Sweden agreed.

Nevertheless, the Swedes were willing to help the Americans this time, but they wanted a special man for a special job. The problem became which man to choose?

CHAPTER 2

During his World War II assignment in Stockholm, Iver C. Olsen had three jobs and one contact with a famous Swedish code name. He worked for the Treasury Department as financial attache of the American legation in Stockholm, for the War Refugee Board as the Stockholm representative and for the Office of Strategic Services, which in 1947 became the Central Intelligence Agency.

For the OSS, Olsen had three assignments. He handled all the finances and accounts of the OSS mission in Stockholm. Olsen also handled "X-2," which involved "interrogating refugees and escapees to Sweden" as well as taking care of S, which meant "procuring intelligence, including dispatching of agents to Norway and to the Baltic area."

In short, Iver Olsen was an American spy.

A progress report dated August 10, 1944, from Olsen to the War Refugee Board shows his heavy involvement in intelligence activities:[1]

With the longer nights now arriving, my Baltic operations are beginning to show results, although they are very difficult. As I cabled you, I lost my man (Algirdas) Vokietaitis, which upset me very much, and had a most serious effect on our Lithuanian operations, to say nothing of losing our best source of Baltic intelligence. He had shipped into Lithuania to complete all the rescue arrangements personally, and the first hint of bad news came when he or anyone else failed to show up at the appointed place when the boat went after him the following week. The same thing happened when the boat went the next week, and it was on the third trip that the evacuees reported he had been captured and shot by the Germans. He was a hell of a fine, fearless fellow and the most skillful operator I had.

Later in the same report, Olsen related his plans to evacuate Finnish Jews to Sweden,[2] which made "almost the entire Jewish community in Sweden mad at me," an irony considering how a Swedish Christian would soon try to help the Jewish people in Budapest. But Olsen explained that the Jewish community in Sweden was delaying helping the Finnish Jews "in the most unconscionable way . . . The following is for your information only," he wrote to the War Refugee Board, "but it is only too true that the Swedish Jews don't want any more Jews in Sweden."

Olsen said Sweden's Jews were comfortably ensconced there, free of anti-Semitism and were "very much afraid that an influx of Jews will not only be a burden to them, but will create a Jewish problem in Sweden."

Washington regularly communicated with Olsen. A series of nine cables and dispatches from March 7, 1944, to June 7, 1944, from the OSS involved Olsen while referring to the establishment of the War Refugee Board and the start of its activities in Stockholm.

Six of the cables came from OSS headquarters in Washington to the OSS in [blacked out] and three from the OSS [blacked out] to OSS headquarters in Washington. They included one message for Olsen, who was known as #799, and whom the CIA said was an "OSS officer assigned to [blacked out]." The cables also mentioned a "Garbo," the codename for the War Refugee Board.[3]

"Instructions for 799 from the War Refugee Board, to be known from now on as Garbo, are contained in a separate communication," said the March 7th cable.[4] This cable went from Washington to Wilho Tikander, #155, who was chief of the OSS Mission in [blacked out], and discussed the War Refugee Board's plan.

"We are in complete accord with this and it represents the initial exploratory action in plan for cooperation between the agencies which may reach out to additional theaters. Garbo sanctions your discreet participation and knowledge of all details but would rather you did not speak of it with the minister just now. Please do everything you can to promote this project." Later, the cable said, "We believe that tremendous aid could be given by Swedish private citizens representing religious and humanitarian organizations if they went on humanitarian missions to the various occupied countries, especially Rumania."

In the same cable, Garbo specified the War Refugee Board's operations and its plan to rescue Jews. This cable also asked to "kindly accord Iver Olsen the warmest reception."

Near the end, the cable said, "kindly take immediate action, as this is a question of life or death to thousands of people. Keep me posted via the War Refugee Board . . . Mr. Olsen of that board will forward your messages on to me."

An OSS cable dated July 1, 1944, which mentions Wallenberg, originated from Richard M. Helms, then an OSS employee (#944)[5] in Washington, who had joined the agency two years earlier. Helms, who stayed with U.S. spy agencies for 31 years, became director of the CIA, the OSS' succeeding agency, in 1966.

Much of the other cables are garbled and barely legible. A March 15 cable told Olsen "you are being depended on in this last and unlimited attempt to save innumerable lives."[6]

Eight days later another cable said John Pehle asked Olsen to be the War Refugee Board's representative in Sweden. Someone at OSS headquarters hoped Olsen could do the job without letting his other duties suffer.[7]

As the War Refugee Board representative in Stockholm, his overt job, Olsen formed a committee of prominent Swedish Jews to advise him on how to help Jews in Hungary. The group, which included Kálámán Lauer, had a plan calling for a Gentile to travel to Budapest on a rescue mission. This person could not represent the United States in a country warring with America, but he could go under the Swedish diplomatic protection. Therefore, he would have a diplomatic passport, money and a plan to issue Swedish passports to get as many Jews as possible to Sweden.

The initial choice was Folke Bernadotte, chairman of the

Swedish Red Cross and a relation of King Gustav V, but the Hungarian government rejected Bernadotte.[8] Lauer then recommended his young associate, Raoul Wallenberg, so Olsen, Lauer and Wallenberg met for dinner at 7 p.m. June 9, 1944, and talked for 10 hours straight until 5 a.m. When they were done, Olsen knew he had the right man. A few days afterward Wallenberg met with Johnson, who reached the same conclusion as Olsen. Next, the Swedish government approved the selection.

While Olsen was instrumental in selecting Wallenberg, he only chose him in his duties as a representative of the War Refugee Board, an American organization, not as an OSS employee. Wallenberg was never recruited and never acted as a spy, though his American handler was a spy.

Did Wallenberg know Olsen was an American spy? Probably not, but one can never be sure.

Before leaving, Wallenberg bargained with the Swedish foreign office, gaining the right to use any methods, including bribery, the right to contact anyone in Budapest and the right to give asylum in buildings belonging to the legation to anyone holding Swedish passes. Wallenberg's demands were so unusual that they were sent all the way to Prime Minister Per Albin Hansson, who spoke with King Gustav V before telling Wallenberg his requests had been approved.[9]

"I wasn't pleased when Raoul left," explained Guy von Dardel, his half-brother, almost 50 years later. "It was an interesting task for him. It was an occasion to show what he was built of. He wasn't able to do much before."

However, "We never understood it would be such a dangerous job."

Ambassador Johnson cabled Washington June 28, 1944, about the "newly designated attache, Raoul Wallenberg," who felt he was "carrying out a humanitarian mission in behalf of the War Refugee Board."[10]

Another cable three days later talked of Wallenberg's interest in substance, not style.[11] "There is no doubt in my mind as to the sincerity of Wallenberg's purpose because I have talked to him myself," Johnson said. "I was told by Wallenberg that he wanted to be able to help effectively and to save lives, and that he was not interested in going to Budapest merely to write reports to be sent to the Foreign Office."

Johnson said the American legation in Stockholm was "very favorably impressed with Wallenberg's ability to act intelligently and with discretion in carrying out any responsibilities that the WRB may delegate to him."

But exactly what? Wallenberg requested instructions from Washington as to which activities he could carry out and to be certain that he had financial support. He received both. In a July 7, 1944, cable, Cordell Hull told Pehle that while Wallenberg "cannot, of course, act as the (War Refugee) Board's representative, nor purport to act in its name, he can, whenever advisable, indicate that as a Swede he is free to communicate with Stockholm where a representative of the Board is stationed."[12]

Hull also gave Wallenberg both the latitude to operate in Budapest and the sword of retribution. The Secretary of State wanted the new Swedish attache to take with him a copy of Roosevelt's statement that promised American reprisals for further Nazi persecutions. "Those who share the guilt will be punished, but . . . helpful conduct now may result in more favorable considerations than actions heretofore might warrant."

To fund Wallenberg, Olsen drew on funds opened by the Joint Distribution Committee, an American Jewish organization, in the Enskilda Bank in Stockholm, a convenient arrangement since the Wallenberg family controlled that bank.

As the American intelligence community later explained in a recently declassified document, "The funds in this account were earmarked for WALLENBERG [sic] and Subject [Olsen] was authorized to draw on this account. Whenever WALLENBERG indicated, through means of letters pouched from Budapest to the Foreign Office in Stockholm, that he needed funds, Subject withdrew the necessary funds from the account referred to above and would send them to WALLENBERG through Swedish Foreign Office channels."[13]

Altogether, Wallenberg had 260,000 Swedish kronor. That included 250,000 from the Joint Distribution Committee, which he used for refugee work. The final 10,000 kronor came from the "U.S. President's secret fund," which Roosevelt used for various discretionary purposes. At an exchange rate of about four kronor to a U.S. dollar, 260,000 kronor translated into around $65,000 in 1944. After adjusting for 50 years of inflation, that amount would have been equivalent to about $540,000 in 1994 dollars.

When Olsen represented the War Refugee Board, he made three separate payments, indirectly, to Wallenberg. Except for the first payment, Olsen deposited the money in the Enskilda Bank in Wallenberg's name or possibly in a joint account held by Wallenberg and Olsen. Olsen gave Wallenberg the first payment in cash via an unnamed third person in Stockholm, and Wallenberg used this money to finance his trip to Budapest. The second and third payments were 50,000 and 200,000 kronor deposited in the Enskilda bank, but Wallenberg used little of the final payment, which was returned to the Joint Distribution Committee.[14]

His finances secure, Wallenberg left Stockholm July 6, first flying to Berlin to see his half-sister Nina, now married to Gunnar Lagergren, head of the Swedish legation's foreign interests section in Berlin. Carrying his clothes in a rucksack, Wallenberg would not even spend two days with his half-sister, insisting on leaving aboard the next train, which was the following day. He told Nina the Nazis were sending 10,000 Jews a day to Auschwitz, and he could not delay. Wallenberg spent the journey to Budapest in the corridor of the crowded train, sitting on his rucksack. He arrived in Budapest July 9, 1944.

By then, the Nazis had shipped 437,402 Jewish men, women and children aboard 148 trains from May 14 to July 8. Each death train to Auschwitz carried up to 4,000 men, women and children—70 to 100 to a car, which had one pail of water and one empty pail for refuse. The trip to Auschwitz took three or four days. When Jews protested about the inhumane treatment, Otto Hunsche, an Eichmann aide, retorted, "There are no more than 50 to 60 dying en route in any single transport."

Eichmann had been too efficient, though, sending at times five trains loaded with 14,000 people to arrive daily at Auschwitz, more than the camp's four crematoria comprising forty-six ovens with a total capacity of 500 bodies an hour could handle. Hoess, the Auschwitz commandant, protested that Eichmann was sending him more people than the death camp could murder in one day. During a conference in Budapest, Eichmann said he had to work fast because of the Russian advances from the east. Hoess and Eichmann agreed on a schedule of two trains one day and three the next.

Only 230,000 petrified Jews remained in the Hungarian capital. Eichmann, with characteristic efficiency, formulated a plan to round up and eliminate the remaining Jews in Budapest, which would have made Wallenberg's mission useless. However, Horthy, the Hungarian regent—emboldened by the Russian army's relentless advance and reacting to criticism from the world press—ordered no more deportations.

Horthy had maneuvered 19,000 Hungarian gendarmes, soldiers and police into Budapest, so Eichmann could do nothing but see his blood pressure rise at the thought of 230,000 human beings escaping his death trains. Four months earlier Eichmann had issued orders forbidding Jews from leaving their homes and made them yield their telephones, radios and cars while children had to relinquish their bicycles. Jews also had their bank accounts frozen, their food rations cut and had to wear a yellow star of David. Hungarian gendarmes had rounded up the Jews, with Eichmann's men acting as supervisors, and put them in local ghettos and concentration camps. From there, they were sent to the gas chambers or war factories where they literally were worked to death.

Back in Stockholm, Olsen lunched with an official of the

Swedish legation in Budapest, who told the American about the unappetizing subject of atrocities:

He said that even he did not believe some of the atrocities until he himself was an eyewitness. He went over to a brick factory where they had over 10,000 Jews herded in an area so small that they were forced to stand up closely packed together for five days, old people and young children alike, without any sanitary facilities. He saw them himself standing there and also being loaded into box cars, eight (he said eight were counted out very carefully) into each car, after which the doors were nailed shut. He said many died just standing in the brick factory. He also said young girls of 14 or 15 were being stolen on the streets, taken into other areas where they had "war whore" tatooed [sic] on their arms. Some of them, young Hungarian Jewesses of good family, had been observed as far away as Hamburg. He lamented very much the total lack of courage among Hungarian Jews . . . even when they knew it was only a matter of a short time before they would be killed.[15]

Prior to Wallenberg's arrival, the Swedish embassy had started to issue a quota of 650 passes to Jews who could show they had business or family ties to Sweden. Wallenberg rapidly began building on that base. As Per Anger, another Swedish diplomat in Budapest, said in a documentary film about Wallenberg, "To start with, he shocked some of us professional diplomats by his unconventional methods, but we very soon found he had the right approach."[16]

Wallenberg realized the Hungarian rulers badly wanted to be recognized as that country's legitimate government. Also, Sweden represented both Hungarian and German interests in several crucial countries when the war had turned against the Nazis and their allies. Thus, influential Hungarians could be manipulated by threats of postwar retribution and promises of Swedish favors if they behaved properly now. Finally, Wallenberg was ready to use bribery or blackmail, if necessary, to save lives.

Wallenberg knew appearances were important in dealing with both the Germans and Hungarians. So, he immediately designed an impressive-looking passport to replace the prosaic one. The new passport was printed in yellow and blue while bearing the triple crown of the Royal Swedish government and covered with stamps, seals and signatures. When unfolded, the passport divided into two pages and four squares with the holder's name and picture in the upper right-hand corner. The passport said, in Hungarian and German, the holder had a visa for Sweden and was under Swedish protection.

Despite the official flourishes, "This was a completely illegal document, of course, from the foreign viewpoint," explained Anger, Wallenberg's colleague.[17]

Nevertheless, the document, or Schutz-pass, gained respect, showing both the Germans and Hungarians the holder had the protection of Sweden, a major neutral power.

On the second floor of the Holocaust Museum, a Wallenberg display stands in one corner. Next to the paintings and pictures of Wallenberg, a glass-enclosed display case contains four Schutz-passes and one legible memory. In the lower left hand corner of one Schutz-pass, the visitor sees—written in pencil—a capital "W."

Initially, the Hungarian Foreign Ministry gave Wallenberg permission to issue only 1,000 passports, but he negotiated the number up to 4,500. Ultimately, Wallenberg, who rented a 16-room office, issued more than 14,000 passports and during the final days before Budapest fell to the Russians, he issued a much simpler version, but that too saved many Jewish lives.

Other neutral nations in Budapest emulated Wallenberg and started issuing their own country's passports to Jews. The Swiss for a while actually issued more passports than Wallenberg while Spain and the Vatican also issued some passes. The Portuguese, representing another neutral nation, issued about 1,000 passports and safe conduct passes to Hungarians, far less than the Swedes, but both countries also provided fictitious employment to Hungarian men and women as secretaries, clerks, chauffeurs, valets, gardeners and other jobs, which extended them the protection due employees of a foreign mission. The Portuguese also gave asylum on their mission grounds to about 80 people, with some staying at the chargé d'affaire's residence and others at a country estate leased by the legation.

A Portuguese diplomat, C. de Liz-Teixeira Branquinho, who lived in Budapest during the Nazi occupation, put Portugal's contribution in perspective when he reached Lisbon.[18] Branquinho, who served as secretary of the Portuguese Legation in Budapest from May 1944 and chargé d'affaires until he left Hungary on October 29, 1944, told U.S. embassy staff members in Lisbon, "the Swedes alone have done a hundred times more in saving lives and otherwise helping Hungarians and other victims of nazi [sic] persecution than all the other neutral missions."

During a two-hour interview at the U.S. embassy, Branquinho told how when he arrived in Budapest "the brutality and barbarism" of the Gestapo horrified him. Though Gentiles suffered, Jews were the main target of persecution.

"Conditions in the jails, detention places and concentration camps were beyond imagination and the way the victims were beaten and tortured was indescribable," Branquinho told embassy officials.[19]

Most of the people, including Hungarian officials, were "horrified and ashamed over what took place in their midst and while they were too terror-stricken and without leadership from within and without to do anything affirmative about it, they tried to help the victims whenever and however they could," Branquinho related.

The Portuguese, Swiss, Spanish, Vatican pass or Swedish Schutz-pass was the answer. Budapest's Jews immediately figured out the plan and hundreds pleaded for these Schutz-passes. Wallenberg's staff ballooned to 250 Jews, who worked in shifts 24 hours a day.

But Raoul Wallenberg was only beginning.

Next, Wallenberg had the Jews quartered in Swedish-protected housing within Budapest. There Jews had food and shelter and received vaccinations against typhus, paratyphus and cholera. He established soup kitchens, nurseries and hospitals in Budapest, purchasing medicine, clothing and food via the funds supplied by the War Refugee Board and the American-Jewish Joint Distribution Committee. By then, Wallenberg's staff had increased to 400 while he only slept, at most, four hours a night. His enthusiasm and energy attracted attention, perhaps too much.

Iver Olsen, the War Refugee Board representative in Stockholm, wrote on August 10, 1944, to John Pehle, one of his three supervisors in Washington, saying, "I get the impression indirectly that the Swedish Foreign Office is somewhat uneasy about Wallenberg's activities in Budapest and perhaps feel that he has jumped in with too big a splash. They would prefer, of course, to approach the Jewish problem in the finest traditions of European diplomacy, which wouldn't help too much. On the other hand, there is much to be said for moving around quietly on this type of work. In any case, I feel that Wallenberg is working like hell and doing some good, which is the measure."[20]

Agreeing via an October 30, 1944, cable was Johnson. "It appears Wallenberg is throwing his full energy into his task and doing remarkably well considering enormous difficulties. Olsen thinks official recognition . . . of Wallenberg's efforts, which would be forwarded through the Foreign office well justified."[21]

Besides praise from abroad, Wallenberg also aroused envy among his own legation. "Really, Raoul was the one who did everything, and his word was everything," said Agnes Adachi, a Wallenberg aide in Budapest during 1944. But his colleagues were "lukewarm" toward him, she said. "They admired him for what he had done, but they were not wholeheartedly, constantly with him."[22]

Lars Berg, another Swedish diplomat in Budapest, added, "Raoul Wallenberg had a very strong will, and he was saying, 'You're talking about protecting Swedes and Swedish property, and I'm talking about saving Jewish lives.'"[23]

At the same time, the Nazis were beset with internal and external problems. Externally, the Germans were caught in a pincer between the Russian advance from the east and the British-American advance from the west. Also, Romania, Hungary's neighbor, had withdrawn from the conflict. Internally, a bomb plot on July 20, 1944, to kill Hitler had failed, but shattered the Germans' arrogance.

Horthy, aware of the German setbacks and pestered by Wallenberg's unceasing demands, dismissed the worst anti-Semites in the Hungarian government and had his new ministers demand Hungarian authorities take over the disposal of Jewish affairs from the Germans. Horthy also wanted Eichmann and his troopers ousted from Hungary.

Since the Germans had lost the precious Romanian oil fields, they wanted to keep the oil production from Hungary's Zala region. They reached an agreement on August 30 with the new Hungarian government that included Eichmann's departure. Humiliated, Eichmann returned to Berlin, where his superiors told him they had more important business than the extermination of the Hungarian Jewish community.

Despite Eichmann's departure, the Jews of Budapest remained in danger. The Hungarians correctly reasoned they had pushed the Germans to the limit, so they proposed they put all able-bodied Jews—males and females—in camps in the Hungarian provinces. There they would work to support the German-Hungarian soldiers. The old, the weak and the young would be put in two other camps while the sick would be sent to hospitals. The camps would be overcrowded and the detainees undernourished. They would face horrendous labor conditions, unsanitary facilities and overall wretched treatment.

However, the International Red Cross, which had done little thus far to help the Jews, inspected the camp sites. After about 45 days, the Red Cross failed to find one site in western Hungary suitable for "accommodation consistent with European standards." The Hungarian government—listening to the Red Cross and Allied protests—dropped the whole plan.

By October, the Russian advance had drawn so close to Budapest that most thought the danger from Nazi deportations had almost passed. If so, Wallenberg could have returned to

Stockholm content with his effort. He had wanted to return to Sweden for a few days in August, but the Germans refused to give him a temporary visa. Nevertheless, in a letter dated October 12, 1944, to Olsen, Wallenberg indicated he only wanted to continue his work in Budapest.

"When I now look back on the 3 months I have spent here I can only say, that it has been a most interesting experience and I believe, not quite without results." Wallenberg told Olsen about the Jews' dreadful situation in Budapest and how that had changed due to the Russian advance and a "natural psychological reaction among the Hungarian people."[24]

To Wallenberg, "We at the Swedish Legation have perhaps only been an instrument to convert this outside influence into action in the various Government offices. I have taken quite a strong line in this respect although, of course I have had to keep within the limits assigned to me as a neutral."

Then Wallenberg wrote Olsen, "It has been my object all the time, to try to help all Jews."

To do that, Wallenberg had to encounter major changes that evoked greater sacrifices and heroic acts from him. Horthy, the regent, foolishly tried to establish a separate peace with the Russians, but the Nazis found out through informers. On October 15, a Sunday, Horthy announced over the radio that for Hungarians the war had ended.

Branquinho, the Portuguese diplomat, watched from his Budapest residence, along an arterial street that led to the main highway to Vienna, as the German garrison first left the city.[25] From around 2 p.m., Branquinho saw the massive amounts of German infantry, motorized units, tanks and artillery flow westward for hours, far more than he had imagined existed in Budapest. These forces did not include the two German divisions ringing Budapest in a half arc on the north, west and south from five to 30 kilometers.

After dark, around 7 p.m., the Germans started to return and this lasted all night. Around midnight, Branquinho heard rifle and machine gun fire and even some light artillery. But it wasn't until the next day that Branquinho learned about the pitched battles in various parts of the capital between anti-Nazi Hungarians on one side and the Germans and their followers on the other.

By Monday morning, October 16th, the Germans were in total control and the Hungarian Nazis ruled Budapest. Since Horthy had failed to leave enough troops to combat the Germans in the capital, the Nazis and the Arrow Cross—the Hungarian fascist party—took over Budapest, putting every Jew in greater peril.

To insure success, the Nazis kidnapped Horthy's son and took him to Germany. Horthy succumbed and let the Arrow Cross, Hungary's fascist underclass, take control of the country and let himself be transported to Germany. Now, the Germans made Ferenc Szálasi, the Arrow Cross leader, as both prime minister and head of the country under the umbrella title of Leader of the Nation. Triumphant, Eichmann returned to Budapest the following day, telling Jewish leaders, "You see; I am back."

Eichmann's new plan involved deportation by foot, making the Jews walk to the concentration camps. Immediately, the fascist Arrow Cross began to round up Jews, spreading fresh terror throughout the community. Several hundred murders occurred along with wholesale arrests, including even Jews under Swedish protection.

Gábor Vajna, the Arrow Cross interior minister, went on radio October 18 and said he would not recognize any letter of safe conduct or foreign passport issued to a Hungarian Jew, threatening to undo everything Wallenberg had done. Wallenberg went into action, working through Baron Gábor Kemény, the foreign minister, who dressed for public occasions by wearing riding boots and a belted pistol.

Against such a man, Wallenberg had three pressure points. 1. The new regime craved legitimacy through the international community. 2. A rivalry existed between Kemény and Vajna. 3. Kemény's wife, the beautiful baroness Elisabeth "Liesel" Kemény.

Wallenberg played the two Hungarians, Vajna and Kemény, against each other. Capitalizing on Baron Kemény's naïveté, the Swedish diplomat told him, "You, Mr. Foreign Minister, are going to be the first foreign minister to Stockholm," which Kemény loved to hear and which the Swedes would never do.[26]

To maintain the charade, Wallenberg daily wrote long diplomatic notes to Kemény. His wife, the baroness, knew why. Wallenberg "wants to make him soft. He was very shrewd, Wallenberg."[27]

Wallenberg knew the baroness was a Jew who fled Austria because of Hitler. Apparently, she did not know the baron was a fascist, but now she carried his child, making her malleable to Wallenberg's pressure.

At a meeting in Pest, the eastern half of the twin city divided by the Danube, Wallenberg told the baroness the national recognition her husband sought would never come if he abrogated the agreement on Schutz-passes. Also, when the Russians captured both Buda and Pest, the Arrow Cross leaders would surely hang without the intervention of a neutral diplomat. Finally, Wallenberg told her that as a Jew she must want to save her people.

The baroness convinced her husband, who tried to sway Szálasi, but he initially resisted, preferring to eliminate all the Jews. Kemény persisted, explaining that if the Arrow Cross re-validated the documents, this would insure the goodwill of the Swedes and Swiss, but only let 16,000 or so Jews out of Hungary. The Arrow Cross could then kill the rest. Szálasi liked that idea.

Wallenberg, who would be satisfied with nothing less than saving as many Jews as possible, insisted to the baroness that her husband make the announcement on the radio so everyone, including the Arrow Cross and public, knew the protective passes were again valid. After threatening to leave him, the baroness convinced her husband to air the change in policy.

Kemény, who had restored the validity of 4.500 Swedish and 7,000 Swiss passes, brought in Wallenberg and the Swiss consul, telling both to repatriate their "nationals" immediately. If not, the passes would be revoked and the Jews treated as badly as any other Jew still alive in Budapest.

Wallenberg agreed, but tried to stall, realizing that if he arranged transport for his Jews they might suffer a fatal "accident" along the way. If they left, he had no further function and no ability to stay and save the thousands of Jews still endangered. Wallenberg knew the Russians, whom he foolishly regarded as his savior, would soon overrun the city and bring down this criminal government. A forward column of "liberating" Russians had entered the city's southeastern outskirts November 2, 1944.

Meanwhile, Arrow Cross thugs—dressed in green uniforms with green shirts, red and white armbands with crossed arrows and wearing black boots—were terrorizing Jews throughout Budapest, beating, robbing and murdering. Eichmann, ever systematic, rounded up Jewish men aged 16 and 60 on October 20, 1944. The ousted Jews had one hour to gather enough food for a three-day march. Some with Wallenberg passports had themselves exempted. Still, 50,000 Jewish men, now little more than slaves, were marched to Budapest's perimeter, where they dug trenches and created other defenses to try and stop the Russian advance. Many perished from overwork or bad treatment.

This eliminated most of Budapest's male population, so Eichmann turned his focus on the women and children, organizing death marches along a 120-mile corridor from Budapest to the Hegyeshalom, at the Austrian border. There, trains took the refugees to the concentration camps and death.

"We went to sleep in the mud, and in the morning when we got up, half the people had frozen to death," said Miriam Herzog, a survivor who now lives in Israel.[28] "Anyone who dared leave the line was shot. Sometimes when I felt I couldn't go on, I'd tell my mother, and she'd hold on to me. Other times she wanted to leave the line, and I held on to her."

Along the way, some Jews took refuge in two barns at Gonyu, one of the designated nighttime rest areas for marchers, where hundreds of women claimed Swedish passports and protection. At the greatest moment of need, Wallenberg arrived and the women rushed to him, pleading, "Save us, save us." In his leather coat and fur hat, the handsome Wallenberg, amid the dirty and lice-infested refugees, looked like he came from another planet.

As the women begged him for their lives, Wallenberg said, "Please, you must forgive me, but I cannot help all of you. I can only provide certificates for a hundred of you. I feel I have a mission to save the Jewish nation, and so I must rescue the young ones first."[29]

To many, that was the first time they had heard the idea of a Jewish nation, which became a reality in Israel.

Miriam Herzog, then 17, was too weak to rise and she didn't even have a Schutz-pass.[30] Nevertheless, Wallenberg "made his way directly to me even though I was far from him. I don't know how he even saw me. He wrote my name at the top of a list, gathered another hundred names and put us into a closed train car and sent us back to Budapest. It wasn't exactly a pleasure trip. We couldn't utter a sound. He bribed the officials where we got on and also the ones in Budapest, but if we had been discovered anywhere on route that would have been the end of us. He couldn't bribe everyone."

Wallenberg had taken the names on a list, and a few days later about a hundred women whose names were thus recorded had been removed from the barn and put on a cattle train back to Budapest. Despite numerous hardships, including a three-day rail trip to Budapest, which normally took three hours, because of the bombed out rail lines, the women survived, thanks to Wallenberg.

Wallenberg and Per Anger kept traveling up and back along the road to Hegyeshalom during those horrible days of November 1944. Wallenberg took vans filled with food, medicine and warm clothing as well as his book specifying the names of Jews to whom he had issued passports while carrying new passports that he would fill in and issue immediately.

Lars Berg, another Swedish diplomat, said the diplomats in his legation went down the road in trucks to try and save the Jews.

"We tried to pick up all the people who had Swedish documents. Wallenberg was more clever than that. He had a typewriter and a secretary on his truck that (typed) out papers as they went along, and he also gave papers to people with a false name, . . . and just took them up on the truck."[31]

During this same period, after an all night drive, Wallenberg arrived at 7 a.m. at Hegyeshalom just as the Arrow Cross was delivering Jews to Eichmann's SS troopers at the railroad station. The starving refugees were dirty and filled with both lice and the fear of imminent death. The Hungarians had divided the Jews into groups of one hundred each. Some had already boarded the freight train and their doors were locked and sealed while others stood on the platform, waiting for orders to enter the empty cars. The SS, Arrow Cross and Hungarian gendarmes walked around the platform, observing their human cargo.

Like a fictional hero, Wallenberg arrived at the last moment, showed his diplomatic credentials and demanded the Arrow Cross guards move aside and let him remove Jews holding Swedish passes. The guards, some of them only teen-age thugs, put their bayonets onto Wallenberg's chest, pushing him away from the refugees. Undaunted, Wallenberg raced to the opposite part of the station, hoisting himself atop one of the sealed freight cars, where he said through the air vents, "Are there any Swedish-protected Jews in there who've lost their passes?"

Disembodied voices screamed "yes" and hands reached through the air vents. Wallenberg raced along the roof, thrusting blank passes into the outstretched hands. The Arrow Cross ordered Wallenberg down, but he stayed until the soldiers fired a volley over his head, and he finally left the roof. In a few minutes, Wallenberg reappeared along with a gendarme officer and a squad of Hungarian soldiers, convinced by his cigarettes and rum to support the Swedish diplomat. Only then did the Arrow Cross let Wallenberg extract the Jews holding Swedish passes, Jews who said they had lost their passes and Jews seized before they could get their passes at the Swedish embassy.

Before he could leave with these survivors, the Arrow Cross demanded that Wallenberg had already listed these Jews in his registry. Wallenberg, who opened the large leather-bound book containing the names of "his" Jews, said loudly, "I have passes for the following people." Looking at a blank page, Wallenberg then read the most common Jewish last names.

The Jews, either hearing their name or understanding the trick, moved forward and said Wallenberg had called their name. As they did, Wallenberg asked them to repeat their full names, which Vilmos Langfelder, his driver, rapidly wrote on a blank pass.

Then Wallenberg pretended to mark off each name in the register. "So here you are. We had to bring it to you," he told one Jew. "Sorry you couldn't make it to the legation on time," he told another.

While saving human beings, Wallenberg also chastised the Arrow Cross. "See, I have a pass for this man, and you took him away before I could give it to him." When confident that he had intimidated the guards, Wallenberg yelled to the Jews, "Which of you has recently lost your Swedish pass? Raise your hand."

Johnny Moser, his assistant, ran through the crowd of Jews whispering, "Raise your hands." The Jews, seeing a chance at survival, thrust their hands into the air.

Now Wallenberg moved through the crowd, touching some raised hands and sending them to Langfelder to get a pass. Pretending to recognize one man, Wallenberg said, "Aha, there you are. I've been looking for you."

"Are you caught without a pass again?" he told another Jew.

To one more, he said, "Why, I just gave you a pass several days ago. Off you go, now," he told yet another.

While he walked through the human forest of hands, Wallenberg repeated softly, "I want to save you all, but they will only let me take a few. So please forgive me, but I must save the young ones because I want to save a nation."

That day, November 23, 1944, Wallenberg saved 300 Jews

from the 3,000 gathered at Hegyeshalom. Of the number saved, 90 percent never had a Schutz-pass.[32]

The Arrow Cross, which had murdered Jews relentlessly, could have easily killed Wallenberg at Hegyeshalom. The fascist thugs had been indoctrinated to think of Jews as subhumans, but here was a brave Christian man. His courage and brazen manner kept him alive.

Not so for the refugees lining the road between Budapest and Hegyeshalom. Bodies, depending on the type of execution, lay in ditches (shooting) or in heaps on the side of the road (hand grenades) or swung from trees (hanging) or squashed (vehicular homicide). Some even took their own lives. Marchers stopped aboard barges anchored in the Danube. A group of observers from the International Red Cross reported that many of these people leaped into the freezing Danube. "Scream after scream piercing the night." The refugees chose death instead of living torture.

By now, the number of Jews left alive in Hungary had dwindled from 225,000 in August to 175,000 in November and Eichmann planned to murder the rest by December. But Szálasi, affected by neutral diplomats' protests and stories of atrocities along the road to Hegyeshalom, suspended the death marches, though Hungarian Jews would still be lent "to the German government for the welfare of the Hungarian nation."

The SS protested, for the survivors were too old and sick to work. Also, since the remaining gas chambers had been closed, the Jews couldn't be exterminated. Nevertheless, Eichmann kept scheming to try and eliminate the last of European Jewry.

On November 27, Eichmann convinced the Arrow Cross government's Defense and Interior ministries to "loan" him the 17,000 people in the Swedish-protected labor brigade. They had stayed in Budapest to dig trenches and remove debris following air raids. These men were the only significant number of healthy Jews left in Budapest, and now Eichmann wanted them to construct earthenworks outside Vienna.

After hearing of Eichmann's triumph, Wallenberg, whose car

the Arrow Cross had stolen again, furiously pedaled on his bicycle toward the freight yards of Józsefváros in eastern Pest. Upon arriving, he raced up the steps of Józsefváros station to find two Arrow Cross guards blocking his path with bayonets. Wallenberg shouted orders and curses at them in German, which neither of the Arrow Cross men knew. Thinking Wallenberg must be a Nazi officer, they lowered their bayonets and he raced through the station's warehouse to the loading platform.

The scene was like Hegyeshalom, but with a major difference. Thousands of Jews stood in columns before the empty freight cars while several others had already been loaded and sealed. But this time the SS, not the Arrow Cross, was in command. The SS officer in charge took out his sidearm and pointed it at Wallenberg, who, as always, was only armed with his wits. Unintimidated, Wallenberg jumped up and down, yelling and swearing in German, "This is an outrage. An outrage. How dare you threaten a diplomatic representative of the kingdom of Sweden."

Wallenberg's perfect German and authoritative manner unsettled the SS officer, who reholstered his gun. Seeing that his bravado was working, Wallenberg kept screaming and jumping. "And this, too, is an outrage," he shouted, pointing at the Jews. "I have it on good authority that among those arrested by you for deportation are Jews protected by the king of Sweden. How dare you rob them of their freedom. Release them at once."

The officer stopped the loading as everyone, Jews and guards, watched this incredible sight. "At once, or I'll lodge a formal diplomatic protest with your superiors," screamed Wallenberg, who knew the Germans feared and respected authority.

The SS officer submitted to Wallenberg's demands. Wallenberg immediately walked down the platform, screaming, "Anyone holding a Swedish protective pass fall out of line and follow me." Dozens of men did so. Wallenberg stopped at one of the sealed freight cars and ordered a guard: "Open it. There may be men inside holding Swedish passes."

The door opened, but the SS officer raced over and said,

"Anyone with a Swedish pass can come out, but if anyone tries to bluff, I'll shoot him on the spot."

Dozens of men made the most difficult choices in their lives and stepped outside, deciding that remaining in the car meant dying. By now, Wallenberg's aides had arrived, holding his registry of protected Jews. Wallenberg sat at a folding table he had brought, checking the passes with those in the registry as the SS officer periodically looked to make sure he was accepting authentic documents.

John Szenes, a survivor who was in one of the cars, said, "I had a passport, but the passport was forged. Wallenberg looked at me and said, 'I know this man well. I gave him the passport personally. Let's not waste our time. The line is long.' The commanding police officer who was present and checked in the register books agreed. He didn't check my passport."[33]

One Jew handed his pass to Wallenberg and whispered, "It's a fake."

Wallenberg said aloud, "Ah, you again. I certainly don't need to check your pass. I remember giving it to you personally just the other day."

However, only about fifty men among the thousands at the station had legitimate Swedish passes. Wallenberg had to do something to save more lives.

"There must be hundreds of men whose passes were stolen by your people when they were collected," he told the SS officer. "I'll take them with me as well."

Befuddled and intimidated, the SS officer didn't object.

Wallenberg yelled to the remaining Jews, "Which of you has documents in Hungarian proving that you once held a valid Swedish pass?"

Several men immediately understood Wallenberg's ploy. First in a trickle and then a flood, they came forward, fetching any piece of paper printed in Hungarian that seemed official.

Wallenberg commanded, "Present those documents to me at once."

About 250 men leaped out of the freight cars and lined up in front of Wallenberg while waving pieces of paper that could save their lives. With great earnestness, Wallenberg examined each scrap of paper, which included ration cards, tax forms, post office receipts and vaccination certificates.

Then solemnly he pronounced, "Yes, obviously you had one. You, too," he told another while pretending to check each piece of paper. Ever a gambler, Wallenberg had correctly guessed that the SS officer, like himself, could not read any Hungarian.

Rapidly, Wallenberg's aides gave these Jews new passes and put the men into trucks along with those holding legitimate passes. That day Wallenberg left Józsefváros Station with about 300 Jews.

He brought them to Swedish-protected houses and then bought a bouquet of flowers for Baroness Kemény, who was being sent to her family's home in northern Italy. The police had told interior minister Vajna the baroness had become a Wallenberg agent. Vajna wanted her arrested, but Szálasi intervened, so the baroness had to leave Budapest within twenty-four hours.

The next day Wallenberg learned the SS planned to deport more Jews from Józsefváros Station. He tried to repeat his earlier performance, but this time Eichmann had placed an experienced aide in charge, who ousted Wallenberg despite his protests. When Wallenberg complained to the German legation, he was told he couldn't be protected "from the consequences" of his actions.

"Several weeks ago a German military truck demolished one of my official cars," Wallenberg said. "Since then, other cars have been the victims of similar 'accidents.' Is this what you mean by 'the consequences'?" Wallenberg was told to return to "peaceful Sweden."

In the next week, Eichmann deported 17,000 men of the international labor brigades from Józsefváros Station. Wallenberg saved just 300. Most of those deported were kept in concentration camps and died of disease, starvation or torture.

Wallenberg had other failures. Horvath Arpad, former chief stage director of the National Theater in Budapest, worked in the resistance movement under the cover name of "Uncle Laci."[34] Several times the Arrow Cross followed Uncle Laci, and one time the Hungarian fascists were so close, he expected to be arrested. Then Wallenberg's car appeared.

Uncle Laci, not knowing who was in the car, flagged down the vehicle and when it stopped, he jumped in and said in German, "Help, help, I am a communist."

The Arrow Cross reached the car and raised their machine gun, but Wallenberg defended this unknown man, who said he was persecuted for his political beliefs. Wallenberg told the Arrow Cross the motorcar is "Swedish territory."

After an exchange of words, the Arrow Cross left. Wallenberg took Uncle Laci to the other end of the city and let him go, but later, Uncle Laci was arrested. Wallenberg intervened at the military tribunal, but "Horvath Arpad perished."

The remaining Jews of Budapest fell in two categories: Protected and unprotected. The unprotected were either too young, too old, too sick or without influence and thus had failed to get protective passes. All unprotected Jews were put into a ghetto, a tenth of a square mile in Pest's Seventh District, where there already were houses carrying the Yellow Star, indicating Jews lived inside. Jews who lived in houses with yellow stars outside the ghetto would have to move in there and give their houses to Christian families living in the area designated for the ghetto.

During late November and early December, 75,000 unprotected and hungry Jews moved into the central ghetto's 243 usable houses. They could only take what they could carry, but Arrow Cross gangs stole most of that. Once inside the ghetto, an average of 209 Jews lived in each house. As in the Warsaw ghetto, a tall wooden fence that the Jews paid for and built encircled the ghetto. A gate stood at each of the four main compass points, guarded by the Arrow Cross and policemen.

Jews could only walk the ghetto streets for two hours a day, and the authorities arrested any Jews found outside the ghetto and returned them there. Eichmann ordered the ghetto sealed December 10, so Jews could enter but not leave.

This concentration of Jews simplified Eichmann's task of extermination. If he could get enough transportation, he could send all the Jews to concentration camps. Or, if the Russians were about to overrun Budapest, he could bomb the ghetto from the air and blast it with tanks. Outside the ghetto, the only Jews left alive in Budapest were 15,000 in hiding, the 35,000 protected Jews living in their own "International Ghetto," also in Pest, and the 6,000 children kept in Red Cross shelters.

Allotted only 4,500 passes by the government, Wallenberg had issued 9,000 to let Jews live in Swedish-protected houses and 14,000 overall. Many more had fake passes, but Wallenberg let them stay there and bribed the Arrow Cross not to oust them.

Amidst all this death and danger, Wallenberg was directly involved in one birth. Tibor Vándor desperately needed help November 3, 1944.[35] His wife was in labor with their first child, but no hospital would accommodate them. Wallenberg took the Vándors to his apartment and while the wife gave birth in his bedroom, Wallenberg slept in the corridor, his coat a blanket.

In the morning, the Vándors asked Wallenberg into his room to see their daughter, a dark-haired child. As that child, Yvonne Singer, later explained, "In the morning, when I was born, my father went outside the door and said to please come in and would he be my godfather, and he accepted and in fact gave me my name."

Originally, Wallenberg chose Nina Maria Ava, but with his permission the name was changed to Yvonne Maria Ava. When the war ended, the Vándors went to Switzerland, Holland and then Canada, where Yvonne grew up as a Christian. She married Ron Singer of Toronto and converted to Judaism, unaware of her Jewish roots. Her parents had only told her she had been born in Hungary during the war. Some years later a relative told Yvonne she had been born Jewish. Though she pressed her parents for details, they refused to talk about the war anymore.

A Toronto Star story on October 20, 1979, specified

Wallenberg's heroics, referring to the Vándors and Yvonne's birth. Yvonne Singer read it and started crying so hard she could hardly read the newspaper. Since then, many other Hungarian Jews in Canada have discovered their links to Raoul Wallenberg and those frightening days in Budapest.

In early December 1944, every Jew in Budapest was again in great danger. Kemény told Wallenberg unless the Swedish government recognized his government before December 14, he would cancel the Jews' protected privilege and give them to Vajna, a death sentence. Wallenberg knew Sweden would never recognize the criminal Arrow Cross government, so he had to stall in hopes the Russians would overrun Budapest.

Perhaps as a hopeful sign, Russian artillery rounds landed in the middle of Budapest December 8 as part of a new offensive to seize the city. As the end came near, Wallenberg told his trusted aides the American War Refugee Board had sent him to Budapest while the American government and private Jewish philanthropies had given some of the funds he used. After the war ended, he planned to use more contributions to start a humanitarian organization to aid homeless and destitute Jews.

The Russian army breached the defenses north of Budapest December 9, cutting off the roads and rails to the north, south and east, with only the west remaining open. Thereafter, most of the Arrow Cross government, including Baron Kemény, had fled west, leaving only Gábor Vajna and Adolf Eichmann to stay.

On December 8, Wallenberg wrote his last letter and had a final confrontation with Eichmann. His final letter, addressed to his mother, spoke of the danger in Budapest and his regret he couldn't spend the holidays with his family in Stockholm.

> Dearest Mother,[36]
> I don't know how to atone for my silence, and yet again today all you will receive from me are a few hurried lines via the diplomatic pouch.
> The situation here is hectic, fraught with danger, and I

am terribly snowed under with work . . . Night and day we hear the thunder of the approaching Russian guns. Since Szálasi came to power diplomatic activity has been very lively. I myself am almost the sole representative of our embassy in all government departments. So far I have been approximately ten times to the Ministry of Foreign Affairs, have seen the Deputy Premier twice, the Minister of the Interior twice, the Minister of Supply once, and the Minister of Finance once.

I was on pretty close terms with the wife of the Foreign Minister. Regrettably she has now left for Meran. There is an acute lack of food supplies in Budapest, but we managed to stockpile a fair amount in advance. I have the feeling that after the [Russian] occupation it will be difficult to get home and I assume that I will reach Stockholm only around Easter. But all that lies in the future. So far, nobody knows what the occupation will be like. In any event, I shall try to get home as soon as possible.

I had firmly believed I would spend Christmas with you. Now I am compelled to send you my Christmas greetings and New Year wishes by this means. I hope that the longed-for peace is not too far distant.
Raoul.

The same day Wallenberg sent this letter he returned to his apartment in Buda just as Eichmann and an aide arrived. Preoccupied with saving lives, Wallenberg had forgotten he had invited Eichmann, who was dressed in a civilian suit, to dinner. Immediately, Wallenberg pretended everything was in order. He took both Germans into his apartment, gave them a drink and went to another room to call fellow diplomat Lars Berg. "I've got Eichmann here, and I've forgotten that I invited him to dinner. Can you set up something this quickly?"

Berg could and did. He and Göte Carlsson, another Swedish diplomat, lived close by in the mansion of a wealthy Hungarian count who some had accused of having Jewish blood. The count fled and left everything—including his houses, servants and antiques—to Berg. With the arrangements in place, Wallenberg told Eichmann and his aide of the change in dining location and walked with them to Berg's house.

While Wallenberg talked of everything but the war and Eichmann relaxed, everyone dined from the count's expensive china, used his silver knives to slice the meat and enjoyed fine wines from his cellar. When dinner ended, Wallenberg carefully steered everyone to the large sitting room for coffee and brandy. He seated Eichmann in a comfortable chair facing curtains the servants had drawn to cover the room's large windows that faced east. As Eichmann played with his brandy snifter, Carlsson, acting on Wallenberg's orders, pulled open the curtains and Wallenberg turned out the lights.

The eastern sky exploded in sight and sound. Without the curtains, everyone saw and heard the Russian advance. The Russian artillery barrage lit up the eastern horizon while the thumps of the guns were audible. Time after time the red flashes of light exploded from the Russian rounds flying westward toward Budapest. The explosions lit the room and as they faded, plunged it back into darkness. Wallenberg, standing near the window, stayed there for several seconds as Eichmann watched from his seat, which no longer felt so comfortable.

Like a teacher talking to a dull student, Wallenberg began to lecture Eichmann about the principles of Nazism. "Nazism is not really a bona fide ideology. It's just the political incarnation of a single basic human emotion: Hate. How can it last?"

Shocked at this assault on his beliefs, Eichmann counterattacked with pat phrases and unrelated thoughts about the "Jewish-Bolshevik menace."

Wallenberg gestured out the window. "Look how close the Bolsheviks are," his voice rising and his demeanor changing. "Your war is almost over. Nazism is doomed, finished and so are those who cling to this hatred until the last minute. It's the end of the Nazis, the end of Hitler, the end of Eichmann."

"All right, I agree with you," said Eichmann in a calm voice. "I've never believed in all of Hitler's ideology, but it has, after all, given me a great deal of power and wealth ... The Russians will take my horses, my dogs and my palace in Budapest. They'll probably shoot me on the spot. For me, there's no escape, no liberation. There are, however, some consolations. If I continue to eliminate our enemies until the end, it may delay, if only for a few days, our defeat. And then, when I finally do walk to the gallows, at least I'll know I've completed my mission."

When Eichmann finished his colloquy, he rose to leave. As he shook hands with Wallenberg, he said aloud, "I want to thank you for an exceptionally charming and interesting evening." Then he lowered his voice and said, "Now, don't think we're friends; we're not. I plan to do everything to keep you from saving your Jews. Your diplomatic passport won't protect you from everything. Even a neutral diplomat can meet with an accident."

Two weeks later, on December 22, the Soviet army breached the Balaton-Danube defense line southwest of Budapest. All roads but two were cut off and the complete encirclement of Budapest was just days away.

Gábor Vajna ordered all Jews in hiding outside the ghetto to go inside or face death. He then fled and left a brother, Dr. Ernö Vajna, another vigorous anti-Semite, in charge of Budapest's defense and the disposition of Jews.

Eichmann's boasts of staying to meet his fate were as false as his Nazi ideology. He also planned to flee, but before going he ordered all Jewish children from the Red Cross shelters into the central ghetto. That way he could kill as many Jews as possible. He told the SS unit left in Budapest that, "No Jew must come out of the ghetto alive."

Eichmann left December 22 on the only open road to the west. Two days later the Russians reached the outskirts of Buda and on December 26, the day after Christmas, the Russians cut the final road open to the west, surrounding Budapest.

Trapped within the Russian circle were 750,000 Christians, 140,000 Jews, 80,000 Germans and Hungarian soldiers, several thousand Arrow Cross soldiers and a few neutral diplomats, including Wallenberg.

With all established order gone, anarchy ruled. Gangs of young Arrow Cross toughs murdered at will, grabbing Jews from the ghetto, homes, streets, hospitals and air raid shelters. These thugs tied rocks to their belts and used them as whips. Execution squads marched Jews to the Danube, where the Arrow Cross played a murderous game. They shackled together three Jews, who were stripped naked, and then shot the middle one in the back of the head. The dead man or woman's collapse into the Danube carried his two companions with him rapidly down the river to their own deaths. This preserved bullets, but sometimes, for amusement, other Arrow Cross hooligans would throw Jews who were still alive into the Danube and then fire at them while betting who could hit the most watery targets. In Budapest, civilization had ended.

But that did not stop Raoul Wallenberg. He went everywhere, threatening, cajoling, bribing and preventing the Arrow Cross from murdering Jews.

Monsignor Bela Varga, a Budapest survivor, said he saw Wallenberg with an Arrow Cross patrol that had captured some young Jewish girls. "Raoul Wallenberg was standing there, and he was speaking with the head of this patrol. We were standing behind him and he put some package into the pocket of the officer. After that, he began to speak to the other soldiers that 'I am the representative of the Swedish king, and these girls are under my protection.' The leader of the patrol commanded them, and they left and the poor girls were crying like babies."[37]

Yosef Lapid, a survivor from those days in Budapest, said "total anarchy was reigning." Wallenberg lacked any way to defend himself "or to protest if they shoot (sic) him right there on the spot," Lapid said. "He was standing up against a group of Hungarian hooligans armed to the teeth, murderers, villains. The fact that he succeeded in commanding them was an exercise of authority that is today very hard to imagine."[38]

The Arrow Cross also brought other Jews into the cellars of Arrow Cross barracks, where they stripped and tortured their captives. The Budapest Institute of Forensic Medicine, which collected some of the bodies, later said, "From the distorted faces of the corpses, the conclusion could be drawn that their sufferings had been ghastly. Very few blown-out brains or heart-shots were to be found; on the other hand, there was overwhelming evidence of the most brutal ill-treatment. Shooting out of eyes, scalping, deliberate breaking of bones, and abdominal knife wounds were Nyilas (Arrow Cross) specialties."

Two particularly cruel Arrow Cross assassins—one female, one male—were Mrs. Vilmos Salzer, who arrived nightly in the cellars wearing riding boots and carrying a riding crop and a Thompson submachine gun. This upper class matron's specialty was burning women's genitals with candles before killing them. A male counterpart was Father Andras Kun, a Minorite monk, dressed in a black cape. This madman's speciality was to hold a crucifix in one hand, a pistol in the other and order executions while shouting, "In the holy name of Jesus Christ, fire."

During those days in Budapest, the life of a Jew depended on the inclination of a teen-age Arrow Cross boy with a rifle. The Arrow Cross thugs began fighting among themselves over jurisdictional disputes or for the spoils of Jewish goods taken during raids. Insane with killing, the Arrow Cross invaded the Swedish legation and shot at Christian men in ambulances that came to aid wounded Jews. No one in Budapest, including Wallenberg, was safe. One local Arrow Cross leader, Miklós Desi-Dregan, had reproduced numerous pictures of Wallenberg and had them on the walls of Arrow Cross headquarters in Buda. He gave them to squad leaders and told the gangs "if this low-class Jew-lover ever sets foot in Buda, shoot him on the spot."

Rather than hide, Wallenberg retaliated as a diplomat, as an administrator and finally as a guerrilla. First, he filed diplomatic protests about the atrocities with the German command and with Dr. Ernö Vajna as well as with the other Arrow Cross officials who in theory controlled Budapest. The terror intensified in late December and early January, so Wallenberg's notes of diplomatic protest became harsher.

The Arrow Cross wanted to move the 35,000 protected Jews from the international ghetto, or the protected houses, into the central ghetto, which was already overcrowded and filled with starving people. Once inside the sealed ghetto, Wallenberg knew they would be subject to a last-minute annihilation. An informant had told Wallenberg that Dr. Vajna planned to exterminate the Jews in the central ghetto with machine guns.

Despite his protests, 5,000 Swedish Jews were marched into the central ghetto on January 5. The next day the remaining 30,000 Swedish Jews had to assemble in front of their homes for their transfer. Wallenberg, at the last minute, made a deal with Dr. Vajna. The Swedish Jews would stay in the international ghetto, and Wallenberg in exchange would give the Arrow Cross government all the food stored in the Swedish houses, keeping only enough to feed his Swedish Jews for three days.

Wallenberg, who had purchased the precious food in the fall, had kept it hidden in the basements of his homes. Now he made this desperate sacrifice, certain the Russians would overrun the capital in a matter of days.

To maintain the myth that the hoodlum Arrow Cross was a legitimate government, Wallenberg wrote a respectful letter to Vajna, confirming their agreement. That made the Arrow Cross leaders think they were a legitimate government among civilized countries and could be recognized by a major neutral power like Sweden.

"We had orders from Stockholm never to do that," explained Per Anger.[39]

While he used flattery with the Arrow Cross, Wallenberg increased his Swedish passes and by the end of December 15,000 Jews held passes he had signed. Many more were kept in the Swedish houses in the international ghetto. Wallenberg's section fed these Jews, gave them medical care and protected them from the Arrow Cross. When possible, Wallenberg smuggled food and medical supplies to the unprotected Jews in the central ghetto.

During this reign of terror, Wallenberg kept issuing passes, which he personally signed. He also kept an information network, alerting him where the Arrow Cross would strike next and where they had taken Jews in other raids. His informants were men of the regular police, the gendarmerie and some of the Arrow Cross. They helped either because they were horrified by the Arrow Cross' appalling acts or because Wallenberg had bribed them or because they feared the war crime trials that would follow the Allied Occupation.

Aided by this information, Wallenberg ran around Budapest halting executions along the Danube, saving Jews from Arrow Cross basements and arranging for guards to protect Swedish houses set for an attack. His courage, administrative skill and street smarts made him the most powerful man in a city of anarchy.

Wallenberg kept his knapsack in the back of his car and slept only when he became too exhausted to continue and then rarely in the same place for two straight nights. He carried a revolver, which he never used, even though the Arrow Cross executed anyone with a weapon. To further confuse the Arrow Cross, Wallenberg dressed his most Aryan-looking Jewish aides in Arrow Cross uniforms and told them to challenge the real Arrow Cross men and seize their papers. These he gave to other Aryan-looking Jews.

Also, Wallenberg bribed policeman to round up Jews with Swedish passes in the central ghetto and march them in a military formation out of the ghetto, past the Arrow Cross and into the Swedish houses. When he heard that Johnny Moser, the young Jewish aide who had helped him at Hegyeshalom, had been captured by the SS for impersonating a German soldier, he had Langfelder go to the SS checkpoint where Moser was held. As they arrived, the Germans were leading Moser away. Langfelder slowed the car and Wallenberg opened the door, shouting, "Johnny. Quick. Jump in." Moser raced into the car, and Langfelder roared away to safety.

To one aide, Wallenberg explained, "I like this dangerous game. I love this dangerous game."

"The Nazis and the Arrow Cross hated him," Anger said. "He was the Jewish hero, the hero of all the Jewish people, and he was the enemy of the Nazis."[40]

Although it seemed impossible, things became worse for the Hungarian Jews on January 7. Pál Szalay, a top police officer of the Arrow Cross, but a Wallenberg ally, told Wallenberg the Arrow Cross leaders who might have kept order had fled and the worst elements had taken over. The next day an Arrow Cross squad attacked a Swedish house where Wallenberg had placed some of his closest aides, who had identity cards and protective passes. The Arrow Cross raiders rampaged through the house, firing their weapons and beating everyone in sight. They had come for Wallenberg, but he never slept there. After a week, 180 of the 280 Jews taken were killed and that represented Wallenberg's biggest setback.

The increased Arrow Cross attacks, the persistent Russian barrage and the taking of power by the worst element of the Arrow Cross hampered Wallenberg's mobility, but he refused to hide. After an Arrow Cross attack on Christmas Eve, the Swedish legation no longer operated and to protect themselves, its diplomats had separated. Wallenberg was the only one who remained in Pest with his Jews. Per Anger, in his last conversation with Wallenberg, tried to convince him on January 10 to come to Buda with the other diplomats, but he refused.

When Anger asked if Wallenberg ever became frightened, he responded, "Sure, I get scared sometimes. But I don't have any choice. I took on this mission, and now I could never go back to Stockholm unless I knew inside myself that I'd done everything to save as many Jews as possible."

Anger continued, "He kept telling me he was afraid. And I

thought that only a man who can admit that is probably genuinely courageous."[41]

On January 11, Wallenberg finally went into hiding, choosing a house on 16 Benczur Street that was protected by the International Red Cross and near the advancing Russian army. Laszlo Ocskay, the Hungarian manager of Socony Vacuum Oil Company, owned the house. Many of his business associates and 25 or so other Jews, mainly rich industrialists, lived there. A German colonel who dined frequently with these cultured Jews protected them and put an SS guard outside the house to keep the Arrow Cross away.

Amazingly enough, as a young man, Eichmann had worked for Socony.[42] After high school, Eichmann, who then lived in Linz, Austria, worked for Socony as a traveling representative. While at Socony, he had traveled, enjoyed life and made friends. In 1933, Socony dismissed Eichmann as part of a company move to cut its staff. Eichmann lied and told his father the company had hired a new Jewish inspector, who had dismissed him for belonging to the Nazi Party. After his firing, Eichmann joined an SS brigade in Germany and devoted his life to war not commerce.

While Wallenberg took refuge in the house on Benczur Street, he went over the postwar humanitarian plan he had created earlier. He felt thousands of Jews who had fled Hungary would try to return and most would be impoverished and without families. As envisioned, his organization would find jobs for these Jews, reunite them with survivors and help those who were penniless. He also wanted to compensate those people who had saved their lives, but lost their possessions during the siege of Budapest.

Ever the humanitarian, Wallenberg wanted to meet with the Soviet Army as soon as possible and visit its headquarters in Debrecen, Hungary, near the Romanian border, to gain the confidence of the Soviet commander. While sitting against the stoves and cold chest in his basement refuge on the morning of January 13, 1945, Wallenberg heard the sound of smashed walls and foreign voices.

Budapest buildings were often connected via underground

passages, cisterns and corridors, some that the Turks had built. The Russians tried to advance through this route to minimize losses and surprise the enemy.

The basement walls of the Benczur Street house rattled and cracked while pieces hit the floor and dust clouds covered the room. After the dust settled, a Russian soldier put his head through a hole in the wall and Wallenberg saw his first Russian liberator. The Russians expanded the hole and 15 moved through into the kitchen. Two whispered to the Jews that they were also Jewish, but to remain silent about that, for they feared the anti-Semites among the Russian ranks.

When Wallenberg found a Russian who spoke German, he explained he was a Swedish diplomat and removed papers from his pocket showing that he, like every Swedish diplomat in Budapest, had been responsible for representing the Soviet Union and protecting its property during the war.

Hours later, the soldier returned with two high-ranking Soviet officers who questioned Wallenberg in a nearby room. Afterward, Wallenberg told the Jews he would accompany the Russians, "but I don't think I shall be away for the night."

The Russian secret police and Army officers interrogated Wallenberg for the next three days. Some of these officers may have belonged to a special political branch of the Russian 18th Army, commanded by Major General Leonid I. Brezhnev. Initially, the interviews were polite, but as they continued the suspicion mounted against Wallenberg. Since Wallenberg spoke such excellent German, the Soviets suspected he was a German or a spy, or both.

Some accounts say Wallenberg tried to make the Russians start a relief program for the Jews in now-liberated Pest. Or, he may have tried to convince his Russian hosts to stop directing fire at the Swedish legation in Buda. Also, he may have discussed his altruistic plans for postwar relief, which the Soviets may have thought threatened their own, and far different, plans. In any event, he exacerbated their suspicions.

When not under interrogation, Wallenberg moved through the liberated areas of Pest, and he visited his offices and friends, including Karl Muller, who had escaped from the Arrow Cross headquarters in Buda by bribing a guard. Muller explained the wretched condition of the Jews in Buda, and Wallenberg said he would go there as soon as possible. Muller warned that Wallenberg's life was endangered because his picture had been distributed to Arrow Cross units in Buda. Wallenberg replied, "My life is one life, but this is a matter of saving thousands of lives."

Which was exactly what he did. As the Russians interrogated Wallenberg, the Germans and the Arrow Cross planned to annihilate the 70,000 Jews in the Central Ghetto. On January 15, Wallenberg learned though his intelligence system that Eichmann's plan to exterminate the ghetto's inhabitants would happen almost immediately. One of Pal Szalay's men said 500 German soldiers and 22 Arrow Cross thugs had gathered at the Royal Hotel. They planned to invade the Central Ghetto and shoot the residents while 200 policemen were being mobilized to guard the ghetto fence and make certain no Jews fled. This would bring to reality Wallenberg's worst nightmare.

Taking Szalay with him for protection, Wallenberg raced to see Dr. Vajna, then listed as Budapest's commissioner of defense. Dr. Vajna knew of the extermination plan, but he didn't care about saving himself or the consequences from any war crime tribunal, so he refused to intervene.

General August Schmidthuber became the only person who could prevent the extermination. Since the SS was now looking for Wallenberg, he could not go there himself. Szalay volunteered in his stead and told the German general that if the extermination occurred, Wallenberg would make certain Schmidthuber was held responsible and hang as a war criminal. The Russians were moving closer by the moment to the ghetto, so the Germans didn't have enough time to find and kill Wallenberg. After some indecision while he probably wondered how the rough rope would feel around this neck, Schmidthuber decided he cared more about his survival than a massacre. He called Vajna on the telephone first, then called a German captain and told them to cancel the operation.

Wallenberg had not been there with Szalay, but Schmidthuber knew of his threats regarding postwar criminal trials. The Jews in the Central Ghetto, through Wallenberg's courageous efforts, had been saved.

Two days later, on January 17, the Russians rolled into Pest and liberated the International Ghetto, where they found 25,000 Jews alive and another 69,000 Jews in the Central Ghetto. After the Russians seized the Buda side, they found about 25,000 more Jews, who came out of their secreted places, in Gentile homes, church cellars, convents and monasteries.

Overall, about 120,000 Jews had survived. Per Anger, Wallenberg's fellow diplomat, gives his colleague full credit for saving the Jews in both the International and Central Ghettos. "How many people did Raoul Wallenberg save? (It's) quite impossible to give an exact figure . . . fifteen thousand to twenty thousand lodged in the safehouses, railway stations . . . His great contribution was that he managed to save the ghetto—seventy thousand."[43] No one knows for sure, but most likely, Wallenberg saved at least 100,000 Hungarian Jews.

Raoul Wallenberg had defeated Adolf Eichmann and saved 100,000 lives. However, at the moment of his greatest triumph, Wallenberg was headed to Debrecen and oblivion.

CHAPTER 3

When Raoul Wallenberg left Budapest on the morning of January 17, 1945, with his driver, Vilmos Langfelder, he planned to meet with Marshal Rodion Malinovsky at his headquarters in Debrecen, Hungary, which is near the Romanian border. Wallenberg thought the meeting was to discuss postwar redevelopment of Budapest, the rebuilding of the city and the resettlement of refugees. Before he left, however, Wallenberg had misgivings and a premonition about the meeting, telling a Jewish relief office in Budapest, "I'm going," he said, but "I don't know if it's as their guest or their prisoner."[1]

Though scheduled to return to Budapest that night, he was never seen again in the free world. Wallenberg and Langfelder started driving to Debrecen January 17, hoping to see the Russian Supreme Command to stop the Red Army from shooting at the Swedish Legation. The Russian NKVD (the secret police, later called KGB) stopped them outside of Budapest and took the pair to Debrecen. At first, the Soviets treated Wallenberg and Langfelder courteously, but that quickly changed.

A Russian major asked Wallenberg for all of his papers.[2]

"I am a diplomat, I can only let you have such papers as I consider it right to let you have," Wallenberg said.

"I said all papers," the major replied.

"That means you arrest us."

"You may consider it that way."

After a few days, the Soviets said that Wallenberg and Langfelder must meet with higher authorities, so the Soviets took them by train and under guard to Moscow via Bessarabia—a Romanian region bordering the then Soviet Union—and then via

Odessa and Kiev.[3] While at a railroad station in Romania, Wallenberg slipped a note to a worker or peasant, asking him to forward it to Sweden. The note said Wallenberg had been arrested and was on his way to Russia.

After stopping briefly at an internment camp for foreigners near Focsani, which is in eastern Romania, Wallenberg and Langfelder changed trains. In Kiev, Wallenberg and Langfelder left the train and a Soviet officer walked them around the town. Then he bought a newspaper and read the latest news of the front to his two prisoners.[4]

During the trip, the guards were polite, but Wallenberg still must have wondered if he were a guest or a prisoner. Since wartime travel was so slow, the 1,500 mile trip to Moscow took Wallenberg and Langfelder two weeks. Upon arriving in Moscow January 31, 1945, the Soviets and their prisoners took the subway to Dzerzhinsky Square, which had a four-story building on one side and a taller modern building next door containing a top floor without windows. Combined, the buildings were Lubyanka, the NKVD's headquarters.

Lubyanka was the Soviet prison system's clearinghouse. There, new arrivals were processed, their fingerprints and photographs taken and a file established. This file, which always stayed at Lubyanka, was a brown, manila folder with the inmate's name, number and status of his case stamped in the top right-hand corner, and it contained the prisoner's travels through the gulag.

Now, both Wallenberg and Langfelder realized their status. They were marched to separate cells and never saw each other again. Then came the interrogation.

Eberhard Muller, the fictitious name of a German vice corporal imprisoned by the Soviets, said he had shared cell 105 with Langfelder, who told him about his travels to Moscow. The Soviets interrogated Langfelder twice, giving him the impression their captors considered them spies.[5]

Most interrogation came at night "through long, subterranean corridors (as prisoners) are brought up to an almost luxurious interrogation room.[6] All the way the guard hits the buckle of his belt," signaling other guards to prevent another transport of prisoners from crossing the corridor and making sure no one sees anyone being brought in or out from interrogation. The questioners operated in an office with a high ceiling, designed for pre-revolution insurance executives. Before the overthrow, this had been the office of the Rossiya Insurance Company.

The secret police accused Wallenberg of spying for the Germans and of helping Nazis escape their punishment for working against the Soviets.

"I am a diplomat and a Swedish citizen," Wallenberg explained. "I was working in Budapest to save Jews from Nazi persecution. I even represented Soviet interests in Hungary."

During the war, Sweden acted as a protective power for the Soviet Union in Hungary and thus expected the Soviets to give Swedish diplomats sympathetic treatment. Furthermore, when the Soviets invaded Budapest, Wallenberg seems to have acted as Swedish chargé d'affaires.

The secret police could never believe that. "What would you be doing working for Soviet interests? We know who you are. You're a member of an important capitalist family in Sweden."

After the interrogation, a guard marched Wallenberg back to his cell and his German cellmates. Wallenberg shared a cell with his former enemy, who populated many of Lubyanka's cells in 1945. Two men incarcerated with Wallenberg were Gustav Richter, a former policeman at the Germany Embassy in Bucharest, and Otto Scheuer, an Austrian lieutenant.[7]

Inside his cell, the guards closely watched Wallenberg and every other prisoner. Every one or two minutes, a guard looked through a peephole to see if Wallenberg or his mates were sleeping, knocking on the wall or getting too close to the single window, a minute opening way up on the wall.

Daily, the guards took Wallenberg and his cellmates to a yard atop the building, where an 18-foot high fence stopped them from looking out, though they could hear traffic on Dzerzhinsky Square while they looked at both the sun and the sky. The prisoners marched in pairs, with their hands behind their backs. An armed guard always watched the prisoners, who were forbidden to speak or stop. They couldn't speak at night either while trying to sleep beneath a two-hundred-watt bulb. Talk was only permitted during the day and inside the cell. Then Wallenberg told his new companions about his exploits in Budapest while constantly worrying that imprisonment would besmirch his name.

Richter, the erstwhile German policeman, consoled him. "In the circumstances, it is certainly no cause for embarrassment. I don't think it will damage your good name."

In March 1945, Wallenberg was transferred to another cell at Lubyanka, where his new cellmates, a man named Willi Roedel and a Czech, Jan Loyda, immediately recognized him from the description given by their previous cellmate, Vilmos Langfelder.[8] Wallenberg was happy to hear Langfelder was alive, but he had left Lubyanka and no one ever heard from him again. Later, a Swiss prisoner told Muller that Roedel had really been chief of the Sicherheitsdienst, Heinrich Himmler's police organization, and boss of the Swiss, who had worked in Himmler's Waffen SS as well as for the Allied Information Service. When Roedel and Wallenberg were incarcerated together, one author wrote, "The Jew murderer Roedel and the Jew rescuer Wallenberg shared a cell."[9]

Supposedly, the Soviets used Roedel, who died in a slave labor camp in 1949, to spy on Wallenberg.[10]

The Soviets transferred Muller to Butyrka Prison on April 6, 1945, and a month later the Czech was transferred to Muller's cell. Only in November 1946 did Muller talk to the Czech about Wallenberg. He explained after Langfelder was transferred from the cell, another prisoner was put there. "That was Langfelder's Swedish boss, Wallenberg."

During his stay at Lubyanka, Wallenberg also met a Finn and a German Admiral, known only as Kraft, according to Muller.[11] The Finn eventually was put in Muller's cell and told him how the Russians had mistreated him because they thought the Finn knew something about Wallenberg and Langfelder. When Muller asked the Finn about Wallenberg, he "beat his chest and screamed, 'What would it help? I know that I will never be free. The Russians will come and kill me. I have heard something and still I know nothing.'"[12]

His fears were justified, for the Soviets dealt harshly with anyone that had met with Wallenberg or met someone who had met with him. Everyone who shared a cell with Wallenberg or Langfelder was sharply questioned by the Soviets about their knowledge of Wallenberg and his experiences in Budapest as well as in Soviet captivity. Afterward, these prisoners were placed in isolated cells with no way to communicate with other prisoners. As the Swedish Foreign Office said, "The treatment accorded these prisoners after they had been questioned suggests that the Soviet authorities sought to prevent as far as possible any further spreading of knowledge of the Swedish diplomat."[13] After the Swedish government protested the Wallenberg case, Muller, the Czech and the Finn were each sentenced on April 24, 1951, to 25 years in prison, but Muller was released in 1954.[14]

A month after Wallenberg arrived in Lubyanka, the Soviets drove him and Roedel across Moscow on the same day the Czech was sent to Butyrka, where he met Muller. Wallenberg and Roedel went to a four-story building that looked like the letter K— Lefortovo prison. There, Wallenberg had a cell, large by Soviet standards—ten feet long by eight feet wide with three beds, one against each side wall and one under the window, a tiny table and a basin with running water. Like Lubyanka, a guard observed them through a peephole, but there not as frequently, only once every two or three minutes.

The Russians repeatedly interrogated Wallenberg, who protested he was a citizen of Sweden, a neutral country, and had represented Russian interests in Budapest. His humanitarian acts did not merit imprisonment. Unlike his efforts against the Germans, Wallenberg failed to achieve any gains against the Russians. His apparent ally had become his enemy.

In the spring of 1946, the Lefortovo guards brought Wallenberg for interrogation, where the secret police accused him of collaborating with the Nazis. Again, he protested and informed them he was a Swedish diplomat. One of his questioners told him, "Your case is quite clear. You are a political case. If you think you are innocent, you must prove it. The best proof of your guilt is that the Swedish government and the Swedish embassy have done nothing for you."

Wallenberg told them he wanted to contact the embassy, but the secret police ignored his requests, telling him, "No one is at all interested in you. If the Swedish government or the embassy cared about you, they would have contacted you ages ago."

When Wallenberg demanded to know what the Soviets would do with him, the Russian told him, "For political reasons, you will never be sentenced."

Back in his cell, Wallenberg felt bitter and betrayed. The Swedes, the Americans, everyone had abandoned him.

Inside Lefortovo, the prisoners had their own language, using the handles of their toothbrushes to knock on the wall for communication. The most popular method was the so-called "idiot system," where one tap meant "A" two "B" and so on. Prisoners also employed the "square system," whereby letters of the alphabet were written out in a square, five letters by five letters, with the "W" deleted. Each letter had two sets of knocks. The first identified which letter in the horizontal column and the second the vertical column. Thus, two taps, a pause and then two taps indicated the letter "G."

All codes and communication were forbidden, and the guards looked through the peephole constantly. Yet with fewer guards at Lefortovo than Lubyanka, the prisoners had more opportunity to knock. To avoid detection, a prisoner usually sat on his bed with a book in one hand and a toothbrush in the other, but concealed behind his back. For further subterfuge, the prisoner would remove his tapping arm from his sleeve and put the sleeve in a normal appearance to avoid suspicion.

To make tapping even more dangerous, the Russians would put spies in the cells to find out what was occurring. A prisoner would never tap unless he were sure of his cell partner. All that made tapping a dangerous and laborious endeavor. Still, the prisoners of Lefortovo had no entertainment and plenty of time. During Wallenberg's early days of captivity, his fellow prisoners called the Swede, "a keen tapper."

If the Soviets caught anyone tapping, the whole cell was put in deep, ice-cold basement cells under the prison and dressed only in underwear for periods lasting from five to twenty-five days, said Dane Mogens Carlsson, who said he spent four years in Butyrka Prison.[15] The bread ration was reduced to 300 grams (10 ounces) daily, and the prisoner received only half a liter of warm soup every third day. This incarceration was "tantamount to a death sentence."

Carlsson was a Communist who sneaked over the Finnish-Russian border, and the Soviets arrested him as a spy and gave him a 28-year sentence for an illegal border crossing. At Butyrka, he shared a cell with Zoltan Rivo and Wilhelm Bergemann in 1950. "Both looked like mummies, grayish-white skin and undernourished," Carlsson said. Rivo was in his 30s and Bergemann, who was 65, said he tapped with Wallenberg at Lefortovo Prison in cell No. 304.[16]

At Lefortovo, the daily bread ration was 450 grams (15 ounces) of pasty bread, nine grams of sugar and half a liter of soup "that filled the cell with a nauseating stench."

Rivo said he shared a cell with Wallenberg in 1951, and the Soviets gave him preferential treatment, providing cigarettes, better food and the right to rest a few hours daily. Other prisoners said this was the cover story the Soviets dispensed via secret NKVD agents to make the gullible think Wallenberg was comfortable. Instead, others insisted the Soviets tortured Wallenberg.

Many foreigners died before the NKVD could interrogate them due to poor food and lack of sleep. This and other discomforts broke the prisoner's mental health, making him sluggish and indifferent, the ideal subject for interrogation. When released,

Carlsson had scurvy and was undernourished. After his release, a story in Berlingske Tidenddi on March 9, 1980, let Carlsson discuss the Soviet psyche.[17]

The Russians do not "acknowledge Western Humanistic and ethical norms but view matters in a purely materialistic way," Carlsson said. The NKVD assumes that Wallenberg's activities have been inspired by political as well as economic motives. Many prisoners said the NKVD was anti-Semitic, which was ironic because the Soviet State Security Service had at least six chiefs of Jewish descent at that level.

Dr. Claudio de Mohr, a prisoner in the Soviet Union for more than six years, said he was imprisoned in Moscow along with other foreign diplomats.[18] De Mohr said he and Wallenberg communicated through prison walls for about three years, and the Italian diplomat was sure Wallenberg was in prison as late as January 1948 when the Soviets transferred de Mohr.

In 1947, Wallenberg was transferred to Vladimir, an ancient cathedral city. When Catherine the Great had ruled, this was the starting point for prisoners marched to Siberia. The Vladimir jail was one of four original buildings and accommodated 600 foreigners.

For prison life, Vladimir was better. Many foreigners—up to 16—shared cells, which helped alleviate the tedium. The prison had a first-rate library with books by authors such as Victor Hugo and Balzac in addition to the obligatory works of Marx, Engels and Lenin.

But Wallenberg was denied many privileges. He could not get packages or letters. If not in solitary confinement, his cellmates were always Russians serving long terms. If they were ever released, the Soviets convinced them to say nothing of Wallenberg. Twice daily, the guard escorted Wallenberg to the toilet, and every ten days Wallenberg and the other prisoners were taken across an open yard to a one-story bathhouse and locked one to a shower stall. If the guards saw a prisoner crossing the open yard unescorted, they shot him.

After Lefortovo and Vladimir, Wallenberg was sent to Vorkuta in Siberia, his fellow 50 prisoners almost all Russians. Previously, Wallenberg had been incarcerated with foreigners, giving him hope of freedom, but now his companions were Russians. As an official herded the prisoners ready for deportation to Vorkuta into one corner, Wallenberg probably realized then he would never see Sweden or live in the free world.

The Soviets sent Wallenberg and the other prisoners to Vorkuta, a town in the northern Urals seventy miles north of the Arctic Circle. Though blessed with oil, coal, gold and other metals, the land is cursed with extreme weather.[19] In December, the sun sets just after noon while 30 degrees below zero is normal and heavy black clouds of coal exhaust turn the snow gray. "We have 12 straight months of winter," they said in the labor camps. "But the rest is summer."

Almost no one wants to work in that climate, so the Soviets used slave labor to mine the area's natural resources. The weather is merciless, killing many prisoners. While Wallenberg was at Vorkuta, the secret police questioned everyone who shared a cell with him in Moscow. Anyone who did was intensely interrogated about anything Wallenberg said, and then they were each put in punishment cells for several months.

In 1948, the Soviets transferred Wallenberg to a labor camp to the north called Khal'mer Yu, where he met Menachem Melzer, a camp doctor who checked prisoners to see if they were fit for construction work. When the guards brought Wallenberg to Melzer, he pressed his stethoscope against the prisoner and said he had a strong heart.

"Your name is Paul, correct?"

"No, my name is Raoul. I'm Swedish."

In January 1951, six years after his imprisonment, Wallenberg was transferred to better surroundings at Verkhneural'sk near the city of Chelyabinsk in the southern Urals, a more comfortable camp for political prisoners, where he stayed for two years. For a while, he shared a cell with David Vendrovsky, a Russian who at one time was a reporter for the European Press Agency in Moscow.

Later, Vendrovsky shared a cell with Abraham Kalinski, once a Polish military attache in Moscow who was serving a 25-year sentence on charges of spying for the United States. When World War II started, Kalinski fled from Poland to London and became a member of the Polish Liberation Army. Quickly thereafter, he became liaison officer between London and Russian headquarters in Moscow. As the end of the war neared, Kalinski heard a great deal about alleged Soviet atrocities against Poland. He said in 1944 he spoke with an American consular officer in Moscow named Paul Michael Dudko,[20] a man for whom the Foreign Service list spells the name Dutko. In May 1944, Kalinski and another Soviet Jew named B. Marko wrote a letter to President Roosevelt, specifying Soviet crimes against the Jews and others that mentioned the Katyn forest massacre, where twelve thousand Polish officers were killed. Dudko received the letter, with instructions to give it to U.S. Ambassador Averill Harriman. But a few days later the Soviets, who had the letter, arrested Kalinski, who said someone named Merkulov at the NKVD seemed aware of Kalinski's conversations with Dudko. That, Kalinski said, made Dudko a double agent, but the State Department also said in 1979 that Kalinski was its "informer" in Moscow.

After arresting Kalinski, the Soviets at some point sent him to Verkhneural'sk prison.

They kept Kalinski in solitary confinement during most of his imprisonment, but periodically, to keep him from going mad, they gave him a cellmate. In November 1951, Vendrovsky shared the cell with Kalinski.

Kalinski, who was happy to have someone to talk to, asked his roommate what other prisoners he had met at Verkhneural'sk. "I have been sitting with a very interesting and unusually sympathetic Swede," Vendrovsky explained. "He is noble and innocent and cannot understand why he is accused of being a spy. He is the former diplomat, Raoul Wallenberg."

Vendrovsky came directly from a prison cell with Wallenberg and a man named Wilhelm Munters, according to Kalinski.

Wallenberg was an "import," which is what the convicts termed people the Soviets abducted from the West. Then Vendrovsky told Kalinski what Wallenberg had told him about his capture:[21]

Vallenberg [sic] had appealed to the Soviet military authorities to allow him to take out the food brought for his wards, the rescued Jews, before the Soviet troops arrived. The next day 5-6 Soviet officers came to see the diplomat and invited him to come to their commander for talks. Vallenberg said that he had some kind of "bad feeling" about it. For an invitation one would have been enough, even a sergeant or enlisted man. And although he knew, he said, "Soviet ways," still he went with them.

When they arrived at the place Vallenberg was put in an empty room whose only furniture was one night table. The officers disappeared. Toward evening a dirty mattress was thrown in for the diplomat and weakened, tired and hungry, Vallenberg fell asleep. In the morning he was awakened by the bitter cold in the unheated room and did some running to warm himself up. For breakfast he was given a tincup of hot water and a piece of doughy bread. Finally, on 20 January Vallenberg and a group of Hungarians were sent . . . to Moscow.

At Lubyanka the young Swede spent about one year "under investigation," then in 1946 was sent to Verkhneural'sk . . . Before he left a judgement rendered in his absence by a special meeting . . . was announced: he was sentenced to 25 years imprisonment "for espionage."

Vendrovskiy [sic], retelling Vallenberg's story, told how at Lubyanka the Swede tried to prove to the investigators that he had done nothing but save Jews from the Germans. Smiling bitterly, David remarked to me that the noble Swede did not realize that saving Jews was a much greater crime than espionage to both the Cheka (KGB) and the Gestapo.

Suddenly one day in 1953, the guards ordered every political prisoner to leave. The prison grapevine beat out this message: Stalin had died in March and Beria, his security chief, was to be killed.

(Beria was executed that December.) Verkhneural'sk needed the space for Beria's friends.

The prisoners were marched to the railroad, where a train with open boxcars awaited them, which must have brought back cruel memories to Wallenberg of his days in Budapest. While waiting to board, Kalinski saw a distinguished looking man in a brown padded jacket who looked vaguely familiar. After a moment, he realized from the descriptions of his fellow prisoners, this was Raoul Wallenberg.

Wallenberg, Kalinski and many other prisoners were returned to Moscow and put in vans that transported them east to Vladimir, Wallenberg's second visit. After seven years, Kalinski met Munters, who had been the former minister of foreign affairs of Latvia, and had shared a cell with Vendrovsky and Wallenberg. Munters confirmed what Vendrovsky said, adding that in 1953 he, Wallenberg and another prisoner named Kupriyanov were eventually sent to Aleksandrovsky, the central prison in the Irkutsk region, when they left Verkhneural'sk Prison.

In 1955, the Soviets removed all the prisoners from the Aleksandrov prison and put them in either Vladimir or Novocherkassk. Kalinksi, Munters and Wallenberg went to Vladimir.

Kalinski said his party was loaded in a "Stolypin" car and sent through Kirov and Gor'kiy to Vladimir.[22] Because Kalinski had a "rank of honor" as a specially dangerous state criminal, he rode in a separate compartment while a guard armed with an automatic weapon watched him. Kalinski could see the other prisoners but not talk to them. Kalinski had a "special convoy," with four guards headed by an officer who was at least a captain. Though frightening, this was a more comfortable journey than the other prisoners, whom the Soviets considered only "dangerous" and transported twenty to thirty in the same kind of compartment without a toilet.

On this journey, Kalinski said that he had heard about Wallenberg but had not seen him.

The Soviets wanted to keep prisoners from having contact with anyone other than their cellmate, but even the most elaborate precautions can fail. In 1955, an Austrian prisoner named Schoggl was mistakenly put in Wallenberg's cell. Wallenberg told Schoggl he had been kept in solitary confinement for many years and asked him, if he were released, to tell the Swedish embassy he had met Wallenberg. Even if he didn't remember his name, just say, "a Swede from Budapest."

The following morning a political officer inspected the cell and became infuriated when he saw Schoggl. He immediately had Schoggl transferred to another cell, where he warned Schoggl never to speak of Wallenberg. Thus intimidated, Schoggl, even when freed in the West, only told his story under the cloak of anonymity.

A year later Simon Gogobaritze, a Georgian social democrat, was moved into Vladimir and his cellmate was Abraham Kalinski. Periodically, from 1948 to 1953, Gogobaritze had shared a cell with Wallenberg. Just after arriving in Kalinski's cell, Gogobaritze put his face against the window and stared out. "It's Wallenberg," he said.

Kalinski looked through the crack in the window and saw that Wallenberg had pulled off his khaki jacket. Now wearing only overalls and an undershirt, Wallenberg grabbed handfuls of snow and rubbed them all over his face, chest and arms. Then he jumped in the air and clapped his hands over his head. Wallenberg ran in place, bent over, did pushups and walked around the walls of the exercise pen, watched by a guard with a submachine gun. Wallenberg was taking an ersatz sauna.

In the succeeding years, Kalinski watched Wallenberg continue to take his unusual saunas and exercise in good weather as well, always accompanied by different Russian cellmates. Kalinski, who was denied the privilege of correspondence, managed to smuggle one message out to the Jewish community in Vienna, which contacted his sister, who had moved from Vienna to Israel.

Later, Kalinski wrote directly to her, saying, "I am living in this hotel and I don't know when I'll move. With me there is an Italian, a Swede who saved a thousand Jews in Rumania . . ."

Budapest may have sounded like Bucharest to Kalinski. In any event, he also wrote, "Those who are here have never committed any crime and have never been before a court."

In her reply, the sister asked "Is there no justice?"

"How can I answer your question," answered Kalinski, "when there is a Swede sitting in prison who has saved tens of thousands of Jews while Gestapo murderers and Russian collaborators with the Gestapo go free?"

Not completely so. Shortly after the war, Wallenberg's enemies among the Arrow Cross had been tried and executed. Those killed included former prime Minister Dome Sztojay and the Laszlos— Baky, Endre and Ferenczy, who had arranged the deportation of the provincial Jews to Auschwitz during the spring of 1944. Also executed were Father Kun, Vilmos Salzer and other local Arrow Cross leaders who had participated in the Budapest reign of terror. Ferenc Szálasi, Gábor Kemény and Gábor Vajna were also executed.

Eichmann, Wallenberg's main adversary, eluded the Allies for 15 years before the Israelis finally captured and executed him. One of the two adversaries from World War II Budapest had been executed, and the other remained in a Soviet prison.

CHAPTER 4

Right after Wallenberg's capture, the U.S. government expressed interest in freeing the Swedish diplomat. But after initial rebuffs from both Sweden and the Soviet Union, the Americans conveniently ignored Wallenberg.

For the next half century, the U.S. government gathered information and expressed platitudes, but never took one step to save Raoul Wallenberg. In fact, after forty years, the federal government moved against Wallenberg, but American intelligence did spy on Marcus and Jacob Wallenberg, Raoul's cousins. As early as 1949, the United States had an opportunity to exchange a Soviet spy for Wallenberg, but refused to consider the idea. Thus, the Soviets imprisoned Wallenberg while the Americans, who had recruited him, and the Swedes, who had sent him to Budapest on a dangerous mission, did nothing to rescue him.

At first, Wallenberg appeared safe but that quickly changed. Three days after Wallenberg disappeared, the U.S. ambassador in Sweden cabled Washington that the Russians had told the Swedish Embassy in Moscow Wallenberg was "safe and sound in that part of Budapest occupied by Russians."[1] A week later the Russians told Alexandra Michaelovna Kollontai, the Soviet Ambassador in Sweden, Wallenberg was in Lubyanka prison in Moscow, which Madame Kollontai relayed to Maj von Dardel.

On January 29, 1945, twelve days after Wallenberg's abduction, Herschel Johnson, the U.S. ambassador in Sweden, sent the U.S. State Department a report saying, "Wallenberg is believed to be safe in the Russian section of Budapest."[2] The cable further said the American embassy in Moscow had contacted the Soviets, but the United States let the opportunity evaporate.

In February 1945, Madame Kollontai, the daughter of a czarist general, told Maj, "Don't worry. According to my information, your son is completely safe. He will come back."

Madame Kollontai, despite her Czarist roots, had commanded the first Soviet antireligious act of the Revolution, the occupation of the Aleksandr Nevsky monastery and held a cabinet post in the first Soviet government. However, she had argued with other Soviet leaders when she led a movement seeking the dismissal of all technical experts trained before the Revolution and the ouster of all nonproletarians from the Communist party. She lost and became the first ambassador to Norway and then Sweden. Once in Sweden, she enjoyed the surroundings, where she could still exhibit her elegance as well as her fashionable dress while enjoying the friendship of such well-to-do people as Marcus Wallenberg, the banker and Raoul's father's cousin. While she lived well in Stockholm, the lives of her husband and many of her friends ended during the Stalinist purges.

The ambassador thus had an affinity for the Wallenberg family, and what she told Maj von Dardel was probably an accurate retelling of her superiors' report to her. Madame Kollontai undoubtedly believed that Wallenberg would be returned home shortly. In Stockholm, few were alarmed about Wallenberg's fate. Staffan Söderblom, the Swedish ambassador in Moscow, had informed his foreign office that Soviet Deputy Foreign Minister Vladimir Dekanosov had told him via letter Wallenberg was safe in Russian hands. The note said, "The Russian military authorities have taken measures to protect Raoul Wallenberg and his belongings." Everyone thought he would be home soon.

Then the news became bad. A radio report on March 8, 1945, on the Russian-controlled radio said Wallenberg had been murdered while traveling to Debrecen. Söderblom asked Dekanosov for information about this, and he said he would check. Meanwhile, Madame Kollontai had been recalled to Moscow for other work. Söderblom communicated with her, and she told him of her earlier discussions with Maj von Dardel.

The War Refugee Board sent a cable to Averill Harriman, the U.S. ambassador in Moscow, on April 4, 1945, asking for help in determining Wallenberg's fate. "The War Refugee Board had special interest in Wallenberg's mission to Hungary because of his outstanding work in protecting Jews and other victims of enemy oppression during the enemy occupation of Hungary."[3]

Edward R. Stettinius Jr., who became Secretary of State when an ill Cordell Hull resigned after the November 1944 election, cabled Harriman on April 9, 1945, telling him to give "all possible support" to the Swedes in the Wallenberg matter.[4] At the same time, Treasury Secretary Henry Morgenthau told the War Refugee Board, "Let Stettinius know that I am personally interested in this man."[5]

But Söderblom basically told Harriman he didn't want any support; the Swedes would handle the Wallenberg affair alone. The Swedes had the Americans withdraw early, hampering any rescue efforts. Though concerned about Wallenberg, the U.S. government only responded with cables, entreaties and then retreated into inaction.

Brigadier General William O'Dwyer, who had become executive director of the War Refugee Board in early 1945 until its dissolution in September of that year, also wrote the Secretary of State April 12 about Wallenberg. A month later George L. Warren, the U.S. government's adviser on Refugees and Displaced Persons, responded that all the cables between Stockholm and Moscow had failed to produce any news about Wallenberg. An April 30, 1945, cable was sent to the U.S. representative in Hungary to get information from the Soviet military authorities. Warren assured General O'Dwyer that the government "will pursue the inquiry concerning Mr. Wallenberg as long as any possibilities of information remain to be explored."[6]

Also on April 12, Harriman had cabled the Secretary of State, discussing conflicting reports from the Swedish legation about Wallenberg. The Swedes first reported him safe in Budapest, but the Swedish mission in Bucharest said Wallenberg had left

Budapest "alone by automobile for an unknown destination and had disappeared."[7]

Harriman's cable then quoted the Swedes as saying, "They have no reason to think the Russians are not doing what they can, and they do not feel that an approach to the Soviet Foreign Office on our part would be desirable." On this same day, President Roosevelt died, so Harriman obviously had other problems then.

When the Swedish Legation from Budapest returned on April 19 to Stockholm, minus Wallenberg, Johnson cabled Washington, "In view of the special interest which the Department and the War Refugee Board had in Wallenberg's mission as well as our own deep anxiety for his safety, it is suggested that the United States Government communicate to the Swedish Government its concern in the matter."[8]

Wallenberg's other American recruiter, Iver Olsen, filed a letter to O'Dwyer on June 15, 1945, saying "sufficient facts now appear at hand to support the conclusion that Hungarian rescue and relief actions initiated by the War Refugee Board from Sweden were the keystones of the most productive steps taken in that area, and paved the way for saving the lives of perhaps 100,000 Jews. The work of Raoul Wallenberg . . . was nothing short of brilliant—to say nothing of being highly courageous."[9]

By June, the American government had a more pragmatic reason for finding Wallenberg. A June 14 cable from the U.S. embassy in Stockholm said the Swedes told the Americans that Wallenberg had "accumulated extensive and well documented records regarding the Jewish situation and related relief activities in Hungary."[10] Supposedly, these records were left in the "chancery in (a) large wooden box near (the) entry to (the) air-raid shelter. These records should prove very valuable," Johnson told Washington. The Swedes suggested that "every effort to obtain them be made by our Mission Budapest." The Americans found neither the box nor Wallenberg, but they did encounter Swedish recalcitrance about freeing its most famous diplomat. During the early postwar years, socialist governments in Sweden tried to avoid provoking the Soviets.

At the same time, the Soviets had much circumstantial evidence to make them doubt Wallenberg was only a Swedish diplomat. "His modus operandi certainly exceeded standard diplomatic practice," said a classified article in Studies in Intelligence,[11] a CIA in-house publication. "The falsification of documents for Jewish refugees, the use of bribes and his successful use of bluff and bravado on numerous occasions were probably known to them."

Additionally, U.S. intelligence contacts asked about Wallenberg's status. A cable from Allied headquarters in Caserta, Italy, in May 1945 said General Bonner Key, who was in the OSS, "asked the Soviet military authorities for information regarding the whereabouts of Wallenberg, (Max) Meier and (Harold) Feller."[12] The last two were Swiss diplomats also seized by the Russians in Budapest, but the Swiss freed the pair via a swap with the Russians. That led to a decades-long—and still unanswered—question. Why didn't the Swedes do the same for Wallenberg?

The cable continued that since the "Soviet authorities may well have conclusive proof of pro-Nazi collaboration on the part of Feller and possibly of Meier and Wallenberg should be of interest to the Department." This reference to collaboration with the Nazis probably referred to Wallenberg's use of bribes to gain the release of Jews and other refugees.

Amid the confusion, the Soviets ignored the American government's constant cables, eliciting a quick surrender from the U.S. legation in Moscow. In a cable dated September 25, 1945, the Moscow mission told Washington since the Soviets disregarded all inquiries about Wallenberg, "We consequently feel that any action here on our part on behalf of Wallenberg, a Swedish national, would serve no useful purpose."[13]

With such a convenient excuse, the American government abandoned Wallenberg to the Soviet gulag.

After several attempts to get a response from Moscow, a functionary at the Soviet legation in Stockholm said in 1946 that Wallenberg was "being taken care of for some foolish things he had done." Another story contended that a Soviet court had convicted Wallenberg as an American spy and sentenced to 25 years.

While the U.S. government ignored Wallenberg, it spied on his cousins, the brothers Marcus and Jacob Wallenberg. A letter dated February 7, 1945, from Morgenthau to Stettinius explained the brothers' activities. A summary accompanying Morgenthau's letter said the family's Enskilda bank had made "substantial" loans to Germany without collateral. Also, the bank acted for German interests in an attempt to conceal German investments in American companies, and Jacob Wallenberg had told the Germans he was willing to sell them a Swedish plant in Hamburg for gold. The United States watched the Wallenberg brothers as part of Project Safe Haven, an intelligence operation to find out where the Germans hid assets in neutral countries, particularly Switzerland, as the war came to an end.[14]

The letter also describes Jacob as pro-German and tries to counter the impression that Marcus was "pro-Allied." It accuses the Enskilda bank of becoming "repeatedly connected with large black market operations," including dealing with dollars allegedly dumped by the Germans.[15] The Wallenberg family's financial dealings with the Nazis were known, but until now the public didn't know the United States spied on the family and discussed it at the highest levels of the government.

Another letter, dated April 14, 1945, said two German officers tried to deposit two million Swedish kronor "with sympathetic Swedes through Wallenberg, the banker" after failing to use the money to buy Swedish navigation equipment for the German Navy. Morgenthau said Jacob "was known to be sympathetic and working with the Germans" and wrote the Swedish-German agreement and served as a member of the "Permanent Joint Swedish-German Trading Commission."[16]

By 1946, a group of Swedish citizens had formed a committee to push the government into action and ask its own questions about Wallenberg. This was the first of the Wallenberg Committees, which eventually expanded around the world.

Söderblom, the Swedish ambassador, thought Wallenberg was dead and didn't want to bother the Russians. The ambassador had a marvelous opportunity to follow through on the matter June 15, 1946, when he had a rare meeting with Stalin. This meeting was kept secret until January 1980 when 1,900 pages of Swedish Foreign Office documents on the Wallenberg affair were released.

During their conversation, Söderblom mentioned Wallenberg.[17]

"You say his name was Wallenberg?" Stalin asked.

Söderblom spelled it out for Stalin on a pad. Then he told the Soviet dictator how the Russians had escorted Wallenberg to Debrecen. Stalin told him the Russians were instructed to protect the Swedes in Budapest.

"Yes, and I am personally convinced that Wallenberg fell victim either to a road accident or bandits," Söderblom said.

"Have you not had any definite information on the matter from our side?" Stalin asked.

"No, but I assume that the Soviet military authorities do not have any further reliable information about what happened after that," Söderblom said.

Stalin, who did nothing about Wallenberg, could easily have reasoned that the Swedes cared nothing about their diplomat. At the same time, an NKVD interrogator at Lefortovo Prison justifiably told Wallenberg, "Nobody cares about you."

Many apparently didn't care. On August 18, 1947, Andrei Vishinsky, Soviet senior deputy foreign minister, in an attempt to end annoying inquiries about this matter, said a search of the gulag had failed to locate Wallenberg. "Wallenberg is not in the Soviet Union and is unknown to us."

The Soviets kept that story for 12 years.

While Sweden and the United States did almost nothing to free Wallenberg, the von Dardel family tried everything—letters, phone calls, talking to returning refugees, but nothing worked. First, the von Dardels tried Sweden and then the United States.

Maj von Dardel, mother of Raoul and Guy, complained about

the coolness and lack of enthusiasm that reigned at the Ministry of Foreign Affairs in connection with the search for her firstborn son. She was upset that the Ministry always assumed Wallenberg was dead. Söderblom, the Swedish Ambassador to Moscow, told her in March 1947 she should not "count on her son being alive."

Guy von Dardel and his supporters met with Minister of Foreign Affairs Östen Undén and his top men during November 1947 in what became an agitated exchange. Undén thought Wallenberg had died in or around Budapest while von Dardel answered that his evidence showed Wallenberg still living, but in a Soviet cell. Undén failed to understand why the Soviets would hold Wallenberg. Mrs. Birgitta de Wylder-Bellander, a vigorous Wallenberg supporter, said the Soviets thought Wallenberg was a spy.

"But then do you think that Vishinsky is lying?" Undén asked.

"Yes, I do," said von Dardel.

That infuriated Undén, who red faced and angry, said, "That is unheard of, that is unheard of" and left the meeting.

Stymied in Sweden, the von Dardels turned to America. Five times in the 1940s, the von Dardels wrote to top officials in the U.S. government or influential individuals, asking for help in freeing Wallenberg. Each time the State Department expressed perfunctory interest, but took no action.

Maj von Dardel, looking for a key to open her son's prison cell, wrote to Eleanor Roosevelt, the President's widow, who then lived at 29 Washington Square West, Apartment 15-A, in New York City.[18] In her letter dated November 30, 1946, Mrs. von Dardel wrote, in English, with only a few minor errors, "knowing your warmheartedness and kindness to all those who suffer I have gathered [sic] courage to write to you."

She outlined her son's remarkable accomplishments, admitting, "I know that as a mother I am no unchallengeable witness." She added that "the fact that a great part of the hungarian jews [sic] have survived can be attributed essentially to one man, working as

the representative of the swedish king and the american president—
my son."

Then Mrs. von Dardel explained to Mrs. Roosevelt that her
son didn't return with the rest of the Swedish legation in Budapest.
She told of feeble official Swedish attempts and next explained
that as a necessary alternative, the Wallenberg family did its own
work to try to find her son. "Privately, we have been able to establish that Raoul Wallenberg is still alive." The Wallenberg family
gave this information to the Swedish Cabinet and Prime Minister,
which promised to do something.

Mrs. von Dardel wanted her letter published in the newspapers and broadcast on the radio, hoping to create "a public opinion in favor of Raoul Wallenberg and of his liberation." She reasoned such publicity would become an engine driving the U.S.
government into action. Then she asked Mrs. Roosevelt to head a
Raoul Wallenberg committee in the United States and enclosed
some relevant newspaper clippings.

Two months later, Mrs. Roosevelt forwarded the letter with a
note to both Andrei A. Gromyko, then the Soviet Union's representative to the United Nations, and to the State Department,
asking to have "someone advise me whether anything can be done
about the enclosed?"[19]

Gromyko wrote back to Mrs. Roosevelt on March 19, 1947,
replying that he had forwarded the note to "our Consulate General for taking [sic] appropriate measures."[20] The Consulate General wrote Maj von Dardel and told the family to talk to the Russian Red Cross in Moscow. The von Dardels had already done that
without receiving any answer until the Consulate's letter arrived,
creating the circle of futility.

Warren, the U.S. refugee adviser, wrote back on February 21,
1947, to Mrs. Roosevelt, returning Mrs. von Dardel's letter and
the clippings.[21] While acknowledging Wallenberg's achievements,
Warren routinely dismissed the matter in a bloodless letter to the
former first lady of the United States. "The last report received in
October 1945 from Budapest was that Mr. Wallenberg had left

Budapest for Debrecen in March 1945 [sic] and that no further word had been received from him."

The Russians seized Wallenberg in January 1945 and two years later the U.S. government still didn't know the correct date. One must wonder either about its sources of information or its interest. In this and several other instances, the State Department and CIA frequently make mistakes—getting names, dates and basic facts wrong in the Wallenberg case. During the last 50 years, the American government obviously has had higher priorities, including accumulating many facts on many topics and—what the heck—everybody makes mistakes. But still the government's frequently inaccurate information on the Wallenberg case, which merited enough attention to accumulate 1,500 documents in the CIA files, undermines its agencies' credibility.

As a Congressional aide said in late 1994, "Years ago, we thought the CIA knew what it was doing."

Warren closed his reply to Mrs. Roosevelt without a commitment regarding Wallenberg. "It does not appear that any official action can be taken until some clue as to his whereabouts is received."

End of letter, end of effort.

After the State Department rebuff, Guy von Dardel, Wallenberg's half-brother, also wrote to Mrs. Roosevelt. Von Dardel, then studying at the Physics Department at Cornell University, in Ithaca, New York, was also trying to "initiate some American action in favor of the release of my brother."

Von Dardel's letter of May 8, 1947, again tried to enlist the former First Lady's help.[22] "I hope I may count upon your further interest and help in this matter." He told Mrs. Roosevelt of his confidence "that something may be done from this country." By then, von Dardel had spoken with members of the now dissolved War Refugee Board, including Olsen, who told him the United States was "very much concerned about my brother's fate as his entire work was initiated and financed by the War Refugee Board . . ."

Next, he appealed to her as "a member of the Human Rights committee [a U.N. group] to help to get my brother the human rights which he has undoubtedly deserved more than perhaps anybody else."

Also, von Dardel included an article by Dorothy Thompson, a prominent journalist, from the April 18, 1947, edition of the Boston Daily Globe. Thompson's article was an open—and frequently pointed letter—to Henry Wallace, former vice president and New Deal advocate. Wallace, the embodiment of the New Deal's "common man" philosophy, served as FDR's vice president from 1941-45, but opposition from party conservatives, particularly Southerners, denied Wallace another term as vice president. He remained in the cabinet as Secretary of Commerce until resigning in 1946.[23]

When Thompson wrote her column, Wallace was headed to Sweden, so she suggested that Wallace, since he had the confidence of the Soviet Union, ask about Wallenberg. Thompson briefly described Wallenberg's heroics in Budapest and his disappearance into the gulag. "Since official channels have failed, your personal intervention with the Russian government might succeed," Thompson wrote. "Sweden—small, and so near Soviet frontiers—finds it hard to do more for her citizen, especially since the new-type, jet-propelled, radio-directed robot bombs were tried out over her territory from the German station at Peenemunde, now in Russians hands."

Thompson, someone whom the von Dardels had already enlisted in their struggle, was a journalistic powerhouse. She had a syndicated column called "On the Record," published for more than 20 straight years in dozens of U.S. newspapers with her anchor the New York Herald Tribune, then a widely circulated and highly respected newspaper. After World War II, Thompson was interested in the problems of all refugees, including Wallenberg.

Following the column to Wallace, Thompson also wrote privately to Mrs. Roosevelt regarding Wallenberg.[24] In a highly unusual letter that compromised her journalistic principles, Thompson told of Swedish reluctance to free its diplomat and tried to convince Mrs. Roosevelt to help Wallenberg by reaching to the highest level of the Soviet Union. Thompson's three-page letter dated May 20, 1947, said, "And may I say now . . . that it is my hope that your position and your long friendship for the Soviet Union, may make it possible for you, alone, to perform an act of signal justice?" Then Thompson explained about Wallenberg's work in Budapest and imprisonment in Moscow. Von Dardel had approached the State Department, which "offered active intervention if the Swedish Government actively requests it," Thompson wrote. "But the Swedish government is obviously not anxious to exacerbate international relations by asking [sic] the intervention of another country in its behalf, even though Wallenberg was, in fact, representing the President of the United States."

Next, Thompson repeated her publicly expressed view that Wallenberg's arrest was a Soviet mistake, which that government would never admit. Privately, Thompson told Mrs. Roosevelt if she were right that Wallenberg's kidnapping revolved around an error, "then little can be served by too much publicity."

To Thompson, only someone like Mrs. Roosevelt, "whose sympathies with the Soviet Union are a matter of record, could, conceivably save Raoul Wallenberg's life, and set at rest the terrible anxieties of his family." Thompson asked Mrs. Roosevelt to write "a personal letter to Stalin, setting forth this case and asking for his personal intervention." For corroboration of Wallenberg's feats, Thompson recommended Mrs. Roosevelt talk to Olsen, and then suggested von Dardel was also available for "questioning." Finally, discarding her journalistic aloofness—and therefore her objectivity—Thompson promised she would "give no more publicity to this matter until I hear of your decision." If the whole affair were an error, "and you are able to straighten it out, I shall keep silent thereafter, for my purpose, I repeat is to help save Raoul Wallenberg." Thompson promised Mrs. Roosevelt, "I shall use what influence I have to keep the story suppressed, *provided* that persons like yourself will take up his case through your own channels."

The former first lady returned a note to Thompson on May 26 that said she had no "'position' as regards the Soviet Union."[25] Mrs. Roosevelt said she had already written about Wallenberg, meaning the letters to Warren and Gromyko.

Thompson, misunderstanding, wrote back to Mrs. Roosevelt two days later, asking to see what she wrote and urging her to get involved on Wallenberg's behalf.[26] "I still have the feeling that if someone whom no one would even suspect of being animated by malice would take up Mr. Wallenberg's case with someone high in the Soviet Union it could conceivably be solved—because I cannot but think that the whole thing was initially an error. I know you have a very warm heart and a strong sense of justice as well as much tact."

That prompted a handwritten letter to Thompson, explaining where Mrs. Roosevelt had sent the letters.[27] "I did not write anything for publication about Mr. Wallenberg."

For whatever reason, Mrs. Roosevelt did nothing further. The von Dardel family, though, did a great deal more.

In early 1947, Guy von Dardel, sent an undated letter to President Truman, again seeking help for his half-brother.[28] Von Dardel appealed to President Truman to help Raoul Wallenberg because "I believe that his fate, apart from being a source of continuous anguish to his family, also touches the conscience of this great democracy."

Guy explained that Raoul worked "under American auspices," but two years of diplomatic efforts to free Wallenberg had failed. Some of the Swedish legation, whom the Russians interrogated, "are firmly convinced that my brother was arrested on the preposterous charge of espionage. This belief is shared by officials of the U.S. State Department and the Swedish Foreign Office," von Dardel wrote. The Russians up to then had not admitted they held Wallenberg, instead permitting Budapest to hold memorial services for Wallenberg and name a street in his honor. "With this convenient ceremony, the curtain of oblivion was to be dropped on the actual fate of my brother," lamented von Dardel.

Then von Dardel cited reports described vaguely as "an ever-larger body of evidence" reaching the Swedish government to indicate the Soviets arrested Wallenberg, and he was still alive. This information put Wallenberg in a Soviet internment camp in Czechoslovakia in April 1945 and then to Bessarabia and next to a camp in the Ukraine. In closing, von Dardel explained diplomacy's failure and his own wishes. "In view of the manifest inability of ordinary diplomacy to cut through the tangle of red tape and misunderstanding that may still be holding my brother a prisoner—more than two years after the completion of his American-inspired humanitarian mission—I ask your assistance, Mr. President in obtaining the true facts."

Von Dardel's letter remained in the White House Central Files-General File, but undated, unacknowledged and probably unseen by the Executive Branch. William D. Hassett, the president's secretary, on March 27 referred von Dardel's letter to the State Department, which was mainly concerned if "von Dardel furnishes any new clues, which could be used?"[29]

Fifteen days later, on April 11, 1947, George Warren sent von Dardel a letter in response to his "undated letter" and again expressed appreciation for Wallenberg's achievements, but minimal interest in helping him.[30] The "heroic efforts of Mr. Wallenberg . . . in collaboration with the War Refugee Board are well known to this Government and are appreciated." Warren added that the U.S. government's efforts "through diplomatic channels have unfortunately not succeeded." He ended with the limp promise that the government was still interested and would advise von Dardel "if any new information is brought to light."

Dean Acheson, then acting Secretary of State, filed a dispatch to the U.S. legation in Stockholm about the letter from von Dardel, someone "claiming to be Raoul Wallenberg's brother."[31] Acheson said the State Department could not verify von Dardel's contentions about Wallenberg being in Estonia. The acting Secretary of State then acknowledged a tepid commitment to Wallenberg.

Since Wallenberg undertook his mission with the active cooperation of the War Refugee Board, the State Department "desires to be of assistance in locating Wallenberg if alive. However, basic responsibility for pursuing this matter must rest with Swedish Govt [sic] whose official he was." To further temporize, Acheson instructed the Stockholm legation to ask about Wallenberg's whereabouts and "if necessary indicate our willingness to support though not to initiate further inquiries."

Even before he received the dismissive letter from Warren, von Dardel sought help from Senator Arthur H. Vandenberg. In 1946, as in 1994, the American voters had empowered Republicans to seize control of Congress, evicting the long-entrenched Democrats and elevating Vandenberg to head the Senate Foreign Relations Committee. The 80th Congress attacked the Democratic president, but then the object of derision was Harry S. Truman, not Bill Clinton.

Like an American politician playing the local angle, von Dardel on March 31, 1947, wrote the Michigan Senator, explaining that his half-brother had graduated from Ann Arbor in 1935.[32] His rhetoric justifiably rising, von Dardel said, "What Raoul Wallenberg did in Hungary in 1944 and the first days of 1945 is one of the most brilliant civil performances of the last war." After outlining Wallenberg's accomplishments and capture, von Dardel said that through unofficial channels and Soviet refugees, "We have been able to ascertain that he is being held a prisoner and put to work for the Russians." He discounted rumors about Wallenberg's death, saying when traced to the source they were "groundless or to result from the speculations of those who saw in his death a convenient end to a troublesome affair." Next, von Dardel pointed out the obvious injustices—a savior who battled the Nazis in Budapest was held prisoner in a country that fought the same enemy.

From an official level, von Dardel said the imprisonment was unjust, for Wallenberg served as a Swedish diplomat and thus deserved "diplomatic immunity." Then von Dardel chided both Sweden and the United States. Since "official Swedish channels have failed to amend this injustice . . . it should be the duty of the United States (which) sent him on his dangerous mission to do the possible and give him back to his country and his family."

In finishing, von Dardel again played the local angle, saying Wallenberg's Michigan link "may to a small degree make him entitled to your interest and help, apart from the general concern which his fate deserves from everyone who appreciates justice and liberty."

Into the mail chute went another letter to Dean Acheson. Vandenberg, who was apparently unaware of Wallenberg's feats, said von Dardel's story of his half-brother was "rather amazing." To Vandenberg, this was probably "one of those 'imponderables' behind the iron curtain [sic]."[33] Nevertheless, Vandenberg asked the acting Secretary of State to "take a 'look' at the enclosure."

Vandenberg, a powerful Republican Senator, merited a two-page typewritten reply from the head of the State Department, but that, too, was a vessel of noncommitment.[34] Acheson talked of seeking more information, but since Wallenberg was Swedish, his government must take "the initiative in inquiries directed toward the Soviet Government . . ."

Acheson also informed Vandenberg that von Dardel, seeking a more direct approach, telephoned the State Department April 14 and "was assured of the Department's continuing interest in the search for his brother."

After two years nothing happened, so Guy von Dardel wrote Acheson, now Secretary of State, careful to date the letter—February 14, 1949—but he probably wrote it a month later because the State Department received it March 22.[35] Much more pragmatic, von Dardel proposed a swap, Valentin Gubitchev, a Russian spy, for Raoul Wallenberg. Gubitchev, a Soviet engineer working at the United Nations, became the first Russian ever to be convicted of spying in the United States. The U.S. government arrested Gubitchev March 4, 1949, along with his alleged sweetheart, Judith

Coplon, at the United Nations.[36] The government said Gubitchev conspired to commit espionage by removing classified government documents concerning national defense. Miss Coplon, a Justice Department political analyst, was accused of attempting to pass these documents to the Russian, Gubitchev. The pair allegedly first met at New York's Museum of Modern Art in September 1948.

Coplon was initially tried in Washington and then with Gubitchev in New York. At the same time, the trial of Alger Hiss, a former State Department employee, was underway, alarming Americans about supposed Communist spies working in the government. During the late 1940s, fear of Communist advances tore at the fabric of American life. Russia had just seized Eastern Europe to become America's new and fearsome opponent. The Gubitchev-Coplon and Hiss spy cases thus became national news, though the Hiss trial eventually became more notable, probably because it boosted the career of a young California congressman named Richard M. Nixon.

In his letter, von Dardel mentioned reading about the recent arrest of Gubitchev and Coplon.[37] That reminded von Dardel how after the war, Switzerland traded some Russians for two Swiss diplomats, Meier and Feller, whom—like Wallenberg—the Russians had taken after conquering Budapest. Von Dardel admitted, this proposed spy swap was an "irregular procedure in peacetime diplomatic relations" and missing American citizens could have a higher priority. "However in my opinion few if any are more worthy of regaining their liberty than my brother by virtue of his courageous humanitarian work." Von Dardel specified how Wallenberg had worked for the American War Refugee Board, entitling him to "all possible help from the American side, even if he is not an American citizen himself . . ."

But von Dardel's effort failed. Five months (July 14, 1949) after von Dardel's dated letter and months before Gubitchev's conviction, the State Department told its Stockholm legation to tell von Dardel the U.S. government "continues to have a sympathetic

interest in the case of his half brother and regrets exceedingly that
its efforts to obtain information regarding Mr. Wallenberg's whereabouts have been unsuccessful." But the U.S. government rejected
any swap of Gubitchev for Wallenberg, "a Swedish citizen."[38]

The spy swap opportunity lingered for another eight months.
A New York jury in 1950 found both Gubitchev and Coplon guilty,
and the judge sentenced him to 15 years in prison and Coplon,
who was also convicted in the Washington trial, to 25 years.[39]
Now, only five years after Wallenberg's disappearance, the United
States had a convicted Russian spy to trade for the hero of Budapest.
Ultimately, the United States gave away its bargaining chip, just
as Sweden would do in a different situation 31 years later. The
American government deported Gubitchev to Moscow, gave him
back to Russia for nothing. On March 20, 1950, he sailed from
New York aboard the liner Batory, a free man.

"Those letters to Truman and others didn't come to anything,"
said Nina Lagergren, puzzled over the U.S. lethargy. "We're used
to people reacting that way in Sweden."

In 1947, Ossian Eriksson, a self-styled soldier of fortune, had
proposed a more daring method of freeing Wallenberg.

Eriksson contended he had smuggled two men out from Denmark to Sweden who had been imprisoned with Wallenberg at a
camp in Kemeri, Latvia.[40] Maj von Dardel talked to Eriksson, but
she was reluctant to share details with U.S. intelligence. Employ-
ing their professional paranoia, the Americans mused that Eriksson
was using the Wallenberg case "as [sic] clever means of penetrating
any operations we may have in the Baltic area or . . . for purposes
of his own gain in linking himself with the American authority in
an effort to procure greater financial support from Mrs. von Dardel."

Translation: The Americans thought Eriksson was a Communist
spy or a ripoff artist.

The Americans also said Eriksson's story about helping free
the men from the Latvian prison had discrepancies. Anti Turunen,
who along with Alf Tyngvik, had escaped from the Latvian prison
camp, had gone by foot to Poland and then were smuggled aboard

a ship to Denmark, but the Americans doubted Eriksson's tale of getting the two to Sweden. Supposedly, Wallenberg told Turunen which people to contact in Sweden about him. Turunen said the camp had 600 prisoners used as laborers, quartered in barracks and in one large five-story building in the compound, which was used as officer quarters, a classroom and for other utility purposes. That was where Turunen served. He said Wallenberg and four Americans plus eight others of the "intellectual group" were quartered there. These men, according to Turunen, were "forced to conduct English classes for the Russian officers."

When Turunen arrived in Sweden on December 20, 1946, he wrote to Marcus Wallenberg, Raoul's cousin, but received no reply. He sent another letter on March 1, 1947, but again no reply. Then Turunen, a Finnish national whom the Russians captured because he fought for Germany in the war, stowed away on a ship to his native country. When Turunen arrived, the Finnish secret police arrested him. The final CIA entry about Turunen only said, "No more word on him."

The other escapee, Tyngvik, said he knew little about Wallenberg and returned to Norway, where the authorities investigated him as a German collaborator. But Eriksson contended he knew a great deal, saying after helping the escapees he had gone to the outskirts of the Kemeri camp, aided by a Latvian peasant named "Taska."[41] During this alleged adventure, Eriksson said he saw Wallenberg and a dozen others headed for the bathhouse outside the compound. Eriksson was thoughtful enough to include a sketch of the compound when he returned to Sweden on February 27, 1947.[42] The surviving copy is barely legible, but the crude drawing does show a compound, officers' quarters and a road bisected by barbed wire. About 5,000 meters from the classrooms, where Wallenberg supposedly taught, is a river, a destroyed bridge where the river and road meet and a pontoon bridge next to the ruined one.

Next, Eriksson went to the Swedish foreign office and proposed the Swedes "fly him to Kemeri area, drop him, give him time to organize an escape and then pick up [sic] group by another plane. The Foreign office, obviously, would give the plan no consideration," the CIA snorted.

Later, Maj von Dardel and Eriksson wanted to talk to the American legation, the CIA reported, "perhaps enlisting their aid" since the United States had recruited Wallenberg.

After the Swedish rejection, Eriksson suggested a small "commando raid" to free Wallenberg and the imprisoned Americans. But this was real life, not reel life, so the Americans ignored the plan and intensified their questioning of Eriksson. When U.S. intelligence pressed him for details, Eriksson "became annoyed and refused to answer questions." Since the Americans doubted his story about Wallenberg's imprisonment, Eriksson made another outlandish proposal: He wanted a camera and 4,000 rubles to get "convincing proof of his story and perhaps other important info. [sic]"

This heightened U.S. suspicion. Eriksson said he was born in Halsinborg, Sweden, but he lacked a passport or other valid identification. For a while, Eriksson worked in a boiler room in Finland and later as a draftsmen in Sweden. Since mid-1946, Eriksson had had no job. He spoke Swedish, Finnish, German and Russian, but American intelligence said, "his manner of speech does not sound genuinely Swedish or does he appear to speak it fluently."

His plans scuttled, Eriksson disappeared.

In 1951, a man named Gheorghe Vas told Swedish authorities in Germany that he had spent four years in the same Romanian prison camp as Wallenberg.[43] The Swedes failed to believe him, but still the Swedish legation in Vienna was approached by someone whose name the CIA has blacked out. This person wanted to "assist in procuring the release of Swedish ambassador Wallenberg." The Wallenberg family instigated the approach and were "prepared to pay a large sum of money for the ambassador's release," according to this document of May 24, 1951. The Swedes were looking for Vas, who said he had "precise information on how Wallenberg could be ransomed or rescued." But they couldn't locate Vas.

As more prisoners of war started drifting back from the then Soviet Union, more started telling stories about seeing or knowing others who had seen Raoul Wallenberg. The prisoners told the CIA, the Soviets have "no scruples in holding as prisoners for years old diplomats, functionaries, officers, without any trial or judgment. Their purpose is to obtain as fast as possible information, revelations and denunciations. They also want to have a certain number of hostages on hand for the eventual exchange of prisoners."

Many ex-prisoners still feared the KGB's totalitarian power and remained anonymous, but some spoke to friends and members of the Wallenberg family. This kept constant pressure on the Swedish government to do something about Wallenberg, but the Swedes abdicated any responsibility. In fact, the State Department felt the Swedish government did little until 1951-52 and then only words, not actions.

Annette Lantos, a Hungarian refugee who as a 12-year-old lived in Budapest during World War II and is now married to a California Congressman, Tom Lantos, has her own theories about why Sweden did nothing to save Wallenberg.

While Gigi, the Lantos' white poodle frolicked on the red carpet, Mrs. Lantos sat in her husband's Congressional office in Washington's Rayburn Building and remembered her days in Budapest 50 years earlier. With her heavy Hungarian accent and perspicacious demeanor, a visitor instantly thinks of Eva Gabor. But Annette Lantos is no actress, rather an intelligent woman, known in Washington for her tours of the Capitol. An aide explained that visitors love hearing Annette's anecdotal and descriptive tour of American history, given in Hungarian-flavored English.

In 1944, Annette Tillemann knew little about the U.S. Capitol and cared only about surviving. "I was a child in Budapest, and the Portuguese Embassy saved me."

Tom and Annette grew up together—meeting when he was 11 and she 7—as their families spent summer vacations together at the Tillemann's summer home just outside Budapest. When anarchy ruled Budapest, Annette Tillemann's family, who ran a jewelry store, went into hiding. The Portuguese, copying the Swedish example, issued a few passes, saving some Jews, including Annette and her mother. But her father "perished because there were not enough Wallenbergs."

The Nazis arrested Tom Lantos for being a Jew and sent him to a "work camp" near the town of Vac. After that, he would have gone to a death camp, but Lantos escaped and returned south to Budapest and found his family and Annette. Just 16, Lantos joined Wallenberg's staff, organizing rescue missions. Blond and blue-eyed, Lantos looked Aryan, enabling him to wear an SS uniform and pass through the fascist lines. He brought food and water to Jews, whom the Nazis and Arrow Cross had imprisoned in the ghetto.

"He was an errand boy," explained his wife.

Lantos accompanied Wallenberg, who carried false Swedish passports and went to trains jammed with passengers headed for death camps, using his bravado to save dozens of lives. During an interview with the Washington Post, Lantos said Wallenberg's authority was "his own courage. Anyone could have shot him to death and not answered for it. He was absolutely unfearful for himself; he abandoned himself totally. In a more civilized, rational and humane way, he was like the primitive aboriginal soldiers who painted their bodies blue, thinking that this would protect them from physical harm. It was as if his courage was enough to protect him."

Just before the fall of Budapest, all the other embassies called back their legations, except for Sweden because Wallenberg knew he had to stay to save the Jews. For that, "All the other ambassadors hated him," said Mrs. Lantos, bitterness subduing her accent and clarifying her words.

"They had to stay for a few Jews," said Mrs. Lantos. Wallenberg's "behavior was inappropriate for a Swede," a people known for their equanimity.

"The Swedes resented him. That's why they didn't save him,"

Mrs. Lantos continued. Furthermore, she added, the Socialist government that ruled Sweden after World War II hated the capitalistic Wallenberg family, hitting Raoul Wallenberg with a double whammy. To the wealthy branch of the family, Wallenberg was a half-breed since his father had died before he was born and his mother had remarried outside the family. But the socialists running Sweden were trying to stifle capitalism and capitalists like the Wallenbergs. Thus, neither the government nor the rich Wallenberg family would help Raoul.

"He was ostracized; the family wouldn't touch him," Mrs. Lantos explained.

Neither would the Swedish government, which lay under perpetual verbal assault from Maj von Dardel. When she came into the embassy, the Swedish officials "would duck into the men's room so they wouldn't have to face this crazy old lady," related Mrs. Lantos, who has been interested in Wallenberg for the last 50 years. She has contacts with many ex-Soviet prisoners and government officials in both the United States and Sweden.

In her view, the Swedish government "hated Wallenberg more than the Russians."

Sitting on a red-padded bench outside a meeting room at the National Press Club in Washington, Birgitta Dahl, Sweden's Parliamentary Speaker, challenged Annette Lantos' contentions. "It's not true that Sweden didn't try to free Wallenberg," she said. Dahl also dismissed contentions that the Social Democrats disliked the Wallenberg family, insisting the Wallenbergs and the government have many contacts.

Furthermore, Dahl added, "I would say the Swedish government is working hard to find out about Wallenberg. We want to know the truth and are not convinced he is not among us." For example, she said, "My mother is five years older than Wallenberg, and she is still alive."

She did admit Sweden could have shown initial trepidation about the Soviet Union during the final days of the war because of the turmoil. Since Sweden's diplomats in Hungry did not arrive

home until April, Stockholm could not know Wallenberg was missing. "If we had known, we would have acted immediately."

She brushed aside any suggestion that Stockholm failed to try
to free Wallenberg. "That's not true."

Dahl pointed out that chaos also gripped Moscow as the war
ended, making it difficult to find out what happened to the Swedish diplomat. "Hopefully, we will find the real documents. We
would like to know what happened."

Then she politely excused herself to give a talk to journalists
and Swedish journalism students at the National Press Club.

Despite Dahl's denials, Annette Lantos feels differently.

After the war, the Swedes repatriated the Baltic people who
had sought sanctuary in Sweden, sending the refugees back to
their native countries—as Russia demanded—and to certain death
by the Soviets. Before the Lithuanians, Latvians and Estonians left,
Wallenberg's mother and sister asked the Swedish government,
which now had some bargaining power, to bring up the issue of
Wallenberg with the Russians, but the Swedes refused.

"The Swedes knew everything about Wallenberg," Mrs. Lantos
contended, "but they keep it under state secret."

CHAPTER 5

Wallenberg, now faced with the chilling thought he could permanently remain a faceless number in the gulag, spent the rest of the 1950s in Vladimir and Vorkuta prisons, probably because the Soviets thought he was an American spy. The CIA had, too, wondered about Wallenberg's involvement with the American government, so the agency had gone to the one person who would know—Iver C. Olsen.

In 1955, Iver C. Olsen had only one job—working as the Washington representative for the New York investment securities firm of Tripp and Co. A CIA agent, whose name is blacked out in the document, called Olsen at his office, 805 15th Street, N.W., and arranged an interview for December 1.[1] The agency wanted specifically to know if Raoul Wallenberg spied for the American government. A search of the agency's files had failed to answer the question about Wallenberg's relation to the U.S. government, but Olsen would certainly know. The CIA, America's main intelligence gathering agency, demonstrated that up to then it had relied on public information—books and articles—instead of stealth or sources to get its facts in the Wallenberg case. True, one of the CIA's four sections—the Intelligence Directorate—analyzes intelligence gathered openly from available sources or obtained secretly via espionage, aerial and satellite photography and interception of radio, television and other types of communication. But the documents indicate the CIA's effort regarding Wallenberg only involved buying what was on the newsstand. Bereft of firsthand information, the interviewer—admitting only secondhand knowledge—said the agency's basic information about Wallenberg came mainly from a book, Raoul Wallenberg—Hero in Budapest, written in

Swedish by Jeno Levai and published in 1948. Olsen confirmed the facts about Wallenberg in the book.

Next, the agent went to the heart of the matter. Did Olsen, at any time, have "any operational contact with, or [make] any operational use of, WALLENBERG [sic]"?[22] Or, was Raoul Wallenberg an American spy?

"Subject replied to both questions with a very firm negative," the agent said in his report.[3]

Olsen then explained that during his days in Stockholm he had three jobs, all for three government agencies. He worked for the Treasury Department as financial attache of the American Legation in Stockholm; the War Refugee Board, where he was the Stockholm representative, and the OSS. At the intelligence agency, he handled the finances and accounts of the OSS mission in Stockholm, interrogated refugees and escapees to Sweden and procured intelligence, including dispatching of agents to Norway and the Baltic area.

Olsen's contact with Wallenberg was "*only* in his capacity as representative of the War Refugee Board," reported the CIA agent.[4] "Subject was extremely emphatic on this point and returned to it on several occasions during the course of the meeting, apparently wishing to insure that there was no misunderstanding on this score."

Olsen wanted to be sure the CIA knew—Wallenberg never spied for America or any other country.

But Olsen agreed he had help select Wallenberg for his mission to Budapest. When Wallenberg arrived at the Swedish legation in Budapest, Olsen gave him money "solely for the purpose of assisting Jews in Hungary."

Next, Olsen explained the nuts and bolts of financing Wallenberg. The Joint Distribution Committee, a Jewish organization, had opened an account in the Enskilda Bank in Stockholm, which the Wallenberg family controlled. The funds in the account were for Wallenberg's use and Olsen could draw on it. Whenever Wallenberg indicated through "letters pouched from Budapest to the Foreign Office in Stockholm, that he needed funds,"

Olsen withdrew them from the Enskilda account and sent the money to Wallenberg via the Swedish Foreign Office. All the money went to help Wallenberg in his refugee work, except for another 10,000 Swedish kronor. That came from President Roosevelt's secret fund, and Wallenberg used that money to travel to Budapest. After Wallenberg disappeared, Olsen told the CIA the account was closed, and the funds, which were "fairly considerable," returned to the Joint Distribution Committee. Olsen concluded the interview by saying he was willing to answer further questions from the intelligence community.

Twenty days later the CIA sent a memo to A. Sidney Buford III, director of the Office of Libraries and Intelligence-Acquisition, about Wallenberg.[5] The writer's name and one passage in the text are blacked out, but he was the executive officer of the Strategic Services Unit, the organization "liquidating the affairs of the Office of Strategic Services."

After a thorough review of the OSS and CIA files and talking with OSS operatives, the executive director reached the "firm conclusion that WALLENBERG [sic] was in fact never employed by U.S. intelligence in any capacity."

Nevertheless, the Soviets, who gave paranoia a human face, probably knew Olsen worked for the OSS and had recruited Wallenberg, so they convinced themselves Wallenberg spied for the Americans, and they imprisoned and kept him imprisoned because, the Soviets reasoned, neither Sweden nor the United States had really tried to free him.

During World II, the United States and Russia, as allies, shared information, including facts about spies. In his book, "The Red Web," Tom Bower wrote that William Donovan, the founder and director of the OSS, had been told in 1942 by President Roosevelt to avoid making the Soviet Union an intelligence target for the OSS and to stop all operations against the Soviets.[6] A year later Donovan attempted to reverse that order. The Joint Chiefs of Staff may have given oral approval, but FDR's policy was to intensify cooperation between the Americans and the Soviets.

Therefore, in December 1943, this policy led to a "high-level agreement between the OSS and the Soviet secret police, NKVD, to exchange information and representatives," Bower wrote. "An internal OSS memorandum dated 4 February 1944, entitled 'Intelligence to be Furnished to the USSR,' stated that Russia 'may be given intelligence which is of distinctive OSS origin and which may be of aid to that country in prosecuting the war against Germany.'"

J. Edgar Hoover, FBI director, stopped the exchange of personnel, but "Donovan obeyed the President and handed over 1,500 pages of Soviet codes which the OSS station in Stockholm had obtained from Reino Hallamaa, the former head of Finnish intelligence who was exiled in Sweden."[7] With all that information, the Soviets undoubtedly knew about the OSS' operations out of Stockholm and probably knew about Iver Olsen, the man who financed Raoul Wallenberg. For the Soviets, who suspected everyone, this was probably enough to indict, imprison and possibly execute Wallenberg.

By the late '50s, most people in Sweden felt Wallenberg was dead and the reason for his death: Espionage. In a confidential U.S. Embassy dispatch from Stockholm, dated February 25, 1957, Joseph Sweeney, First Embassy Secretary, said, "A current explanation to why Wallenberg was liquidated by the Russians was because that they believed he was an American spy. Rudolph Philipp, the Secretary of the Wallenberg Committee—a group of prominent Swedish citizens—once claimed that Wallenberg had been on a secret mission for President Roosevelt."[8] Philipp, a Jewish-Austrian journalist who had fled Hitler and settled in Stockholm, wrote a book in Swedish about Wallenberg right after the war. An enthusiastic Wallenberg supporter, Philipp also contended in his book Wallenberg had been on a secret mission for FDR.

Lars Berg, press attache at the Swedish Legation in Budapest, had said the Russians believed Wallenberg was an American spy and they were suspicious of his activities in Budapest.[9] Berg felt the Soviets tried to collect evidence against Wallenberg, saying he had spied for the Germans. Now Wallenberg's case had become such a matter of prestige that the Russians didn't want to release him and hoped the Swedes would forget him.

Many Swedish officials said that Wallenberg knew former American Minister Herschel Johnson, and he supposedly picked Wallenberg for his "dangerous mission," said Sweeney, who also didn't know all the facts about Wallenberg's selection.[10] In any event, Sweeney said he lacked "concrete evidence" if Wallenberg were involved in espionage or on a "secret or confidential mission for any foreign power."

Though Wallenberg couldn't communicate with the outside world, his former inmates did for him. For example, in 1956, Aftonbladet, a Stockholm newspaper, reported Hausel Mersonent, who had been in the Soviet prison system, said prisoners at Vladimir told him that Wallenberg was in a neighboring cell.[11] The Swedish Foreign Ministry spoke with Mersonent before Prime Minister Tage Erlander left on a trip to Moscow, but nothing developed from this information.

An unnamed U.S. source in Munich met on February 19, 1957, with two Estonians, Romulus Mandel and Elmar Lipping.[12] Mandel said he had just met with someone named E. Wallenstein, a German, who had recently returned from Soviet incarceration. Wallenstein told Mandel he had served in the German embassy in Bucharest and the Soviets arrested him in Romania, sentencing him in 1947 to 25 years in prison. Wallenstein served some of his time in Vorkuta, where he met Wallenberg in 1955 or 1956.

A man named Emil Brugger, a Swiss citizen, spent ten years (1948-58) in Soviet prisons.[13] During Wallenberg's 42nd birthday, August 4, 1954, Brugger said he had kept in contact with Wallenberg by tapping in Vladimir Prison. Via this prison pipeline, Wallenberg had given Brugger a message, "Wallenberg—First Secretary in the Swedish Mission in Budapest, taken in 1945." In reply, Brugger said he had been captured in 1948. Wallenberg asked Brugger to contact Swedish authorities if the Swiss were released, for the Soviets allowed Wallenberg no correspondence.

Several other prisoners who came back from the gulag confirmed that Brugger, while imprisoned, mentioned this contact with Wallenberg.

Brugger told the Swedish Embassy in Vienna that he had evidence Wallenberg had lived at least into the 1950s. Erik Braunerbielm, first secretary of the Swedish Embassy in Vienna, said Brugger had told him about Wallenberg. Braunerbielm, who had to handle screening and security duties at the embassy, provided information on December 3, 1958, to the CIA's agent in Bern about the Wallenberg contact.[14]

"Brugger allegedly told the Swedes that Wallenberg had communicated his presence to Brugger, also a prisoner in that prison at that time, by means of pipe rapping," the CIA agent in Bern said in a memo. "Braunerbielm said his Government is constantly trying to find traces of Wallenberg's possible existence and wished to evaluate Brugger's reliability."

Two German citizens, H. T. Mulle and G. Rehekampf, were incarcerated in Soviet prisons, respectively, from 1950 to 1956 and 1945 to 1955.[15] Each said they learned at different times "through one and the same co-prisoner in the Vladimir Prison that Wallenberg was in . . . Vladimir at the beginning of the 1950s. This Soviet co-prisoner has been characterized as a trustworthy and reliable person by a great number of former prisoners who have returned from Vladimir."

Besides the believable, there were the impostors, who periodically surfaced, seeking money, notoriety or military intelligence.[16] In 1955, a man with three names and an unconvincing story appeared in Vienna. He called himself Rohan (the CIA file omits the first name) and said he could provide information about Wallenberg. Sven Allard, the Swedish Minister in Vienna, said that Rohan's real name was Jaromir Alexander Balcar, and that Balcar was a petty criminal, liar and possibly a Czech agent. His story was a fabric of lies, based on newspaper reports. Similar impostors appeared throughout the years, necessitating an American or Swedish interrogation and then a quick dismissal.

To trace Wallenberg through the Soviets, the Swedish government sent 15 written and 34 oral notes and reminders delivered in Moscow without results until February 6, 1957.[17] Then the Soviets, who for ten years said they knew nothing of Wallenberg, admitted they had imprisoned him, but now they said he had died in the gulag.

Andrei Gromyko, Soviet deputy foreign minister, handed an eight paragraph, two-page note to Swedish Ambassador Rolf Sohlman in Moscow, saying an extensive investigation uncovered in the archives of the medical department of Lubyanka Prison a handwritten document dated July 17, 1947, and signed by Colonel A.L. Smoltsov, chief of Lubyanka prison's medical department.[18] This document was addressed to Viktor S. Abakumov, state security minister. It read, "I report that the prisoner Walenberg [sic], who is known to you, died suddenly in his cell last night probably as the result of a myocardial infarction [heart attack]. In connection with our instructions that I maintain personal supervision of Walenberg, I request instructions as to who shall make the postmortem examination to establish the cause of death."

After Smoltsov's signature and date came a handwritten notation: "Have personally informed the minister. Order has been given to cremate the corpse without postmortem examination."

Gromyko's memorandum blamed Wallenberg's death on Abakumov, Stalin's state security chief, who supposedly kept Wallenberg in jail and lied to the government about the case. Abakumov was chief of SMERSH (whose initials mean "death to spies"), a unit of the Soviet intelligence agency. In 1954, the Supreme Court of the Soviet Union condemned and executed Abakumov as a "tool of Beria." In closing, the memorandum said the Soviet government "presents its sincere regrets because of what has occurred and expresses its profound sympathy to the Swedish Government as well as to Raoul Wallenberg's relatives."

Gromyko's report, released just after then Premier Nikita Khrushchev denounced Stalin, specified that Abakumov, who had imprisoned Wallenberg, was a friend of Stalin's. The new Soviet regime tried to blame the old for Wallenberg's "death."

This memorandum, undercut by repeated sightings of Wallenberg, convinced few people. At the time of his "death," Wallenberg was only 34 years old and in apparent good health. The men who had escorted Wallenberg from Budapest to Moscow were missing and protest petitions Wallenberg had filed to the Russians were unavailable. Just before he "died," Wallenberg had been transferred to Vladimir Prison, 120 miles northeast of Moscow, according to testimony of former prisoners. The U.S. embassy in Stockholm suspected subterfuge. Every word of the Soviet message was weighed and impacted with vagueness, explained Joseph Sweeney, First Secretary of the Embassy in a February 25, 1957, correspondence to the State Department in Washington.[19] For instance, the message used phrases such as, "the conclusion should be drawn," allowing the Soviet government "free to adopt another interpretation if it chooses," Sweeney cautioned.

Sweden answered the Soviet explanation with a sharp note to the Russians. R. Hichens Bergstrom, the assistant director of the political section of the foreign office, freely translated the diplomatic language: Sweden said to the Soviet Union, "We think you are lying."

Prime Minister Erlander held a press conference the day after the Soviet note on Wallenberg, complaining that the Soviet reply "contained such meager information."[20] The Swedish Foreign Office also had testimonies from 19 ex-prisoners of war, mainly German, Austrian and Italian who shared prison cells with Wallenberg or Langfelder or claimed they were in communication with him by the prison code of "tapping" in Lubyanka or Lefortovo prisons. The Swedes requested the remains of Wallenberg's body, but the Soviets—conveniently—said it had been cremated. However, the usual Soviet practice then was to bury dead prisoners with their number plate affixed to one leg. If the Foreign Office had failed to issue a firm note, influential Swedish citizens would have publicly objected, putting a political strain on the Swedish government.

Public opinion, including the only Wallenberg committee then in existence, united in supporting the Swedish government's response to the Soviet Union, but the opposition press in Sweden blasted Foreign Minister Östen Undén for "alleged passiveness" and lack of interest to find Wallenberg just after the Russians seized him, the U.S. embassy said in a cable to Washington. Some Swedish weeklies said Undén in 1947 supposedly accepted Soviet assurances as evidence that Wallenberg was not in the Soviet Union. But that was ten years earlier and in 1957 Undén was responsible for the sharp note to the Soviet Union.[21]

"Rather than quieting Swedish public opinion," Sweeney said, "this statement by Gromyko has further activated the demand here for the full story on the fate of an almost idolized Swedish citizen fallen the victim of a totalitarian police state."[22] The strong Swedish protest note "is still another indication that Swedish-Soviet relations are at a low ebb."

In the same message, Sweeney told Washington that while "few commentators doubted that Raoul Wallenberg must now be dead," they didn't believe the Soviet explanation. The existing Soviet regime tried to blame Wallenberg's arrest and imprisonment on Stalin and his henchmen, now all dead, but the Swedish press blasted the memo, the Russians, everybody within its inky range.

Sweeney interpreted the press criticism for Washington: Such treatment of a neutral diplomat reflected on the entire Soviet Union, "with its inherent terror and disregard for human life, irrespective of who may for the moment be the rulers." Sweeney speculated that the Soviet Union released the note as part of "the new Soviet campaign to woo the Nordic countries." But the Swedes rejected the Soviet advances. Instead of healing Soviet-Swedish relations, the Gromyko note "significantly worsened" them, Sweeney said.

In 1959, two Swedish Supreme Court Justices, Ragnar Gyllenswärd and Per Santesson, said that in their opinion and thus under Swedish law, Wallenberg was probably alive at least during the early 1950s in Vladimir Prison.[23] The Soviets were still lying about Wallenberg, but if not dead where was he?

Kalinski, who was released October 22, 1959, saw Wallenberg before he left and thought he "looked young and fit." That drastically changed.

Apparently desperate after 15 years of imprisonment, Wallenberg went on a hunger strike, a precursor of the tactics used by Russian refuseniks in the 1980s. In a way, Wallenberg's hunger strike worked. He became sick and was transferred to Moscow, where he came under the care of Dr. A.L. Myasnikov, chairman of the Soviet Academy of Medical Science and chief of the Department of Internal Medicine at Moscow's University Hospital. Myasnikov knew a professional colleague, Nanna Svartz, an internationally known physician, from Sweden.

In 1961, she was in charge of the Department of Internal Medicine at the Stockholm University clinic as well as on the staff of Stockholm's Karolinska Hospital. That facility's administrator was Fredrik von Dardel, Raoul Wallenberg's stepfather. Svartz' private patients included Prime Minister Erlander, his wife, Aina, and Maj von Dardel, Wallenberg's mother. In the 1940s, Svartz also treated Madame Kollontai, then the Russian ambassador to Sweden.

The female doctor traveled frequently to Moscow for scientific conferences and knew Myasnikov.[24] Because of her involvement with the Wallenberg family, Svartz decided to ask Myasnikov about Raoul Wallenberg. She accompanied Myasnikov on his rounds at Moscow University Hospital, and then they went to his office and talked, using German, a language they both knew well. After a few minutes, Svartz said, "I must tell you that I have been asked by the director-general of Stockholm's Karolinska Institute, Fredrik von Dardel, to see what I can find out about his stepson, Raoul Wallenberg."

Myasnikov spoke in a low tone. "As a matter of fact, I know a great deal about the Wallenberg case. The person you're speaking of is in a very bad way. He's been at Vladimir for quite some time, and now he's in the mental hospital. He's extremely tired, nervous and depressed, and he's also lost a good deal of weight; he needs to rest."

Finally, credible evidence that Wallenberg was alive.

Myasnikov added that he had recently examined Wallenberg at the same hospital where they were talking. Despite Wallenberg's condition, Myasnikov said he had found it "enjoyable" to talk to him. Svartz sensed an uneasiness in Myasnikov, who perhaps wanted to help but feared for his own safety. She asked if she could see Wallenberg. "I'll be returning to Sweden soon. Since I'm a doctor, why not let him return to his native country under my care?"

Myasnikov refused. "There are 'things' that have to be completed here before he can go," he said.

They continued to talk, and Myasnikov went out and brought in a colleague, a Dr. Danishevski, who was interested in the case. But when Svartz mentioned she had renewed her acquaintance with Vladimir Semyonov, the Soviet deputy foreign minister, Danishevski recommended she try diplomatic avenues to get Wallenberg freed. Svartz had once saved Madame Kollontai from dying of pneumonia in the 1940s when Semyonov had been the ambassador's deputy. Svartz returned to her hotel, got Semyonov's telephone number from the Swedish embassy and called him, but he was out.

Svartz left Moscow for Stockholm, where she spoke to Prime Minister Erlander, who wrote to Khrushchev. The Swedish ambassador Sohlman delivered the letter to Khrushchev February 25, 1961. Khrushchev gave the ambassador a hostile reception. He said there was nothing to add about Wallenberg and then threatened Sohlman. "If Sweden insists on bringing up the Wallenberg affair again and again, it must mean Sweden is intentionally trying to worsen relations with the Soviet Union."

Svartz returned to Moscow in March 1961 and asked Myasnikov in the presence of a third doctor if she could see Wallenberg. Coldly, he responded, "That can only be decided at a higher level. Provided, of course, that he is not dead."

When they were alone, Myasnikov told her, "Why did you have to repeat to your government what I told you in the strictest confidence? . . . Khrushchev himself called me in and shouted at me for saying anything about Wallenberg. In fact, he was so enraged that he pushed me, and I fell down a flight of stairs."

Next, Svartz telephoned Semyonov, the deputy foreign minister, but he was always unavailable to her. She left Moscow again without Wallenberg.

Some accounts contend that because of this 1961 incident, Khrushchev ordered Wallenberg moved from Moscow to Wrangel Island, one of the most desolate spots in the world, to avoid detection by the West. For that, Wrangel Island was excellent. The island, an icy Siberian dot about half the size of Long Island, is 300 miles inside the Arctic Circle and 100 miles north of the Siberian mainland as well as 270 miles northwest of Cape Lisburne, Alaska. Though desolate, countries have argued over it for more than 100 years. The crew of a New England whaler discovered the island in 1867 and named it for Baron Ferdinand Petrovich von Wrangel. Von Wrangel, a lieutenant in the Imperial Russian Navy, had led failed expeditions looking for the island 25 years earlier. In 1881, the United States claimed it after Captain Calvin Hooper stuck an American flag and built a cairn, where he put a record of his visit. American, Russian and British expeditions hunted, trapped and surveyed the island during the next 40 years. Eventually, an Alaskan company bought it from the U.S. government and started a trapping operation. The Red October, a Soviet gunboat, landed there in 1924, and the Soviets arrested the American representative of the Lomen Reindeer and Trapping Corporation and incarcerated him in Vladivostok. The Soviets said he died there of pneumonia.

The Soviets like Wrangel Island, for 100 miles of the Arctic Ocean separate the island from the mainland. Wrangel is literally in the middle of nowhere, making it one of the most secret places in the world. This is the ideal spot for a nuclear submarine base, a school for spies or for hiding prisoners that might embarrass mother Russia. However, the CIA contends its intelligence gathering and later satellite photography show there never was a prison camp on Wrangel Island. Accounts from prisoners, including some who have testified before Congress, dispute that.

In any event, Wrangel has no regular mail service and communication with the outside world is almost impossible, but incredibly someone managed it. An Italian hunter in 1971 shot down a goose and attached to it he found a rubber tube with a piece of paper. Though old and faded, some words were legible, "SOS . . . Italian officers . . . island beyond the Arctic Circle."

As Wallenberg suffered, possibly on Wrangel Island, Svartz persisted in her attempts to free him. She returned to Moscow in 1962 for another meeting and found Myasnikov. This time fear had replaced anger. He pretended not to understand her German and turned his back on her. In 1964, Myasnikov wrote to Svartz in answer to new stories about Wallenberg, created when Andrei Gromyko visited Sweden. Myasnikov denied any knowledge of Wallenberg and said miscommunication probably resulted from his poor German, a language he and Svartz constantly had used for communication.

When Khrushchev visited Stockholm in June 1964, Expressen, the biggest Swedish newspaper, printed a headline and article in Russian on the front page. The headline said, "THE QUESTION: WHERE IS RAOUL WALLENBERG?"

Again, Khrushchev was livid. He told Prime Minister Erlander, "If I had suspected that the subject of Wallenberg would be brought up, I should never have accepted your invitation to visit Sweden." Khrushchev remained annoyed over the Wallenberg matter during his time in Sweden. While in Gothenburg on the last day of his visit, Khrushchev saw that someone had put cut flowers at the base of a statue of Charles XII, a Swedish king who had raided Russian territory in the eighteenth century. At a post-luncheon speech in Gothenburg's Town Hall, Khrushchev noted the bleak parallels. "Sweden again wants to declare war on the Soviet Union."

Erlander realized the Wallenberg matter had ruined Khrushchev's visit. The Soviets didn't realize that for Sweden's citizens Wallenberg was an important matter, not a Cold War pawn.

In July 1965, Svartz again returned to Moscow and saw Myasnikov, who once more denied he had ever treated Wallenberg or knew of his whereabouts. Four months after this discussion, Myasnikov unexpectedly died, though he appeared to be a man of good health in his sixties.

CHAPTER 6

The two nations—Sweden and the United States—that could do something to rescue Wallenberg during the 1950s, '60s and into the '70s did nothing. Swedish leaders, content to let the Soviet jailers steal Wallenberg's life day by day, belonged to the Social Democratic Labour Party, which dominated Swedish politics in this century, holding power for 44 straight years, from 1932-76 and again from 1982-91. Economically sunk in the Depression of the 1930s, the Swedish people turned to the Social Democrats, which pulled the country up and into a social-welfare state.

Per Albin Hansson, a store clerk with minimal formal education, became the four-time premier of Sweden from 1932 to 1946 and its economic savior. Hansson started measures for construction of public works, aid to agriculture and financial expansion as well as unemployment insurance and old age pensions. His plan worked, so the Swedish people kept the Social Democratic party in power for almost a half century. One could draw parallels to President Franklin D. Roosevelt's election in 1932 and the start of his New Deal legislation to pull the U.S. economy out of the Depression and give the Democratic Party a 20-year grip on the American presidency.

During the war, Hansson ruled through a coalition government while retaining Sweden's neutrality. When Germany attacked the Soviet Union in 1941, the Nazis demanded transit rights to let a division of German troops from Norway to Finland. Fearing its powerful neighbor, Sweden succumbed. After the war, Hansson resumed the total rule of the Social Democrats. The programs included tax reorganization to obtain wider distribution of wealth, which meant trying to take money away from capitalists like the

Wallenberg family. In that socialist atmosphere, Swedish bureau-crats apparently devoted minimal attention to freeing the country's famous citizen, Raoul Wallenberg. The Swedish government asked the Soviets for information on Wallenberg, but many Swedes felt not hard enough. The Swedes nudged, not pushed the Rus-sians, either out of simple nuclear fear or dislike of Wallenberg, or both.

"The Social Democrats could have done much more," Nina Lagergren complained. "They could have been forceful in their behavior when they still had the chance."

When asked why the Social Democrats failed to do more, Mrs. Lagergren responded tersely: "Ask them."

The only other possible rescuer lay 4,000 miles west across the Atlantic Ocean, but the U.S. government always had more important matters. Every day of delay meant another reason to do nothing to help Wallenberg. At the same time, the Soviets had Wallenberg, knew they had him and told no one. Of course, this was the age of Stalin, where Russians were killed or put in prison daily without reason or remorse.

The State Department and the CIA seemed more interested in gathering information from Swedish government actions, newspaper reports or recent books about Wallenberg rather than taking any action to free him. Instead of a fearless rescuer, the U.S. government became a dispassionate observer.

For example, during the mid-1950s, a man named Nikolay Nefedov met a merchant in Hamburg named German Krisko, who has just left the Soviet Union after spending about 10 years in Lubyanka and Vladimir.[1] Krisko felt his kidnapping by Smersh was linked to Wallenberg's. Krisko lived in Riga, Latvia, but right before the start of World War II, he went to Yugoslavia and became involved in commercial operations. As the war continued, Krisko moved to Hungary and as the conflict came to a close, he worked as an interpreter in the Swedish Embassy in Budapest. Trilingual, Krisko was fluent in Russian, German and French, but the embassy only needed his Russian skills, for after Hungary declared war on the Soviet Union, the Soviet delegation left Budapest and the Swedes looked after their interests.

Krisko said he met Wallenberg frequently to translate documents and requests as well as acting as translator for Soviet refugees, who were "former" Soviet citizens fleeing the relentlessly-moving Red Army that had pushed the Germans back through Poland, Romania and now moved into Budapest. Though the Soviet refugees sought protection against the fascist Germans and Hungarians, Nefedov still referred to them as "former Soviets" because, "to the great amazement of the Swedes, (they) did not at all want to return to the socialist 'paradise' and naively requested that they be sent to Sweden."[2]

Nefedov and Krisko became friends and when they met later in Germany, they saw each other daily, where they returned to his "road of sorrow" and the Wallenberg kidnapping. Just after the Soviets seized Budapest, four Smersh agents dressed in regular Red Army uniforms grabbed Krisko near the Swedish Embassy, threw him into a car and transported him to the outskirts of Pest. After questioning him, the Soviets put him in a cellar filled with prisoners of all nationalities "packed in like sardines: Greeks, Spaniards, Rumanians, Yugoslavs, and others."[3]

Two days later the Soviets took Krisko to an airport and put him on a big transport airplane with several dozen other prisoners. After several hours, the aircraft landed at a Moscow airport and the prisoners were taken to Lubyanka, where the Soviets put Krisko in solitary confinement for three years. In that three-year-span, the Soviets interrogated Krisko weekly the first year, the questioning decreasing with time. His many interrogators included Abakumov.

While the Chekists accused Krisko of spying for three countries—first Sweden, then England and then the United States—the interrogation centered on Wallenberg's activities. Specifically, the interrogators wanted to know what Russians had spoken with Wallenberg, who had sought help and what help Wallenberg had given. Also, the Soviet investigators wanted to know what part Wallenberg had taken in rescuing Budapest's Jews.

Though Nefedov doesn't specify, Krisko somehow found out—apparently from his captors, for Krisko remained in solitary confinement—that Wallenberg was also a prisoner in Lubyanka. The Soviets, trying to force Krisko to confess, did tell him that Wallenberg had confessed the day before. After surviving three years in Lubyanka's confinement, Krisko was transferred to Vladimir. He received no trial, but stayed in difficult circumstances for more than ten years. Finally, Konrad Adenauer, chancellor of West Germany, gained the freedom of German prisoners of war and those deported during the war, so Krisko as a German subject went from prison to a repatriation camp and then to West Germany a week later.[4]

When he arrived in Germany in the mid-1950s, Krisko went to the CIA office in Frankfurt and told the agency all he knew about the Wallenberg kidnapping. The CIA took his testimony but repeated the now threadbare refrain: Wallenberg is Swedish, not American, and the CIA could do nothing.

Next, Krisko went to Stockholm, but the Swedes barely showed any interest in his tale. Nefedov explained Swedish recalcitrance: "don't anger the Kremlin in any way."

In contrast to minimal governmental activity on two continents, the Swedish populace maintained its fervent interest in Wallenberg. Sweeney, the American diplomat in Stockholm, explained to Washington in 1957 the Swedes' acute interest in Raoul Wallenberg. "Neutral during the war, Sweden did not experience, as many of the belligerent nations did, mass disappearance of nationals, so that the fate of one single Swedish citizen particularly one engaged in humanitarian relief work, went to the heart of the general public."[5]

The Swedes were especially upset, feeling the foreign office had failed at an earlier stage to conduct "its investigation concerning Wallenberg with the necessary concern," reported the U.S. legation in Stockholm.

When private citizens formed Wallenberg committees, that translated into "implied criticism" over the Swedish government's handling of the case, creating clashes between the committees and Foreign Minister Undén, "who appears to have attached more faith in the Soviet assurance that (it) could discover no information about Wallenberg than subsequent events warranted," the U.S. legation said.

During the 1950s, the Swedes kept pressing the Soviets for information about Wallenberg. At one point, the Swedish government urged the Soviets to "make a speedy investigation in order to determine whether Wallenberg has been detained in the Vladimir Prison." In response, the Soviet Union replied March 6, 1959, that it has the "honor to state that its memorandum of February 6, 1957, contained all information concerning R. Wallenberg."[6] But beneath the surface, the Swedish government cared little about Wallenberg, regarding him like a wayward relative best left in prison. A U.S. government agent, possibly CIA, met with a Swedish agent in late 1956. Both names remain classified, but though the document, dated December 7, 1956, is frequently blacked out, part of the conversation is revealed and that reveals Sweden's ennui with Raoul Wallenberg.[7]

First, the Swedish agent talked of his dissatisfaction with the Swedish Ambassador to Moscow, Rolf Sohlman, who had both a Russian wife and a love of Russia. Sohlman liked Moscow and wanted to "spend the rest of his life there," the American quoted his Swedish counterpart as saying. "There were strong overtones of pro-Soviet views on the part of Sohlman in [blacked out] statement that this man is quite useless for accurate reporting purposes and that serious consideration is being given to kicking him upstairs into a Swedish Ambassadorship at the United Nations." This view conflicted with the official line from the Foreign Office, where Sohlman was regarded as a great Russian expert. In fact, the Foreign Office wanted to keep Sohlman in Moscow "because of his great value."[8] If indeed Sohlman loved Russia and wanted to stay there, why should he endanger his position with annoying inquiries about Raoul Wallenberg?

The American agent's interest percolated when the Swedish agent mentioned Wallenberg, but the Swede's views lowered the boil. "He said the Foreign Office energy in pursuing this case was largely the result of the strong pressure of public opinion both through the press and through the special Raoul Wallenberg association . . . [The Swedish agent] made it clear . . . that the Swedish government expects another rejection for their latest note to the Soviet Union on this subject, and that the Swedish Government would be left with no recourse but to publish a White Paper." The Swedish agent continued that "such publication might be somewhat embarrassing to the Foreign Office because of its probable revelation that until approximately 3 years ago the Foreign Office had not pursued the question with sufficient vigor, although since that time the Foreign Office has been extremely vigorous in its notes of protest and inquiry."

Still, the Swedish agent said a year before he had spent three months in Germany interrogating German returnees from the Soviet camp at Vorkuta and was "satisfied of the positive identification of Wallenberg and certification of his presence in Vorkuta by at least one German who had been Wallenberg's cellmate."

Therefore, this agent was "positive that he could trace Wallenberg's actual existence up to a certain date," sometime before 1949. "I am not at liberty to tell you the exact date" when Wallenberg's actual survival was last certified, he told the American.[9] In any event, the Swedish agent was certain Wallenberg had died by then (1956). Washington added the report to its growing file on Wallenberg.

A stalemate. Sweden was unwilling—or afraid—or both, to push the Soviets beyond paper protests; the United States avoided the affair by saying Wallenberg was a Swedish citizen, even though an American agency had recruited him, so the Soviets— unencumbered by any pressure—kept Wallenberg in the gulag, retaining their story that he had died in 1947. To put the situation into schoolyard terms, the smaller and frightened schoolboy Swede kept launching puny protests against the Soviet bully while America, the bully's physical equal and normally the schoolboy's ideological ally, stood by only taking notes.

The Soviet-Swedish-American stalemate continued into the 1960s, creating crises—both foreign and domestic. "The Wallenberg case has been the most persistent issue of contention between Sweden and the USSR since the war," George R. Andrews, second secretary for the U.S. Embassy in Stockholm reported to Washington, which monitored the situation.[10]

After Khrushchev ended his visit to Sweden in June 1964 and repeated the Soviet position that Wallenberg was not in the Soviet Union, Prime Minister Tage Erlander said on June 26, 1964, "We are deeply disappointed that the Soviet Union has not felt able to do more about this matter," adding the Swedish government did not intend "to give up our efforts in this matter."

The U.S. Embassy learned confidentially Khrushchev was extremely unreasonable and obdurate and annoyed that Erlander kept asking about Wallenberg. Erlander, Hansson's political soulmate, had little in common with the Wallenbergs, though he graduated from Lund University in 1928, the same school where Guy von Dardel later taught physics. In 1933, Erlander became a member of the Riksdag (parliament) as a Social Democrat. He served in many posts and in 1945 he ran the Ministry of Education and Church Affairs in Per Hansson's government. When Hansson died in 1946, Erlander became prime minister and chairman of the Social Democratic Party. He remained in both positions until he retired in 1968 and championed social-welfare legislation.

During the campaign prior to the Swedish September 1964 elections, "The bourgeois opposition has criticized the Social Democratic Government for not doing enough to clear up the mystery (of Wallenberg)," Andrews told the State Department.[11] The bourgeois opponents urged the government to make public the confidential evidence, showing Wallenberg was still alive after 1947 when the Soviets said he died in Lubyanka. The bourgeoisie wanted to pressure the Russians to release Wallenberg or more information about him. The Swedish Socialists, who held power, refused, fearing if they released such information, that would irritate the

Soviets and reduce the chances of freeing Wallenberg if he were still alive.

Nevertheless, Erlander wrote to Premier Kosygin on February 11, 1965, but that drew a negative reply from the Soviet Ambassador in Stockholm. When Erlander visited the Soviet Union in June 1965, he once more discussed the Wallenberg case with Kosygin, but nothing happened. After Erlander returned, he decided to relent to the opposition proposal on releasing a White Paper.

Released on September 16, 1965, the White Paper reviewed Wallenberg's mission in Hungary and discussed his arrest and imprisonment in the Soviet Union.[12] Always the politician, Erlander gave the opposition the White Paper only a few hours before he released it to the press, apparently for a double-barreled effect. First, Erlander hoped this would stifle any contentions that his political opponents had forced the Socialists into such action. Second, he wanted to show the Soviet Union the White Paper "represents a considered step by the government, acting upon its own initiative."

The Swedish government issued the White Paper "to reply to opposition criticism that it has not been active enough in pursuing the question with the USSR. While the Wallenberg affair will continue to be a definite irritant in Swedish-Soviet relations, it will not affect the operations of Swedish neutrality policy," Andrews reported to Washington. The U.S. Embassy in Sweden saw the White Paper as a "surprisingly strong effort to put pressure on the Soviets to be more cooperative in the matter."

The most sensational information in the White Paper involved the previously mentioned statement by Dr. Nanna Svartz about her trip to Moscow and meeting a Soviet doctor who said Wallenberg was still alive. A month later, the standoff remained. The Soviets were obdurate and even scornful toward the repeated Swedish requests for information. Prime Minister Erlander could have dropped the matter or the Soviets could have "sought to allay Swedish suspicions by providing specific information or by appearing more solicitous of Swedish feelings, but neither did so," Andrews reported to Washington October 4, 1965.[13]

Andrews, in the U.S. legation in Stockholm, put his spin on the White Paper. The document "represents an effort to put public pressure on the Soviets, while at the same time seeking to avoid giving undue offense."[24] Additionally, the White Paper is "in effect also an admission of despair on the part of the Government that there can be a successful resolution of the Wallenberg case."

To the U.S. diplomats in Stockholm, the White Paper represented "more of a gesture towards Swedish public opinion." The Swedes all along had only planned a limited effort on Wallenberg's behalf, said Andrews.

"Whatever the frictions in Swedish-Soviet relations engendered by the Wallenberg affair the Social Democratic Government is highly unlikely to let them affect its concept of Sweden's neutral and non-aligned role in the East-West conflict."

Erlander tried to convince the Soviets that the Swedes cared about Wallenberg. "The fate of Raoul Wallenberg has deeply engaged Swedish opinion . . . We have sought to convince the Soviet leadership of the extraordinary seriousness with which Swedish quarters look upon this question."

The prime minister said "an essential part" of Swedish negotiations with the Soviet leaders concerns the Wallenberg case. "Unfortunately, the result has been negative."

In 1965, Prime Minister Kosygin said a new investigation uncovered documents showing that Wallenberg had been cremated. The Soviets kept insisting Wallenberg was not in their country, not in prison, not in the hospital or anywhere else, Erlander said. Then he promised, "As long as there is a possibility, this effort must continue and be pursued."

To Erlander and the Swedish Government, Wallenberg's release was not worth an all out effort. The Swedes feared the Russians too much, even more than the bourgeoisie opponents, whom they hoped to mollify by releasing the White Paper. The Swedish government contended it kept chasing every lead. From 1945 to 1965, the Swedes sent at least 30 demarches to the Soviet government. "We have left no trace unexplored, however vague it may have seemed."[15] Sweden said it worked via diplomatic channels or personal contacts. "Intensive checking of all material and thorough internal considerations have taken place all the time," including talking to returning prisoners about Wallenberg. Government officials tried to make contact with the prisoners of war returning from the Soviet Union who might have been in Vladimir Prison. The testimonies of the former prisoners and Dr. Svartz created the foundation for the representations to the Soviet Union. The Swedish government felt only through contact at the highest level of the Soviet government could an arrangement be completed to free Wallenberg.

While the politicians temporized, the indefatigable Maj von Dardel only knew her first born son was imprisoned and she would try almost anything to liberate him. So, in 1973, Wallenberg's mother again tried to arouse American interest by writing to a top government official. Sven Strömberg, a Swedish radio correspondent in London, used the Freedom of Information Act in 1979 to uncover a relevant letter to Henry Kissinger and its resulting developments. On May 4, 1973, Mrs. von Dardel wrote to Kissinger, then Secretary of State, asking him to find out the truth about her son.[16]

"I now ask you, who through your outstanding efforts, have freed thousands of prisoners, to against the background of my tragic uncertainty about what really happened to my son after he was imprisoned to inform me if you have the possibility to do something which can shed new light on my son's fate, and if he still is alive to bring him back to freedom."

Almost four months later—August 21, 1973—the letter reached Kissinger with an attachment. Five political and diplomatic experts at different levels of the State Department researched the case and recommended a positive reply. They included a memorandum that described the Wallenberg case, an unsigned letter to

Maj von Dardel and a cable ready for sending to the U.S. Embassy in Moscow, telling the legation to start a new investigation.

The proposed letter said, "In view of the humanitarian nature of the case and your son's efforts for the Hungarian Jews during World War II, the United States Government is prepared to make inquiries regarding you [sic] son's fate of [sic] the Soviet government through the American Embassy in Moscow. At such time an answer is received, we will communicate it to you promptly."[17]

The cable from the State Department in Washington to the American Embassy in Moscow ordered the U.S. ambassador to contact the Foreign Office in Moscow and request available information about Wallenberg. The cable had been readied and typed on a telex tape to be sent to the telex system that connects the headquarters in Washington with the U.S. embassy in Moscow. Only Kissinger's approval was required. That never happened, and neither the cable to Moscow nor the letter to Mrs. Von Dardel was sent.

On October 11, 1973, the subordinates received a three-word answer, "rejected by Kissinger." Kissinger gave no explanation for his rejection. Inquiries to his office received the response of "no comment."[18]

When Lena Biorck-Kaplan, chairperson of the American Wallenberg Committee, pressed Kissinger for an answer, he maintained he never knew why the letter was disapproved. His staff members could use his signature, Kissinger said. The U.S. Secretary of State at last muscling the Soviets on Wallenberg could have produced some answers about or freedom for the hero of Budapest. Instead, again nothing occurred.

Stig Ramel, head of the Nobel Foundation, on February 20, 1974, wrote Kissinger on behalf of Mrs. von Dardel, requesting information from Kissinger about her son. Kissinger replied he knew all about Wallenberg's feats, but a check of the files revealed nothing that would provide help on the case.[19]

Strömberg thought Kissinger took no action to help Mrs. von Dardel in retaliation for Sweden's criticism of America's involvement in Southeast Asia, particularly its bombing of Cambodia. In a March 18, 1979, article in Dagens Nyheter, Strömberg wrote about the fractured relations between Washington and Stockholm due to "Sweden's increasingly critical stand against U.S. Vietnam policies."[20] Kissinger, himself a Jew once persecuted by the Nazis, became "particularly insulted because of the allusions to Nazi-like crimes against Vietnam," Strömberg wrote.

The Americans particularly disliked Swedish Prime Minister Olof Palme for his outspoken criticism of the Vietnam War. In 1968, Palme joined the North Vietnamese ambassador to Moscow in a Stockholm demonstration against U.S. participation in the Vietnam War. That infuriated the Americans, but Palme accelerated his criticism, comparing President Richard M. Nixon's order to bomb Hanoi to Hitlerian acts.

Palme, once a close adviser to Erlander, dominated Swedish politics for 20 years, serving as head of the Social Democratic Party for 17 years, including 11 as premier.

Domestically, Palme advocated social equality and employed high taxes to give generous medical, educational and recreational benefits to Sweden's citizens. He disregarded opponents' demands to cut taxes, aid competition and reduce welfare spending, contending this would create a society of "egoism and sharp elbows."

Therefore, the American government had little desire to help the Swedes in the Wallenberg matter or much of anything else while the Socialist Swedes hardly had common ground with the capitalistic Wallenberg family. Once again, Raoul Wallenberg had no national ally.

CHAPTER 7

Other Soviet prisoners—Shifrin, Kaplan and Kalinski (the noted) and Solzhenitsyn (the notable)—became linked, directly or indirectly, to Wallenberg during the 1970s-80s and explained his travail to many in the West, including the Senate Internal Security subcommittee.

Abraham Shifrin was the chief lawyer of the Soviet Defense Ministry for the Contract Section after World War II, a high position for a Jewish lawyer in Stalinist Russia.[1] Suddenly the Soviets arrested and incarcerated Shifrin, who contends his only crime was his religion. His colleagues invented a story of subversive activity (in 1953) and without charges or a trial to answer these charges, Shifrin was sent to a labor camp for detention. Internal exile. Stalin had placed many Jews in such camps, holding them there for years. Sadly, Shifrin's father had been imprisoned in Siberia and died there after a ten-year sentence. Shifrin, who now lives in a small community near Jerusalem (Zichron Yaakov), himself spent 10 years in the camps, where he met several prisoners some of whom said they had known Wallenberg.

The Soviets sent the younger Shifrin to the camp at Potma (Dubravlag), Camp 7. There he got books, some in English and translated one, "Exodus," by Leon Uris, from Russian into English, a task that helped keep Shifrin sane. At Dubravlag, Shifrin said he first learned about Wallenberg as a Swedish prisoner being transported from camp to camp, including Wrangel Island, the remote camp far above the Arctic Circle. Other men returning from Wrangel Island told their prison colleagues about seeing Wallenberg there. They told of their suffering in the bitter cold Arctic winters, and they also spoke of Wallenberg as the Swede who stayed fit by rolling in the snow. The prisoners knew of his heroic mission in Budapest, but they could not understand why he was in prison. After his release, Shifrin came to Israel in 1972 and met with Soviet émigrés, including Yefim Moshinsky, who said they were imprisoned with Wallenberg or knew other prisoners who had contact with him.

A year later Shifrin spoke to the Senate Internal Security sub-committee.[2] He told the subcommittee on February 1, 1973, that ten years earlier he heard from prisoners who had just arrived from a camp on Wrangel Island that there was a special group of high ranking foreign military and other official prisoners on the island, including POWs taken in 1945.

During his testimony, Shifrin said another source (Moshinsky), whom he met in Israel, and prisoners he met at Camp No. 7 told him the Wrangel Island POWs were used for medical experiments.[3] Other former Soviet prisoners, when repatriated, vaguely referred to Wallenberg's internment in a Soviet mental hospital as well as in the familiar trio of Soviet prisons—Lubyanka, Lefortovo and Vladimir.

Moshinsky contended he had met Wallenberg twice—first when he arrested him and second when they were both prisoners on Wrangel Island.[4] During the invasion of Budapest in January 1945, Moshinsky was a Soviet military officer and one of those arresting Wallenberg. Later Moshinsky was betrayed as a Zionist and sent to Wrangel Island in 1953, where he said he again met Wallenberg. Until 1962, when he said he left that Soviet prison, Moshinsky contended Wallenberg was still there. After Moshinsky's release, he went to Israel and corresponded with Wallenberg's mother.

His accounts to various people remain questionable. Moshinsky produced letters with personal greetings allegedly written by Wallenberg and smuggled out of the prison camp, but Guy von Dardel has said they are not authentic. Other witnesses feel differently about his story, but not the U.S. government. In a February 2, 1978, document, the State Department said the Swedes interviewed Moshinsky, but doubted many of his statements. "He was, for example, unable to identify Wallenberg in photographs."

Nevertheless, as "Koslov," Moshinsky's pseudonym, he signed an undated statement submitted to Congress, making two obvious errors—the age of Wallenberg, who was 32 during his days in Budapest, and how he saved the Jews there. In his statement, Moshinsky supplied dreadful details to Congress about supposed Soviet torture techniques at Wrangel Island.

The camp on Wrangel Island was an experimental camp where experiments were conducted on living people. The experiments were in the form of injections, diets, oxygen tests on people who were long declared dead but were alive at that time (1962) and were working very hard in the camp. The guards and the administrative staff were former convicts . . . The camp also had a military guard for a special camp in which people were trained for spying abroad. That camp was headed by Ivan Ivanovich Shevilov, a veteran NKVD trooper. There were also many others, including Italian war prisoners. There was also Raoul Wallenberg, who had been Swedish consul in Budapest during the war and who under the German occupation, aided by money, helped Jews escape from Hungary, through Switzerland, into other countries. When the Russians entered Budapest, Raoul Wallenberg was immediately arrested at the request of the military commandant of the city of Budapest and sent by special train to Moscow. He was 27 years old, and was a handsome educated young man.

These are a few of the many facts which I knew, having witnessed them personally. Unfortunately, I cannot sign my real name [to the statement] as I still have some close relatives in Russia.

Annette Lantos, wife of the U.S. Congressman, said her sources—prisoners released from the gulag—confirmed that the Soviets tortured Wallenberg throughout his imprisonment.

Why?

"Because they had him."

In even, but sad tones, Mrs. Lantos continued. "I think they used him for medical testing, not tortured him, worse than that.

They experimented on him. He was in terrible shape. If they can get ahold of a man instead of a monkey, they're very happy."

Interested in more details, I eagerly asked Mrs. Lantos if I could meet with the released prisoners.

"They won't talk to you," she said, an iron edge in her voice. End of request.

The Spotlight, a weekly newspaper so far out of the mainstream that it has carved its own channel, printed a three-part series in February 1978 discussing alleged torture methods on Wrangel Island.[5] Although the Spotlight, a weekly publication of the far right-wing Liberty Lobby, lacks the believability of the New York Times, the CIA put two of the Spotlight's stories in its files on Wallenberg. Furthermore, Robert K. Dornan, an ultraconservative Californian who served in Congress until he lost the 1996 election, encircled the forced labor issue as part of his sphere of interests. The Spotlight quoted Dornan as saying, "The Russians probably still have labor camps on Wrangel Island."

One article in the Spotlight said Wrangel is "the site of three super-secret Russian concentration camps where KGB agents carry out incredible human experiments on thousands of prisoners held captive there."

A Spotlight "probe" supposedly unearthed that "thousands of prisoners of war—including high-ranking German, Spanish and Italian officers thought dead since World War II—have been secretly imprisoned on Wrangel Island." The newspaper said Soviet "'scientists,'" under the KGB's direction, "carry out inhuman medical and scientific experiments on the prisoners." Also, the KGB operates a special training camp there for foreign espionage agents.

Next, the Spotlight discussed Shifrin's testimony before Congress, where he supposedly said the Soviets had an atomic reactor in one concentration camp on Wrangel Island "and they make experiments on live prisoners with radiation."

In another concentration camp, the Spotlight quoted Shifrin, who used Moshinsky as his source, as testifying, "They have experiments with physicians on the people and in a third they have submarines and they have experiments with live people under water."

Shifrin, back in Israel in 1978, told the Spotlight that, "Unspeakable deeds are perpetrated there, beyond the Arctic Circle, and they are being perpetrated today! By the time, we learn all there is to know about them, they will have passed into the realm of history, and nobody shall be unduly disturbed by these past horrors." Later, the Spotlight said Moshinsky testified before Congress that guards and the administrative staff at Wrangel Island were ex-convicts. "The camp also had a military guard for a special camp in which people were trained for spying abroad."

Coupled with Shifrin's testimony was a July 28-29, 1970, article in Der Bund, based in Bern, Switzerland, about "Penal Camps with Special Conditions," which included Wrangel Island.[6] The article explains, "In the vernacular these camps are also called 'death camps' because practically no one is released from them." They can't survive the "'special' conditions."

Shifrin's testimony in 1973 motivated the CIA to fresh inquiries. Someone whose name the CIA blacked out in the documents tells the director that two people, whose identities are kept secret, are "still pursuing every lead, no matter how tenuous," about Wallenberg, but the pair had just about "exhausted possibilities."[7]

A deputy was sent to Israel to interview Shifrin, who impressed the agent, but he couldn't evaluate information from a "sub-source" "Kozlov," who was really Moshinsky, that Wallenberg was held on Wrangel Island. Kozlov claims he served as a medical attendant on Wrangel Island, but Shifrin believed Kozlov could have had a KGB mission at Wrangel. After ten years of imprisonment in the gulag, any prisoner has earned the right to paranoia.

However, the CIA said its records showed no "punitive camp" at Wrangel now.[8] The CIA agent who monitored the Soviet prison labor camp system said, based on the "most reliable intelligence information available," he had no evidence that a labor camp ever existed at Wrangel Island.

Still, in the early 1960s, a special construction group built an

airfield on Wrangel Island, so it is possible the Soviets could have
assigned prison labor to help. The CIA mused that the prison
labor would have had no means of escape and any prisoners used
in construction may have been moved from the island afterward.[9]
By the CIA's definition, this fails to qualify as a punitive camp,
making one ask how bad or how long must the punishment become
before it descends to "punitive"?

The CIA speculated that Shifrin might have supplied the information for the Der Bund article. Next, the CIA tried to discredit Shifrin, explaining that a recent Soviet émigré, himself a
prisoner in the Soviet labor camps, said much of "Shifrin's information is inaccurate." The CIA agreed. "Based on the documentation at our disposal, it is our considered opinion that Shifrin's
information should be considered less than totally reliable and
should be weighed carefully. He does not appear to be completely
stable and does not conduct research on a scientific basis."

Reliable or not, storyteller or fabricator, after Shifrin surfaced
in the 1970s, he told a colorful tale about Raoul Wallenberg, Leonid Brezhnev, Jewish diamonds and greed. A Russian documentary film with English subtitles shows Shifrin, a publicist in Jerusalem who had become the de rigueur interview for the Wallenberg
story, specifying why—in his opinion—the Soviets captured and
imprisoned Wallenberg.[10] When the Soviets invaded Budapest,
the first wave of the 18th Russian army ransacked Wallenberg's
office. That safe contained all of the jewels of the Jewish families;
emeralds, diamonds, rubies—millions of dollars in precious stones.

A besieged people again, the Jews had no one to whom they
could give their diamonds. So, they gave them to Wallenberg, who
put them in his safe, promising to hold them until they returned
as free men. They had no one else to trust.

After the Soviet troops stormed Budapest, Leonid Brezhnev,
who headed the political section of the 18th Army, was the first
brigade to move into Budapest. Then Shifrin mentioned Yaakov
Leontevich Menaker, a guard involved in spy activity during the
Russian liberation of Budapest. Anders Hasselbohm, the

correspondent for Aftonbladet, said Menaker had reliable information that Brezhnev's soldiers confiscated Wallenberg's money, jewelry and diamonds, which he had used to finance the release of Jews from the Nazis. Menaker also emigrated to Israel and met with Shifrin and others involved in the Wallenberg campaign.

In the documentary film, Shifrin rhetorically asked about Wallenberg's imprisonment. "Why is he kept imprisoned? He has no value in the Soviet Union. I am shocked for this is a question without an answer."[11]

Then Shifrin tried to answer. "I met a man, a person called Menaker who had been an intelligence sergeant in the 18th Army, which captured Budapest, and he tells me that their intelligence squad was subordinated to the head of the political division, Leonid Brezhnev."

The patrol was sent to Budapest and met Wallenberg there, who was happy to see them, Menaker told Shifrin. Next, Wallenberg had gone with them to Brezhnev and told him about his activities. Supposedly, Wallenberg then told Brezhnev about a huge amount of jewels, which many Jews had entrusted to him.

According to Shifrin, after Brezhnev heard Wallenberg's story, he sent him and a patrol back to Budapest. A Soviet captain returned with a sack full of jewels for Brezhnev, "and thus it was obvious that Brezhnev like a common crook had designs upon the diamonds," Shifrin said. "Why shouldn't they give up Wallenberg? You may say that Brezhnev ruined the party and the country, but to admit that the leader of the Soviet government, the leader of the Communist Party was a common pickpocket who stole the diamonds; this is impossible."[12]

Shifrin said Menaker knew about Brezhnev's involvement and his greed in taking the jewels from the safe in Wallenberg's office. Brezhnev held onto the jewels and made a deal with Beria that they would both be silent about the cache of diamonds while keeping Wallenberg as a hostage. Supposedly, gold, diamonds and emeralds were inside Wallenberg's Budapest safe. Brezhnev allegedly stole them to pay for his ambitious and unusual climb to power, from a modest military beginning. After Budapest, Brezhnev returned to Russia with a suitcase full of diamonds, making him a rich man. This loot—mainly diamonds, some emeralds and gold—was allegedly worth a few million dollars. The theory continues that Brezhnev then arranged for Wallenberg's arrest in Debrecen and made a deal with Beria, then the head of the KGB.

Beria would keep Wallenberg out of sight, lose him in the KGB prison system. For that, Brezhnev allegedly promised to share the diamonds with Beria in return for his complicity and Wallenberg's indefinite imprisonment. After that, Brezhnev arranged with Gromyko's help to have Beria killed as the Stalinist era was ending. Wallenberg became a prisoner without his own name, without papers, forever lost in the Gulag Archipelago. Wallenberg got a new name and Brezhnev got all the diamonds for himself. Beria was dead, but Brezhnev remembered Gromyko's help and kept him in power. Brezhnev then used some of the diamonds to advance through the Soviet political system to the top while Wallenberg stayed imprisoned, where he will remain until the last survivor of that era—Brezhnev, Beria, Khrushchev, Gromyko and Gorbachev—has died.

Incredible story, but it has a factual polish.

In February 1982, Brezhnev's daughter, Galina, became involved in a bizarre scandal involving diamonds, corruption and a circus performer named Boris the Gypsy.[13]

As part of a corruption crackdown, Soviet police arrested a flamboyant circus performer known as Boris the Gypsy, whose real name was unknown, and that led to the arrest of the nation's main circus official, Anatoly A. Kolevatov. In Kolevatov's apartment, Soviet police discovered diamonds and foreign currency worth 1.2 million rubles, then equal to almost $1.7 million. Both Boris the Gypsy and Kolevatov were friends of Galina Brezhnev, then 53.

Unlike America, Russia had no free press, so all information on this affair came from underground sources. But The New York Times reported February 27, 1982, the police questioned Galina after Boris the Gypsy had implicated her. Galina denied the charges and that may have ended her involvement in the inquiry.

Rumors swirled in Moscow that Galina, a tall beauty when young, had fallen in love and married a famous circus performer, Yevgeny Milayev, who gave her lavish gifts. Supposedly, Galina's father (Brezhnev) opposed the marriage and made his daughter end the union. Which raises the question: Was Boris the Gypsy really Yevgeny Milayev? That remains a mystery. With the circus performer eliminated as a suitor, Brezhnev arranged in 1971 for Galina to marry Yuri M. Churbanov, then a prosaic young officer in the Interior Ministry.

Russian newspaper accounts say nothing about the diamond incident. After ruling the Soviet Union for 18 years, Brezhnev died November 10, 1982, leaving Galina vulnerable. Moscow was filled with stories about Galina's fortune, which could have come from the Brezhnev diamonds or gifts from Milayev—or both.

The career of Churbanov, Galina's husband, rose and fell with Brezhnev. By 1980, Churbanov had risen to First Deputy Minister of the Interior, making him the country's second-ranked police officer. But in 1984, two years after Brezhnev died, Churbanov was demoted and three years after that, in 1987, he was arrested on corruption charges. In December 1988, Churbanov was convicted of receiving the equivalent of $1 million in bribes related to fraud in the cotton industry in the central Asian Republic of Uzbekistan. The Soviets sentenced Churbanov to 12 years of hard labor, and Galina divorced him. He was released in 1993.

A few years earlier, Galina won a lawsuit in Moscow, claiming a variety of valuables confiscated when her husband was put in prison.[14] Galina said the valuables—money, a Mercedes sedan, furniture, chandeliers, antiques, a country house and stuffed animals—belonged to her and not to her husband. During the court case, which was reported by the newspaper Komsomolskaya Pravda, Galina said, "The Mercedes was a gift to my father from some government official. I had a driver's license and I drove the car. My father wasn't in the habit of giving gifts to my husbands."[15]

She said the cash, totaling 65,492 rubles, or about $111,000 at the prevailing exchange rate, came from her father's estate. Galina said she had bought the country house, valued by the court at 64,000 rubles, or about $108,000, by using money from her mother and by selling a sable coat and earrings of sapphire and diamonds. Those are all plausible explanations, or Shifrin could be right. Galina, who died on June 30, 1998, at the age of 69, may have made her fortune using the Brezhnev diamonds stolen from Wallenberg's safe.

That would mean the Russians imprisoned Wallenberg only because of avarice.

While many doubted unknown prisoners like Shifrin, they believed the famous—Alexander Solzhenitsyn, the Russian author who won the 1974 Nobel prize for literature. Solzhenitsyn himself was imprisoned in the Gulag Archipelago, which he used for material and his book title. During his trip to Sweden to receive the Nobel Prize, Solzhenitsyn visited Raoul Wallenberg's mother and told her to keep trying to free her son.[16] While in Sweden, he held a press conference and answered questions on a variety of topics. A reporter from Russian Thought asked about Wallenberg. The report appeared in the January 16, 1975, edition.

In response to a question about Wallenberg's fate, Solzhenitsyn said, "No, I heard nothing about him when I was a prisoner, or for many years after that. This just shows how vast is the Gulag Archipelago, and how many hidden places there are. There are many such secret places, where prisoners are isolated forever, where no word ever trickles out, so that no one knows about these people.

"I happened to meet another Scandinavian who called himself Erik Arvid Andersen. When I tried to find out something about him here in Sweden and to learn who his relatives are, I came across the Wallenberg story."

Solzhenitsyn then never met Wallenberg, but he used Andersen as a character for his book.

During the same press conference, Solzhenitsyn discussed his meeting with Maj von Dardel, who still couldn't free her son.

"Yesterday I saw Wallenberg's mother. It was heartbreaking to see this old lady, who has been waiting for her son for twenty-nine years."

Solzhenitsyn continued, "Please weigh and consider the full meaning of what I am saying—twenty-nine years. Wallenberg was arrested at almost the same time I was. I served my entire sentence, both imprisonment and exile, was set free for a number of years, as you know from my published writings . . . But this man has been in prison for twenty-nine years and is still there today!"

Solzhenitsyn said he did not challenge the witnesses who said they saw Wallenberg, but he explained that because of the Soviet system, these sightings must be indirect testimony.

"Wallenberg's mother has information on who was in prison with her son, and when. I do not for a minute doubt the authenticity of her data. In the Gulag Archipelago, if a man said he was in prison with someone else, that is the truth. Fourteen witnesses are listed here, and it is evident that he has been kept in secret confinement, but occasionally someone or other saw him briefly and this is how the information seeped out.

"But there is a difference: If a man is arrested in the West or the Third World, it is open knowledge in what prison he is held and how he is being treated . . . But Wallenberg is in a Soviet prison, so all we have is this kind of indirect testimony from people, some of whom conceal their identity either because they are still in Eastern Europe or because they have relatives there . . . And so, since they are so well hidden in Russia, since prisoners are so well concealed and kept incommunicado, no one tries to free them; I have heard that our Prime Minister Olof Palme considers that there is too little information to justify spoiling relations with the Soviet Union on account of Wallenberg."

Solzhenitsyn then suggested that the Jewish community mobilize to free Wallenberg.

"We must hurry, hurry to have him released . . . That is a powerful public opinion movement able to force our government to save this man. And here I think that Jewish world opinion could be very helpful. Here is why I say this: you probably know that Wallenberg, as an official of the Swedish embassy in Budapest, rescued Jews from death by getting them to the West. According to that date, he saved over twenty thousand Jews in this manner, and I think that Jewish public opinion, which has been so effective in defending Jewish people in the Soviet Union imprisoned for one, three or five years, could come out strongly for Wallenberg and save him."

After this, Solzhenitsyn felt he couldn't do anything further. The Wallenberg family appreciated his efforts, but he no longer was involved.

Throughout the Wallenberg file, other famous names tantalizingly appear and then fade like apparitions. In a CIA memo dated November 20, 1970, a memorandum for SB in headquarters tells someone whose name is blacked out that two documents from July and November 1970 say another person whose identity is secret met the chairman of the Swedish National Police Board. During that conversation, the chairman requested that Svetlana Aliluyeva, Stalin's daughter, be asked about Wallenberg, but there is no further indication if anyone talked to Svetlana.[17]

Simon Wiesenthal, the famed Nazi hunter, became involved in 1970 and he wrote a letter February 12, 1975, to Senator Henry Jackson, who has since died. "To millions of Swedish citizens and to thousands who have survived Soviet Russian barbarity, the case of Wallenberg has become a sort of trauma. To know that we can do nothing to bring light into the fate of a man who fell victim to his own good deeds is almost unbearable."[18] Again, nothing happened. Wiesenthal located an Austrian Jewish doctor, the aforementioned Menachem Melzer, a former Communist, who said he had treated Wallenberg while both were prisoners in the summer of 1948 at camp Khal'mer-Yu in the Komi republic.

During the 1970s, the Soviets apparently transferred Wallenberg around various camps, including to Butyrka, which is 18 miles from Moscow. As Wallenberg wandered from prison to prison, more famous names and unknown witnesses kept appearing with stories about him. From nowhere came Leon Uris. A declassified document dated September 28, 1976, from a person, whose name was blacked out, to the CIA director, said author Leon Uris is "either writing or plans to write book about Wallenberg case. Can HQS confirm this?"[19]

No one could because Uris, made famous by "Exodus," confined his book length writing to other subjects.

The State Department surpassed the Uris error when in a February 2, 1978, document it gives Wallenberg's background and said he is "(not related to the industrial Wallenbergs)."[20] The same document that discusses Uris mentions "Wallenberg's aged mother," who—three years from her death—pressed the Social Democrats, who had been voted out of office in 1976 after 44 years in power. Though the former government just lost the election, Mrs. von Dardel wanted the old regime to keep after the Soviets about her son. She thought the new government would want to review the case and expose "mistakes" of the Social Democrats in how they dealt with the Wallenberg case.[21]

Two of the most credible witnesses involved in the Wallenberg case were Jan Kaplan and Abraham Kalinski, both prisoners themselves.

Kaplan, a Russian friend of Kalinski's, had been imprisoned in 1975 for both illegally buying diamonds and currency violations, tactics used by Russians trying to get their money out of the Soviet Union. Kaplan, once an administrator of an operatic conservatory, was sentenced to Butyrka prison. When released after serving about two years due to a heart condition, Kaplan called his daughter, Anna Bilder, who had emigrated to Israel in 1973. While in the prison hospital, Kaplan told his daughter he had shared a cell with a Swede. When asked how her father had tolerated the imprisonment, Kaplan said, "Two years—I guess that's nothing—the Swede has been imprisoned for more than thirty years—and he is still living." Kaplan said the Swede was "in pretty good condition." Due to the lack of Swedes in the gulag, Kalinski, who had become aware of Kaplan's predicament, thought the prisoner thus described had to be Wallenberg. The only other Swede was the previously mentioned Erik Andersen, whom Kalinski called "crazy."

Unfortunately, Kaplan tried to smuggle out a letter to his daughter about Wallenberg. He finally found a foreign tourist who promised to send it to Mrs. Bilder, but either the tourist was a KGB spy or someone intercepted the letter. In any event, the Soviets came to the Kaplan's Moscow apartment in February 1978, searched the premises and took away Jan Kaplan, who disappeared forever into the gulag.[22]

Understandably, other ex-Soviet prisoners with information about Wallenberg refuse to be identified. Even if they have fled Russia, many still have relatives living there, fear the authorities and choose to channel their information through people like Annette Lantos.

Kalinski provided information putting Wallenberg in Butyrka prison's sick ward as late as 1975. He had heard about Jan Kaplan, calling his daughter in Israel to get Kaplan's home telephone in Moscow. When he called there, Kaplan's wife, Eugenia, answered and said he was unavailable. That was because Kaplan was back in prison, but she confirmed he had mentioned meeting a Swede in Butyrka in 1975.

Despite the risk, Eugenia, Kaplan's wife, smuggled out a letter in 1979 to her daughter, explaining what had happened to Jan Kaplan. After wondering what to do, Bilder spoke with Kalinski, who told her to take the letter to the Swedish embassy in Tel Aviv, which made a photocopy and forwarded the original to Stockholm. After the Swedes assured themselves of the letter's authenticity, they generated another note to the Soviets in August 1979, asking to reopen the Wallenberg case and requesting an interview with Jan Kaplan. In return came the Soviet response: "No further information."

While Wallenberg's fame grew internationally, an Israeli Minister-Counselor named Yanai, who had been imprisoned at Lubyanka in 1945, cautioned the State Department about Kaplan and other reports emanating from Russia, feeling the Soviet Union was full of "cranks, people with fantasies, and people who seek publicity for themselves in hopes that it will facilitate their efforts to emigrate."[23] Indeed, it seems some Russian émigrés in Israel tell stories to hear themselves talk while others may have been or still remain Soviet agents.

Kalinski, the Pole and Kaplan's friend, became another popular interview subject, but he had more credibility than Shifrin. After the Soviets "rehabilitated" Kalinski and released him in 1959 following 15 years in prison, he lived in Vladimir until 1968 when he moved to Moscow, working as a translator and engineer while all the time trying to leave the Soviet Union. That took 17 years. During this time, Kalinski married a Russian and became a Soviet citizen.

While still trapped, but not imprisoned in the Soviet Union, Kalinski met his former Vladimir cellmate, Simon Gogobaritze, whom the Soviets released in 1967. A year later Kalinski went to Fiflis in Georgia and the two ex-prisoners shared memories of their bondage. Gogobaritze told Kalinski Wallenberg was still in prison when he left. In 1976, the Soviets let Kalinski emigrate to Israel, where he worked as a chemical engineer. Kalinski didn't realize Wallenberg's importance until he moved to Israel. Wiesenthal suggested the 1980 Olympic Games, planned for Moscow, should be stopped unless the Soviet Union released Wallenberg. This thrust the Wallenberg issue into prominence and Kalinski read about the Swedish diplomat. "I had the name somewhere in my head."

Next, he talked to the Israeli authorities, who sent him to the Swedish Embassy in Tel Aviv, where in November 1978 he explained his indirect encounters with Wallenberg. The Swedish Ministry of Foreign Affairs thought the conversation so worthwhile that it contacted Kalinski, who by then had gone to the United States to sue this country. Kalinski sued the U.S. government for $1.5 million, charging it betrayed him to the Soviets, which led to his imprisonment. As part of that effort, Kalinski tried to see Averill Harriman and George Kennan.

Leif Leifland, Swedish under secretary of state for foreign affairs, and Sven Hirdman, head of the department, met Kalinski

December 20, 1978, in New York. That conversation yielded a report to the Soviets January 3, 1979, seeking a renewed investigation about Wallenberg, but nothing happened.

Despite the Soviets' nondenial denial, Kalinski felt Wallenberg remained in the gulag and had a chance for an unpleasant, but long life. "I can tell you," Kalinski related, "that those who survive prisons live for a long time." Since the Soviets never put foreign prisoners in camps, Wallenberg avoided such places.

While hardly Club Med, the Soviet prison system could provide survival, according to Kalinski. "In prisons there isn't as hard work, there is less hunger, there it is easier to survive. From what I heard, the person who was seen in (Butyrka) was in good health. The sick ward is for light sicknesses, but prisoners from different places come there.

"And Wallenberg isn't old—he would have been 63 years old then."

Kalinski's report to the Swedish government prompted many newspaper stories. The Dagens Nyheter newspaper put the Wallenberg situation into bold relief in a page one story January 23, 1979. The Wallenberg case "continues to throw a shadow over the Soviet authorities conduct," the newspaper reported. "One has the strong feeling that they feel that with the great suffering of the Soviet society during the Second World War in mind Sweden ought to stop interesting itself in one single human fate."

Then the Dagens Nyheter blasted the Soviets for their "nonchalant rebuff" in response to inquiries on Wallenberg. The Soviets made no effort to investigate any new information, the newspaper complained.

When Maj von Dardel, then 87, heard about Kalinski's statements and the Swedish note, she concluded her conversation with Swedish journalist Eric Sjöquist by crying. Guy von Dardel, then a professor of physics at Lund University, told Expressen, Sjöquist's newspaper, "We must not be satisfied with the Russian answer to the Swedish Government's note."

While in New York to sue the U.S. government, Kalinski—

described as a small, round, pleasant man with the Polish liberation medal on his blue jacket—stayed with his relatives in Queens and gave a press conference that Swedish journalists voraciously devoured. Kalinski—his briefcase bulging with evidence, reports and articles—answered questions calmly in a Manhattan hotel. Why, asked the Swedish journalists, didn't Kalinski say earlier that Wallenberg was possibly alive as late as 1975?

"Dear God," Kalinski said and stroked his slightly graying hair. "I was certain that Wallenberg had gotten out long ago. Without the notice in the Israelian [sic] newspaper I would still have been thinking so."

The Swedish press described Kalinski "as the most genuine witness since Professor Nanna Svartz among the numerous who have reported on Raoul Wallenberg."

Kalinski did an article in Russian for the Novoye Russkoye Slovo magazine's January 28, 1979, issue, which the CIA translated.[24] In this story, Kalinski charged when the KGB wants to confuse people "who are following the trail of Chekist (KGB) crimes, it spreads widely varying rumors, creating great confusion." He contended this "Goebbelsian tactic" convinced Wiesenthal, who refers to stories by people who said they saw Wallenberg in a "special camp for foreigners."

"There are no such camps and never were," sniffed Kalinski. "No camp can be as rigidly isolated as a prison." In fact, "isolation and secrecy can be raised to devlish [sic] perfection."

After Ronald Reagan's administration swept into office in January 1981, the CIA kept monitoring developments on the Wallenberg case, but what seized the U.S. embassy's attention the same month were the Wallenberg hearings in Stockholm, which the Swedish foreign office regarded as a serious forum for information. Gohan Berg, the Foreign Ministry's Wallenberg expert, told embassy officials January 21 the Ministry had begun the "arduous" task of independently assessing the information.[25] That was necessary before the Swedish government could undertake further measures on the Wallenberg case.

About 350 people attended the hearing in Stockholm sponsored by the Swedish Wallenberg Association. Attendees included Marcus Wallenberg, the patriarch of the Swedish banking empire, the British and Israeli ambassadors, Elizabeth Moynihan, wife of Daniel Moynihan, the Democratic Senator from New York, and Simon Wiesenthal.

Wiesenthal told the gathering, "I'm saying that Wallenberg is alive unless the Soviet officials prove the opposite.[26] The story about Wallenberg's death has been proved wrong by more than 20 witnesses who confirm that they have seen him after this time. Some of them have even talked to him." After that, Wiesenthal said he had information from a confidential informant that a Soviet general named Kuprianov died in 1979 after the KGB interrogated him about stories in the western press concerning times in the 1950s when Kuprianov saw or met Wallenberg in the Soviet prison system.

Other specific testimonies attracted governmental attention. Andre Schimkevitsch claimed he shared a cell with Wallenberg in Lubyanka in December 1947.[27] Lena Biorck-Kaplan of the Wallenberg Committee read a statement by Leo Milton, whose "confidential source" in the Soviet Union had news about Wallenberg as recently as February 1980, who at that time had supposedly been sent to Kirov after a tooth extraction. Biorck-Kaplan also quoted a pseudonymous "Mr. Ivanov," a Russian lawyer who said the director of a prison camp in Mordovia bragged in 1972 that one of his important foreign prisoners included a Swede who had been in Soviet camps more than 20 years.

Gideon Hausner, chairman of the Israeli Wallenberg Committee and the prosecutor of Adolf Eichmann, said he had had no convincing evidence that Wallenberg had died.[28] To the contrary, Hausner believed there was "considerable material" to contradict the Soviet version of Wallenberg's demise. Then Hausner said President Roosevelt had appointed Wallenberg to his mission in Budapest, adding, "We don't want to relieve America of the responsibility to pursue the case."

Into the diplomatic pouch went all the materials given out at the hearings.

Berg, the governmental expert on Wallenberg, saw a "downside" to all the fresh publicity about Wallenberg, fearing this would spawn a "profusion of information from unreliable sources—perhaps motivated out of vanity or uninformed emotion." That would make it difficult to discern the truth from the falsehoods.

"The Soviets, if they are clever," Berg said, "might promote the profusion of such unreliable and conflicting information."[29]

As in 1945, the Americans abrogated their responsibility regarding Wallenberg. "It is our assessment, based on Berg's evaluation and that of other Swedish officials, that it continues to be appropriate to take our lead from the GOS [Government of Sweden] in the Wallenberg case," wrote U.S. Ambassador William C. Hamilton.[30] He added "the most constructive thing" the U.S. government could do "to supplement the quiet, careful GOS efforts to clarify Wallenberg's fate" is to respond to requests for help in following up leads. Hamilton also wanted to watch the Wallenberg committee's movements to establish an international group that would try to directly approach the Soviet government.

The American government barely tried to rescue Wallenberg, but it never stopped gathering information about him. For example, after all the discussions about the Soviets keeping Wallenberg ensconced in a mental hospital, the CIA—prompted by the Swedes—in 1982 prosaically collected facts about a Moscow psychiatric clinic.[31] The Chief of the Soviet/East Europe Division supplied the information to the CIA's deputy director, telling him to give it to the Swedes, at his discretion.

This hospital is eight kilometers south of the Kremlin, across the Moscow River. Since there were no fences around the dispensary compound, this was probably an outpatient clinic, the CIA concluded. "Ordinary psychiatric hospitals (OPHs) normally are surrounded by walls, and the more severe special psychiatric hospitals (SPHs) by security fences," the agency reported. The dispensary was apparently a two-story building in a compound with three five-story structures that appeared to be apartment buildings.

Instead of sneaking someone inside the hospital or using an informant to get information, the CIA used an 11-year-old Moscow telephone book. Upon reading the 1971 reverse Moscow phone book, the CIA found 19 private listings for the hospital's address, 28 Sevastopoljskih prospekt, indicating private dwellings in the compound. Taking a seven-year-leap forward, the CIA consulted a 1978 Moscow phone book and found listings for a "registrar, domestic assistance, head nurse, head physician and Medical Labor Mast." In case anyone wanted to call, the telephone numbers were also listed.[32]

Putting down its phone books, the CIA then talked to émigrés who said that outpatient psychiatric clinics were used to "detain and 'assess' Soviet political dissidents on a short-term (days or weeks) basis. Political dissidents are usually detained for longer periods (weeks, months) of 'evaluation' at OPHs."

One example was Vladimir Bukovskiy, who was detained in many OPHs and later confined in an SPH. "Long-term incarceration of political dissidents or prisoners usually occurs at SPHs, prisons or labor camps, which are all to various degrees guarded facilities," the CIA said. "Soviet practice with foreign prisoners is to isolate them in these more secure facilities, usually a prison or a labor camp."

The CIA's analysis? Sources identified "Psycho-neurological Dispensary No. 13 as an institution associated with the detention and examination of dissidents. It is their judgment that this dispensary or outpatient clinic, has probably been used for screening and temporary detention of dissidents, but that it is not used for long-term imprisonment, nor to detain or confine foreigners."[33]

Nevertheless, the CIA said, "It is conceivable that a political prisoner might be detained at the No. 13 dispensary/clinic. It is highly doubtful that Raoul Wallenberg was kept there on a long-term basis since (1) we have no independent evidence to that effect, (2) it is against Soviet practice to use such clinics for anything but short-term detention, (3) it is against Soviet practice to intern foreigners in facilities other than prisons or labor camps, and (4) Wallenberg's case is of such notoriety that we would not expect the Soviets to hold him in a minimum security facility in a city to which foreigners have easy access." But since the Soviets detained political prisoners for short-term assessment at psychiatric clinics, the CIA felt, "We would not rule out the possibility that Raoul Wallenberg was held briefly in Dispensary No. 13—either for assessment or in transit."

But, cruelly, now Wallenberg's worldwide notoriety may have killed him.

CHAPTER 8

Annette Tillemann Lantos thrust Wallenberg into the American psyche in 1979, using an electronic chat with the president of the United States. That became yet another effort in the 1970s-1980s to rescue Wallenberg. After escaping from Hungary to Austria in November 1944 with her mother—but without her father whom the Arrow Cross grabbed from a safehouse and murdered—Annette returned in 1945, but then left for the United States in 1948. Tom Lantos left Hungary in August 1947 and moved to the United States on an academic scholarship at the University of Washington. He graduated in 1949 and received a master's degree from the same school a year later. In 1953, Lantos earned a doctorate from the University of California, where he was a Phi Beta Kappa. He married Annette, and they settled in San Mateo, California, where they had two daughters. Lantos became a consultant, a television news analyst and commentator and also worked as a foreign policy adviser to the U.S. Senate. At one point, he was a legal aide to Joseph Biden, a Democratic senator from Delaware.

Meanwhile, Annette tried to raise the national consciousness about Wallenberg, but few Americans knew or cared about him. "Wallenberg was the means of teaching our daughters about the Holocaust," Mrs. Lantos said. He gave heroism a human face.

While her daughters were in high school, a teacher invited Mrs. Lantos to talk to the students about the Holocaust. When she started, "the students were bored and inattentive—after all, I was talking to them about ancient history—but by the time I finished they were moved to the point of tears. This was the beginning of a new career for me."

She began talking to high schools and organizing others to do likewise, considering this work a memorial to her father. Then the Lantoses thought Wallenberg was dead, but on November 7, 1977, an item in the New York Times said Simon Wiesenthal had located Wallenberg alive in a Soviet mental hospital. Mrs. Lantos called the Swedish Consulate General in San Francisco and received a distressing reply.

"Yes," the Swedish official replied. "I am familiar with the name although I don't know if the report is correct or not. But why are you interested? In our diplomatic courses, Wallenberg is cited as an example of what a Swedish diplomat should not be. He brought great shame upon Sweden."

Stunned, Mrs. Lantos later said she learned if a Swedish diplomat while training showed Wallenberg-like characteristics, he was advised to leave the foreign service.

"Wallenberg was charged with the ultimate diplomatic crime: to save lives. He arrogated authority to himself. He held a minor position and had very little authority, but he used the power of the Swedish government to back him in his negotiations. His legend, it turned out, was preserved in Sweden, but it was a tale of infamy," Mrs. Lantos said.

Next, she tried Amnesty International, but that organization said Wallenberg had died and the group devoted its energy to the living. After that rebuff, she tried to get public officials, newspaper columnists interested, but nobody cared.

In 1977, Mrs. Lantos had helped form a Free Wallenberg Committee "to try to acquaint the world about him," but the media ignored the group. "No newspaper would print a paragraph on him," complained Mrs. Lantos.

"'Thirty-two years ago a man disappeared into the gulag? So what?'" came the reply from America's media.

"He's one of the great heroes of our time," said Mrs. Lantos.

Still, only inky silence.

She tried to enlist the help of Wilhelm Wachmeister, the Swedish ambassador, but he was "unfriendly to me and my husband.

He said it's none of our business and stop meddling in Swedish affairs."

Undaunted, the Lantoses bought ads in the San Francisco Jewish Bulletin and the New York Jewish Week, telling Wallenberg's story. The ad campaign provided a lead for Elenore Lester, a New York Times reporter who did a story for the magazine section and later a book about Wallenberg. The exposure also brought numerous letters and responses to Mrs. Lantos, who recommended people write or call the President, their congressmen, the Secretary of State or even the Soviet government. She wanted to involve President Jimmy Carter, who had made human rights a touchstone of his administration, "but who was I to get to the president—a French teacher and housewife, married to a college professor."

She got her chance in the fall of 1979. During that summer, Nina Lagergren and Guy von Dardel came to Washington to attract American support for their half-brother. Nina and Annette met with Secretary of State Cyrus R. Vance, who said the American government had raised the issue with the Soviets and awaited a reply.[1]

A deputy assistant secretary of state named Barry and a Soviet chargé named Vasev met July 21, with the American official asking the Soviets to take a fresh look at the Wallenberg matter.[2] But Vasev parroted the stale Soviet response about how Wallenberg had died in 1947, and Vasev had nothing to add. Barry countered that many people had said they had seen Wallenberg alive long after 1947. Vasev dismissed these accounts, reducing them to the level of Elvis sightings by characterizing them as third hand. He "asserted the Soviets would not say [Wallenberg] was dead if he was not."

Vasev wanted a leap of faith from his Western comrades. The inconclusive meeting ended with Vasev saying he would report the conversation to his superiors in Moscow.

While in Washington, von Dardel managed to meet on August 30, 1979, with the European Soviet Director, listed in the CIA documents as "Shinn."[3] The then secret document, dated

September 1, 1979, and signed by Vance explained that once more von Dardel sought the American government's help. This time he asked if computer printouts were available that had the names of Soviet and foreign prisoners who had died in the gulag during and after the Second World War. Shinn said that "regretfully" they did not exist. But he suggested the possibility of interviewing former Soviet defectors from that era, now living in America, to get "insights at least on the Modus Operandi of those times vis à vis Wallenberg." Shinn assured von Dardel that the State Department would "make every effort to follow up on this" but little happened.

The same summer von Dardel and Lagergren went to Israel, where they met with both Kalinski and Menachem Begin.[4] The Israeli Prime Minister promised to open the Mossad files on their half-brother and to ask President Carter to bring up the Wallenberg matter with Brezhnev, the Soviet leader, at their Summit meeting in Vienna June 15-18. The U.S. delegation asked the Soviets, but they ignored the request. Despite the rejection, Mrs. Lagergren said all this "put Wallenberg into the world spotlight; he became an international public figure. U.S. committees were formed and hope began."

After these face to face meetings, Mrs. Lantos had her aural audience with the President of the United States on October 13, 1979.

She had heard an announcement on National Public Radio that President Carter had scheduled a radio news conference, where he planned to take questions from citizens in their homes. "I sent ten picture postcards, but you could only put your name and phone number, not the question," for Carter wanted the questions to be spontaneous.

"My phone rings two weeks later," she said.

Fog and fate had intervened. Mrs. Lantos had planned to pick up her mother, who was flying in from Vancouver, but the famous San Francisco fog kept the plane from landing and Mrs. Lantos at home to take the call.

"My card was the third one selected out of 24,000. I had two minutes to present my case to President Carter."

At last, after more than 34 years, Annette Lantos, the Hungarian refugee whom Raoul Wallenberg had helped save, now had the nation's attention to talk about her hero.

She did, telling the president of Wallenberg's amazing efforts in Budapest and his capture and disappearance into the Gulag Archipelago. Then she asked if the President would use his influence with the Soviets to free Wallenberg. To her amazement, Mrs. Lantos discovered Carter knew about Wallenberg.

Carter listened and said, "We have raised the case with the Soviets, and we will continue to take every appropriate opportunity to pursue it."

After years of frustrating effort, Mrs. Lantos heard the president of the United States make a commitment over national radio to do something. "As soon as I put down the phone, the Chicago Tribune, San Francisco Chronicle and Los Angeles Times started calling."

Ten minutes later the Chronicle had a reporter and photographer at her door. Newspapers, magazines, television stations all wanted to know about Wallenberg. Now the media, which would print or air nothing about Wallenberg, wanted to know everything.

"Nobody ever heard anything of this. Now it became newsworthy," said Mrs. Lantos, amazed at the lemming-like reflexes of journalists.

The resulting media attention led to the unearthing of documents that proved Wallenberg worked on behalf of the U.S. War Refugee Board in the final months of World War II. President Carter later wrote Mrs. Lantos, explaining the Soviets' refusal to deal with the U.S. government on the Wallenberg issue because he was a Swedish citizen and Sweden's responsibility. Again, nothing happened.

However, the more the Swedes protested about Wallenberg, the more the Russians growled. A dispatch from the American Embassy in Sweden to the Secretary of State dated November 10,

1979, said Soviet deputy foreign minister Zemskov had complained about the Wallenberg case on his visit to Stockholm the prior month.[5] The Soviets found Swedish Prime Minister Ullsten's letter to Kosygin and other "repeated thrusts" from Swedes as totally unacceptable to Soviets.

The U.S. embassy related that "Zemskov said with some force that GOS (Government of Sweden) stop gossip to further irritate Soviet government."

Leifland, the Swedish permanent undersecretary, told Zemskov to separate the Swedish government from the private effort of the Wallenberg family in Sweden and other countries. While blaming the Wallenberg committees for any aggressive action to free Raoul Wallenberg, Leifland did say the Soviets had misled the Swedish government. That prompted Zemskov to say, "It was not so remarkable that the Soviets had taken Wallenberg in Budapest," the American Embassy said. "He said there were strong indications that Raoul Wallenberg was an American spy."

In 1979, the new Swedish Government tried to work out a spy swap for Wallenberg, but the deal failed and he remained incarcerated.

The dismay over Sweden's inactivity accelerated. Kalinski's January 28, 1979, article in Novoye Russkoye Slovo specified the lack of Swedish commitment toward Wallenberg.

In 34 years the Swedish Government has done surprisingly little to rescue Wallenberg even though Sweden has had, for more than 30 years, irrefutable proof that he was abducted by Soviet Chekists and is now in their hands. I stated that "quiet diplomacy" could not help in this matter. The experience of the last 20 years has demonstrated that in relations with the Soviet authorities only broad publicity can help. It is common knowledge that criminals fear the light of day.

Unfortunately, even today the principle of "not upsetting the Kremlin" is fairly widespread in the free world even though its bankruptcy has been demonstrated many times.

Kalinski's article gave birth to a companion piece by Nefedov, who had befriended German Krisko.[6] Nefedov's story appeared in the February 15, 1979, issue of the same magazine, where he first blamed the Soviets, but then blasted the Swedes for Wallenberg's endless incarceration:

Naturally, it is (the) Soviet leaders who are primarily responsible for the tragic fate of Raoul Wallenberg. However, their guilt does not take away the responsibility of the socialists sitting in the Swedish government for the fate of their diplomat. When information was received about the Soviet crime, they did everything possible to see that Wallenberg's kidnapping did not receive wide publicity, fearing an international scandal, and hoping to straighten things out on the sly. The instance with Krisko is evidence of this. Rather than widely publicizing his information and setting up a press conference, the Swedish bureaucrats hurried to get rid of him, announcing that a special commission to investigate the Wallenberg matter would visit Krisko in Hamburg. As to be expected, no such commission ever showed up. (In 1974), Krisko suddenly died of a heart attack in Hamburg . . .

Thus, even when it had become quite certain that R. Wallenberg was still sitting in a Soviet jail, the Swedish government limited itself to timid protests rather than presenting an ultimatum about the immediate release of their perfectly innocent diplomat and threatening the severance of diplomatic relations. But as numerous examples showed, the Soviets only laughed at toothless protests.

Then, in early 1980, Stockholm released 1,900 pages of documents on Wallenberg, covering the period from 1944-49, but this merely gave the Scandinavian press an opportunity to use the Swedish government as a punching bag. "Negligence bordering on cold indifference characterized the attitude toward the Wallenberg case of the Swedish Ministry of Foreign Affairs," said an article in the Berlingshe Tidende of Copenhagen by Jens Thomsen on February 1, 1980. "The suspicion that Raoul Wallenberg's Swedish relations have entertained for years that Raoul Wallenberg was sacrificed in favor of a good Swedish-Soviet relations has been confirmed in the seven volumes of documents with a total of 1,900 pages that were released by the Swedish Ministry of Foreign Affairs yesterday."

A Christian Science Monitor story on July 22, 1980, agreed. "Until recently, the Swedish government had made only halfhearted attempts to get to the bottom of Wallenberg's disappearance. Sweden's postwar socialist government was afraid of stepping on Moscow's toes and repeatedly passed over opportunities to raise the issue or exchange prisoners. Sweden turned down several offers of assistance in the case from the US."

These 1,900 documents, which included Ambassador Söderblom's conversation with Stalin where the Swede said Wallenberg probably had already died, were 10 to 15 percent of the total material about Wallenberg. Only one man in the Swedish Foreign Service, chargé d'affaires, Ulf Barck-Holst, made "energetic efforts" for Wallenberg with the Soviets, Thomsen said in his story. Barck-Holst asked the Soviets in December 1946 about an exchange for Wallenberg. He wanted Stockholm to get a Russian answer to the suggestion, but the Swedish bureaucrats did nothing.

The Thomsen article added that "despite the continually growing stacks of documents in the Swedish Ministry of Foreign Affairs, Wallenberg was more or less forgotten."

Sweden's newspapers accelerated the body blows to the Swedish governmental bodies, saying the foreign office acted in a manner both "pusillanimous and naive re Soviets during whole history of affair."

"It is useful to recall that Sweden in those days both felt threatened by the USSR and harbored sincere hope that it eventually would be possible to open fruitful relations with the Soviets," according to a March 9, 1980, article in the Berlingske Tidenddi of Copenhagen. In the government's defense, the Swedes contend they have tried ever since Wallenberg was captured to make the Soviets tell them what happened to the diplomat and will indefinitely continue the effort. The Swedish protests have included sharp notes and verbal complaints to its vastly more powerful neighbor.

Something more definitive happened on November 4, 1980. During Ronald Reagan's electoral landslide, Tom Lantos, a Democrat, ousted a sitting Republican and won a Congressional seat, one of the few Democrats to win anything that day. One of his campaign promises was to introduce legislation to make Raoul Wallenberg an honorary citizen. Lantos was elected to each succeeding Congress—surviving even the second Republican landslide in 1994—and when the Democrats controlled Congress, he had become chairman of the Subcommittee on International Security, International Organizations and Human Rights.

After his initial election, Lantos immediately proposed the Wallenberg legislation, but he had to overcome Washington's political inertia even on such a seemingly harmless bill. Edna Mitchell, then a Congressional staffer, now a college professor, recalled the travail necessary to get the legislation through Congress. As a Congressional fellow, Mitchell worked for Elizabeth Holtzman, a New York Democrat in the House, but Holtzman, trying to move up to the Senate, lost to the Republican, Alfonse M. D'Amato, in 1980. Adrift, Mitchell decided to go with this Congressional freshman from California, Tom Lantos.

"In 1981, I helped run with the idea of citizenship for Wallenberg," explained Mitchell, now the director of the Women's Leadership Institute at Mills College in Oakland, California. Until then, only Winston Churchill had become an honorary American citizen, and powerful arms of the American government wanted to retain the status quo. Both the Justice and State Departments opposed citizenship for Wallenberg.

"My contacts among Holtzman's ex-staffers told me (Lantos) was a freshman and shouldn't be pushing this," Mitchell remembered. "I passed that on to Tom."

More specifically, the State Department feared citizenship for Wallenberg would offend the Soviets. "If he were alive, the Russians would use this as evidence that (Wallenberg) was an American spy and that would worsen relations," Mitchell recalled.

The State Department knew Wallenberg had American money

but never acted as a spy. Still, in the early 1980s, America regarded the Soviet Union as a formidable, nuclear foe. Additionally, the Justice Department did not want to grant citizenship "to someone who doesn't ask for it," Mitchell said. Incredibly, she recalled, "Some people on the House side said, 'What if he's alive and wants Social Security?'"

While interviewing Mitchell in the Rayburn House Building in Washington, I stopped writing in my notebook, looked at her and asked if she, or rather, the House members were serious. Absolutely, responded Mitchell.

Then, apparently to discredit the plan whether Wallenberg was alive or dead, the House people complained that, "We don't give citizenship to dead people," Mitchell said even though no one knew if Wallenberg were dead.

With all these roadblocks, the legislation remained stalled until March 29, a Sunday, when President Ronald Reagan—an inveterate television watcher—saw a TV documentary about Wallenberg. Mitchell's sources told her the documentary intrigued Reagan, who asked his Secretary of State, Alexander M. Haig Jr., to do something about the Lantos bill.

The next day Reagan was shot.

While recuperating from the assassination attempt by John W. Hinckley Jr., President Reagan had concerns besides Lantos' bill. "It stopped everything," Mitchell said. "There was no forward progress. After (Reagan) recovered, he didn't stop it, but it was not a hot item."

Originally, the Lantos staffers thought the bill would go through by May, but Reagan's indifference set the bill back until October. The House and Senate eventually passed the legislation unanimously, for in open session how could anyone oppose a hero of the Holocaust? The petty concerns were for horse trading in the cloakrooms.

At 2:35 p.m. on October 5, 1981, President Reagan spoke at the signing ceremony, putting the bill into law. While Lantos, his wife, Annette, and Guy von Dardel and Nina Lagergren listened in the White House Rose Garden, the President said, "We're going to do everything in our power so that your brother can sit beneath the shade of those trees and enjoy the respect and love that so many hold for him."

Annette remembers standing in the Rose Garden and watching Count Wilhelm Wachtmeister, the Swedish Ambassador whose face was "wreathed in smiles." A few years earlier he had rebuffed the Lantoses, now he and his wife stood behind Reagan at the ceremony.

"In spite of the celebration, my heart was breaking because Wallenberg was still in jail," Annette lamented. "I wondered, as we drove back to the Capitol from the White House, if in some remote corner of the Soviet gulag, the man whose humanity we were honoring today might hear about it and know that all he did for us and for so many others had not been forgotten."

Instead of the promise made that October afternoon, the U.S. government did little—and sometimes seemed to obstruct efforts—to free Wallenberg. "When (Wallenberg) became a U.S. citizen, I thought the Americans would have done more," Nina Lagergren said. "We had hope. This implied more action, but it did not come to pass."

Nevertheless, twenty-two days after Wallenberg became an honorary citizen the Swedish government had the opportunity to free Wallenberg, but it bungled the chance.

A Soviet submarine ran aground October 27, 1981, on the Swedish coast, within some barrier islands close to the Karlskrona Naval base. The next day a fishing boat discovered the Soviet sub in restricted waters, and Swedish naval vessels surrounded the diesel-powered ship, demanding to know why it was there. Initially, a stalemate developed between the two countries. Sweden refused to let either Soviet or Swedish ships pull the sub, an old type with a crew of 55 that was sometimes used for intelligence gathering, off the mud until the captain, Pyotr Gushin, submitted to questioning about the incident.

Gushin discussed his predicament by radio with Moscow, but

he refused to speak with the Swedes without the presence of Soviet diplomats. A big Soviet fleet assembled outside Swedish territorial waters and demanded the Swedes let the Soviets pull their sub free before an approaching storm struck. Despite the threat, the Swedes refused to let other Soviet ships into the area or make Swedish tugs yank the Soviet sub free until the Swedes had investigated the vessel and talked to the captain. A Soviet salvage tug moved into Swedish waters October 29, probably to retrieve the submarine, but Swedish vessels blocked its access. The same day an unidentified submarine was seen within Swedish waters, but it disappeared after helicopters armed with depth charges pursued it.

The Swedes suspected their ancient enemies, the Russians, had been violating their waters with submarines for a long time, but now they had prima facie evidence. Here was a wonderful electronic image for the world's television sets. Every network showed images of the Russian sub trapped within Sweden. This was an international embarrassment, a colossal faux pas. The Swedes had the submarine, a huge bargaining chip. What would the Russians trade to release the submarine? To many, the obvious answer was Raoul Wallenberg.

Raoul Wallenberg committees, both in Sweden and aboard, as well as individual citizens appealed to Stockholm to intern the Russian submarine crew until Moscow released Wallenberg. But, as always, the Swedes ignored the pleas.

Swedish Foreign Minister Ola Ullsten said October 31 the government was "not going to link these two cases together."

Leif Leifland, undersecretary of state at the Swedish foreign office, verbalized about the possible sub swap for Wallenberg. "This was discussed and immediately rejected by the government because we found, and I still think, that a serious government does not enter into that kind of blackmail."[7]

Armed with sophisticated radiation detection equipment, Swedish experts checked the Soviet vessel from the outside. The Swedes found typical radiation emitted by uranium 238 coming from the forward part of the vessel, where the torpedoes are normally kept. U-238 is not the isotope used in making nuclear weapons, but the Swedes thought U-238 was used to shield U-235, which was used in nuclear weapons. The obvious conclusion was that the submarine had nuclear torpedo warheads.

Amid all this international turmoil, the Swedish Foreign Minister appeared on ABC's "Nightline" and in response to an inquiry about a "trade," he said that "would certainly not serve any useful purpose."

On November 2, the Soviet captain left his ship to tell his tale aboard a Swedish naval vessel with two Soviet diplomats present. Gushin blamed a storm and a malfunctioning gyrocompass for his penetration into Sweden. Swedish officials rejected his explanation, saying the sub required skilled navigation to go as far into the archipelago near the Karlskrona base on the southwest coast. While Gushin was away, the deputy commander sent out distress signals because he feared high winds from a storm in the Baltic Sea would sink the submarine. Swedish tugs pulled the submarine to a safer spot, but still within Swedish waters.

Despite the evidence provided by naval investigators, appeasement prevailed. On November 6, eleven days after the Soviet sub had invaded Sweden, the "neutral" Swedish government ordered one of its tugs to take the submarine out of its territorial waters. Because of rough seas, the tug disconnected and the sub proceeded under its own engines to a waiting flotilla of Soviet naval ships. Another lost opportunity.

Ullsten said the matter was over. "There will be no further protests. We have made unprecedented protests in the strongest possible language."

Soon after the incident, Nina Lagergren said, "We are terribly disappointed. Mr. Ullsten said there could be no link between Raoul Wallenberg and the Russian submarine; however, his refusal to link the two made it clear that the two should not be separated."[8]

Congressman Lantos said the sub incident was a "global embarrassment" to the Swedes, who could have leveraged this to obtain Wallenberg's release or an accounting of his whereabouts.[9] Instead, the Russian bully frightened the timid Swedish schoolboy.

More than a year later Journalist George Will excoriated Sweden about the sub incident. Using his syndicated column in the Washington Post, Will quoted a Swedish official as saying his country was working on the supposition that Wallenberg was still alive. Will wrote, "Sweden's lethargy concerning the case—lethargy born of cowardice—hardly constitutes 'working.'"[11]

Wilhelm Wachtmeister, the Swedish Ambassador to the United States, swiftly launched a letter that the Post printed. His rebuttal called Will's nasty remark "grossly unfair," though he admitted, "in retrospect it may be argued that mistakes have been committed particularly in the very beginning, when official Soviet assurances that Mr. Wallenberg was under their protection were taken at face value too long." But for the next 38 years, the Swedish government has "pursued this [Wallenberg] matter with a vigor and perseverance that probably exceeds what any government has done for one of its citizens."[12]

That failed to satisfy Will, who replied in another column that although Sweden found "neutrality profitable between 1939 and 1945, after the war it discovered morality, and ever since has been urging it on others, especially the United States . . ." After criticizing Swedish Prime Minister Olof Palme for not discussing Wallenberg during a 1976 meeting with Soviet Premier Alexsei Kosygin, Will mentioned Sweden's failure to take advantage of the trapped Russian submarine. "Cringing neutrality has not noticeably immunized Sweden from the aggressive disdain of Soviet submarines," Will said.[13]

Wachmeister again raced to his typewriter, and the Washington Post again complied. Will "continues his polemics against Sweden by suggesting—in apparent seriousness—that the Swedish government should have kept an intruding Soviet submarine—and supposedly—its crew in order to extract information about Raoul

Wallenberg," Wachmeister said. "We do not believe that hostage taking as a means of foreign policy is either legal or effective."[10]

Then Wachmeister defended Prime Minister Palme against Will's verbal assault, specifying Sweden's aid to developing countries, protection of the environment and respect for human rights. "We are rather proud of our record in the defense of these principles," Wachtmeister said, adding that would continue to navigate Sweden's foreign policy. "And, I repeat, the efforts to clarify Raoul Wallenberg's fate will continue."

When Birgitta Dahl, Sweden's Parliamentary speaker, was asked in 1995 why Sweden failed to link the sub with Raoul Wallenberg, she replied she was "not in a position to comment." Dahl explained that in Sweden the speaker nominates the prime minister and acts as head of state if the King is out of the country. "The speaker represents all of Sweden," so that kept her from talking about the sub linkage or any potential spy trades.

Endlessly, the CIA kept researching its files, looking for intelligence links between the United States and Wallenberg. Every time the CIA found nothing.

A March 23, 1983, memo from a CIA analyst whose name is blacked out talked about a briefing involving an analyst from the National Security Council, whose name is also blacked out, concerning Wallenberg.[14] "After a one day session, she [National Security analyst] concluded that there was little information in those files which might be of interest to the NSC."

The CIA analyst then gave his colleague from the executive branch of government further material from other government agencies, including numerous documents from the Department of State. Using this material, the NSC analyst again looked through the files and again found no linkage.

In a handwritten note dated March 25, 1983, she said, "No new information on RW's whereabouts or whether he is alive— Nothing to indicate he was OSS agent, indeed the contrary. CIA files do not reveal anything of substance beyond what is in public domain . . ." The analyst then explained how the CIA has "responded fully on every State Dep't urging for info—nothing of substance has been withheld."[15]

Sonja Sonnenfeld, a Wallenberg activist from Sweden, met with Dennis C. Blair of the National Security Council in the spring of 1983.[16] Sonnenfeld wanted support from the American government to locate Wallenberg, but Blair, in turn, wanted only to get enough information from the CIA to satisfy Sonnenfeld. He only told her he had no information relating to Wallenberg's whereabouts.

That generated an internal CIA memo on April 6, 1983, that said the "Agency has no analyst assigned to the Wallenberg case per se," showing the CIA's long-term lack of interest in the matter.[17] The NSC analyst said the CIA, though most of its information was in the "public domain," this couldn't be released "because of the sensitivity of liaison relationships with foreign intelligence services and the necessity of protecting sensitive sources and methods."

In her letter to the U.S. government, Sonnenfeld indicated the Wallenberg matter occupied great interest in Washington. Hardly. The CIA quoted the NSC analyst as saying, "The Wallenberg case has not been treated as a matter of high priority for US intelligence collection, and properly so, given other pressing needs for intelligence on Soviet matters, and given the vigorous efforts of the Swedish government on Wallenberg's behalf."

The CIA didn't care; in fact, many of the documents in the CIA files came from the State Department, and "the CIA role has largely been one of responding to State inquiries."

Like an obedient child, the intelligence agency said, "Nothing of substance has been withheld from State in these exchanges."

To conclude the memo, the CIA said it had no new information on Wallenberg's whereabouts or if he were still alive. Its files also showed material "on several key public sources which cast doubt on their credibility." The agency then explained the War Refugee Board's link to Wallenberg, but again said "there was no official OSS association with Wallenberg."

The CIA also didn't know if "it is Soviet practice to deliberately keep prisoners alive at all costs," and it couldn't "judge the authenticity of the 1957 Soviet reply about Wallenberg's death."[18]

Therefore, America's greatest intelligence service knew little and cared less about Raoul Wallenberg.

During the 1980s, two Secretaries of State, Alexander Haig and George P. Shultz, did raise the Wallenberg issue with the Soviet foreign minister but nothing happened. When Shultz gave the opening address in Stockholm on January 17, 1984, at the Conference on Disarmament in Europe, he mentioned that day was the 39th anniversary of Wallenberg's abduction.

In his book, "Turmoil and Triumph: My Years as Secretary of State," Shultz writes his speech "began with a tribute to Raoul Wallenberg . . . The Soviets claimed he had died shortly after the war, but we did not believe that."[19]

Despite all the evidence, Russia maintained its story that Wallenberg had died of a heart attack in 1947. Wallenberg had become a cause célèbre, which may have led to his death, according to Annette Lantos. "I think he died in 1981, around the time when he became internationally famous."[20]

Almost every year during the 1950s, '60s and '70s, "We had a lot of information. In 1981, it came to an end. They killed him because of the atrocities they committed against him," she said.

Her voice low, but serrated with emotion, Mrs. Lantos explained how during her tireless efforts, "We thought we could get him back." Like everyone else, though, they failed.

A CIA document filed on October 3, 1983—which describes a 3 a.m. visit by a KGB agent, a mysterious Norwegian arms dealer, a Briton and a Swedish judge—portrays a kinder conclusion. Gunnar Linnander, a retired justice of Sweden's highest court, worked part time as an arbitrator on assignments for the International Chamber of Commerce in Paris, reported the author of the memo, an unnamed CIA agent working in the Office of Soviet Analysis. Linnander knew the analyst since the judge was a U.N. adviser to the foreign ministry of Nepal from 1960 to 1963 during a leave from his work in Sweden's judicial service while the CIA analyst then worked as a journalist in New Delhi.

During August of 1983, Linnander wrote the CIA analyst saying he would be in New York the following month on an arbitration case and wanted to visit the agent and his wife as they had done in prior years in Hong Kong and Washington. In his letter, Linnander said he had discovered some interesting information about a Sasha Pavlov, whom he thought was the No. 2 man in the KGB, and he wanted further identification about him. After checking the unclassified file on Soviet officials, the analyst wrote to Linnander that there were two Aleksandr (Sasha) Pavlovs among senior Soviet officials, but neither was listed as with the KGB.

Upon completing his arbitration hearing in New York, Linnander flew to Washington October 1, a Saturday, and spent two nights with the agent's family before leaving for Stockholm, the same day the agent filed his report.

"Although he did not say so specifically, I had the strong impression that his main purpose in coming to Washington was to tell the Wallenberg story that he related to me Saturday night," the analyst said. "He knew I had gone into the US government, and before telling me the story he checked with my wife to confirm his suspicion that I now worked for the Agency."

To cover himself, the agent explained that his Aug. 15 "Outside Activity Approval Request" on Linnander's possible visit permitted the agent to reveal his true identity. Then he told Linnander's story.

At the end of May or in early June, Linnander traveled to Geneva, where his wife, Margareta, lives part of the time as the representative of the combined Swedish aid agencies working with the United Nations and other international organizations. During a social meeting with a Briton, Wallenberg's name arose.

"'He died two months ago,'" the Briton told Linnander.

Understandably, Linnander was curious about one of his country's heroes and a contemporary, for the judge was born in

1914, two years after Wallenberg. Linnander mixed in the same social circles as the Wallenberg family, knew several family members as well as Nina Lagergren, Wallenberg's half-sister, and the judge also knew about Wallenberg's heroics and his imprisonment.

Linnander pressed the Briton, whose name the judge would not divulge, and he explained his information came from a Norwegian arms dealer who lived in Geneva. The Briton arranged a luncheon a day or two later where Linnander could talk to the Norwegian without revealing he wanted to discuss Wallenberg.

The two Scandinavians met at a yacht club on the lake and talked in English, though the Briton understood their languages. During their discussion, the Norwegian contended he knew and worked with President Ferdinand E. Marcos of the Philippines and Prime Minister Zulfikar Ali Bhutto of Pakistan. Marcos was still in power then, but Bhutto had been executed four years earlier.

"Linnander found him convincing rather than exaggerating," the CIA agent reported.

As Linnander maneuvered the conversation to discuss the Wallenberg family as important bankers, the arms dealer replied with as much "personal knowledge and apparent access to the family" as the judge had. The arms dealer especially knew Henry Wallenberg, then in retirement from the family business and living in the south of France. Finally, the Swede asked the Norwegian about Raoul Wallenberg.

"'Oh, he's dead. He died two months ago under house arrest in a forest near Moscow.'"

To Linnander, this meant a natural death, though the arms dealer failed to specify. At that time, Wallenberg would have been 70.

Linnander pushed for more details. In response, the Norwegian told the Swede that at 3 a.m. two months earlier Sasha Pavlov, whom he identified as the KGB's No. 2 man, visited him at his home in Geneva. Pavlov, whom the Norwegian knew, pounded on his door until the arms dealer finally let him inside. The KGB man had been drinking but was not drunk, according to the Norwegian. Pavlov wanted more liquor and over another drink he told the arms dealer that Wallenberg had died.

Then Linnander wanted to know why the KGB had told the Norwegian. "The Norwegian presumed that he was intended to pass along word to Henry Wallenberg," the CIA analyst reported. The arms dealer thought the KGB wanted him to tell Henry Wallenberg, but he hadn't because he didn't want to get involved in the case or the publicity that has encircled it.

"The Norwegian's motives in having told the Britisher and then repeated it to Linnander were not clear to Linnander, he told me, but Linnander speculated he was possibly considered a good channel back to the Swedish establishment," the CIA analyst said.

Linnander promised the Norwegian he would not reveal his name. Then the judge pressed the arms dealer for more information about Raoul Wallenberg, but he gave him nothing more of value. When the Briton and the Swede drove back together to Geneva, he told Linnander he had warned the Norwegian—while the Swede was in the bathroom—to say no more, for he had said enough.

The Swedish judge felt awkward about this meeting, which he had not discussed with anyone in the Swedish government. He feared a disclosure to a friend in the cabinet would mean a leak to the press and a public attempt to identify and interview the Norwegian, which Linnander felt would break his pledge to guard the man's identity. Linnander considered taking the story to the Swedish attorney-general, who has somewhat of an independent position under Swedish law, but he hesitated. One reason was that the judge remained uncertain about Pavlov's identity.

Though Linnander did not ask the CIA agent to report what he said, "I assume he intended that I should do so," explained the American. Linnander did ask for a better identification of Pavlov, so he could better evaluate the story. The American and the Swede discussed the possibility that Pavlov was the KGB's No. 2 man in

Geneva, someone who could wander around Geneva at 3 a.m. and contact arms dealers.

Linnander then mentioned that the United States had named Wallenberg an honorary citizen "some years ago [two years earlier]. He seemed to be implying that the US government should take interest in this report," the agent wrote.

The CIA analyst told his superiors "Although it might never be possible to be certain about the story, coming as it does after so many other conflicting official and unofficial Soviet accounts of Wallenberg's fate, a surfacing of the story in Sweden would be to US advantage in reminding the Swedish public of a case that had periodically soured Swedish-Soviet relations."

In 1979, four years before the latest report of Wallenberg's death, Maj Wising Wallenberg von Dardel, Raoul's mother, died after spending the last 34 years of her life relentlessly—but unsuccessfully—fighting for the release of her beloved first born son. Maj von Dardel died at the age of 87 and her second husband, Fredrik von Dardel, died two days later at the age of 93.

The couple's two children, Guy and Nina, now alone carried the burden of trying to free their half-brother. Neither Sweden nor the United States would do anything of value to rescue Wallenberg while the Soviet Union insisted he had died in 1947. Since writing letters, making telephone calls, forming committees and even obtaining honorary citizenship on behalf of Raoul Wallenberg had failed to free him or uncover his whereabouts, the von Dardel children needed a new weapon. Unknown to them, an idea—strong as a cudgel—lay in the middle of the American continent.

CHAPTER 9

Marvin W. Makinen, an American foreign exchange student from the Free University of Berlin, was touring the Soviet Union alone on July 27, 1961, when the KGB arrested him on a street in Kiev. The Soviets charged Makinen with possession of sensitive photographs. To this day, Makinen declines to comment on the circumstances of his arrest.

During a closed military trial, the Soviets found Makinen guilty of espionage and sentenced him to eight years in prison. They put Makinen in Vladimir prison, where he spent 20 months. While incarcerated in Building No. 2, he shared Cell No. 33 with a Soviet prisoner, who told Makinen about the accomplishments of another inmate, known cryptically as "the Swede from Budapest."

From late December 1961 to March 1962, Makinen shared his cell with the Soviet prisoner. "When I once asked him whether other foreign prisoners had been in Vladimir, he told me there had been a Swedish prisoner, but that he knew no further details."[1]

Two cells away from Makinen in No. 31 sat Francis Gary Powers, the U-2 pilot shot down over the Soviet Union on May 1, 1960. After the Soviets traded Powers in February 1962, Makinen stayed in Cell No. 33, but Powers' cellmate remained alone in No. 31. When Makinen's cellmate was transferred to a labor camp in March 1962, the Soviets transferred the American to Cell No. 31. Still living there was Zygurd Kruminsh, a Latvian and Powers' former cellmate.

"We occupied Cell No. 31 together for the next 10 months, whereupon he was released from prison by a pardon of the Supreme Soviet," Makinen said. "Since I had heard of a Swedish prisoner through my first Soviet cellmate, I asked Kruminsh whether he had ever known of this person. Kruminsh told me that several years earlier while he had been a prisoner trustee in Building 2, he had met a Swedish prisoner. He claimed that he did not learn the prisoner's name and that he thought that he was no longer in Vladimir. My estimate of his contact with the Swedish prisoner was 1956-59."

In July 1963, the Soviets transferred Makinen to a labor camp at the village of Leplei in the Potma region of the Mordovian Autonomous Republic, which is about 300 miles southeast of Moscow. He arrived a month later. "After approximately one week there, a prisoner inquired from me who had been my cellmates in Vladimir," Makinen remembered. "He had previously been in Vladimir and had been transferred himself to the labor camp about six to ten months before me. When I told him of Kruminsh, his comment was clear, 'That son of a bitch, Kruminsh. He got to sit with all the foreigners. He sat with you; he sat with Powers, and he sat with the Swedish prisoner van den Berg.'"[2]

After about 28 months in prison, Makinen was released in October 1963, exchanged for two Soviet spies. Then 24, Makinen wanted to start his medical studies at the University of Pennsylvania, but he could not forget about the mysterious Swede. In 1964, a year after his release, Makinen's interest heightened following a visit to the Swedish Embassy in Washington for a debriefing regarding the prison references to the Swedish prisoner in the Soviet cell. The Swedish Embassy, in turn, had learned from the U.S. State Department, which had interviewed Makinen after his release, about his link to the Swede.

While talking to the chargé d'affaires, Makinen learned that the Swede was actually a diplomat from World War II Budapest who had saved thousands of Jews. As the Swedes showed Makinen to the embassy door, the chargé d'affaires requested, "Mr. Makinen, we would appreciate it if you would not talk about this."[3]

"Why? What was this? It was the one statement that made me think 'Who was this person?'" said Makinen, who didn't solve that riddle for another 16 years. At 3 a.m. April 1, 1980, Makinen finally got his answer.

After arriving home late from his laboratory at the University of Chicago where he had been conducting experiments with liquid helium, Makinen had a glass of orange juice and went to the living room to read the New York Times Sunday magazine. When he turned to page 21 and saw an article titled "Hero of the Holocaust," he was immediately engrossed.[4]

"I was just so floored. I mean I was taken by this article. As I started to read, all those neuronal connections started to come into play," said Makinen, a soft-spoken scientist.

"Van den berg. Wallenberg, that's it. That was the first time I'd made the connection. I had known nothing. Wallenberg was not then a household name," Makinen said.

The article mentioned that Wallenberg had a half-brother, Guy von Dardel, on sabbatical at Stanford University's Linear Accelerator Laboratory, where he was doing research on elementary particle physics. The next morning Makinen telephoned von Dardel and explained how he had been incarcerated at Vladimir and had heard vague references about a Swedish prisoner whose identity was kept secret.

Shortly thereafter, von Dardel and Makinen met between flights at Chicago's O'Hare International Airport. In less than a year, von Dardel asked Makinen to speak at the first international Wallenberg hearing in Stockholm. The meeting, held in January 1981, was designed to highlight the most recent evidence that Wallenberg might still be alive and, if he were, to make the Soviet Union release him.

"There was no way I could have said no nor would I have wanted to," Makinen explained. Still, until then, he had never publicly spoken about his imprisonment. Makinen had never mentioned it to his two sons, who in 1981 were nine and six years old. Rarely did he even mention it to his wife, Michele, a clinical social worker.

For Makinen, who eventually became chairman of the

biochemistry and molecular biology department at the University of Chicago for five years, this had been "background" for 17 years.

"Much of the hard, harsh experience I hadn't resolved totally; I just sort of kept it repressed," he said. "Still, I find it extremely heavy, a painful process. What happens to people who've been through these kinds of experiences is that one little word evokes such a fountain of emotions, of different emotions and associations that you become immobilized."

Before going to Sweden, where his admission would cause an international stir, Makinen had one important task in the Hyde Park section of Chicago. He had to tell his sons or they might learn of this from someone reading a newspaper or from one of their friends or teachers. As Makinen gave his sons their baths one night, he explained how he had been a prisoner in the Soviet Union. While there, he had heard about another man who had been imprisoned for more than half his life—if he were still alive—for no reason.

That job done, Makinen told 800 people at the Wallenberg hearing about his experiences. When he returned to Chicago, he didn't look for ways to become involved, but occasionally von Dardel would confer with him.

During one of these conversations in the early 1980s, Makinen suggested a novel way to free Raoul Wallenberg—sue the Soviet Union.

"The idea for a lawsuit . . . I certainly saw it as a feasible path," Makinen recalled about a dozen years later during a telephone conversation from his university office. "I can't really say I came up with it originally. I got interested while speaking with a lawyer named Luis Kutner."

Kutner, a Chicago lawyer for more than 60 years and now dead, was one of the most prominent human rights attorneys of the 20th Century, undertaking several famous cases. For instance, Kutner helped win the release of the poet Ezra Pound from a mental ward after World War II.[5] At the request of Pope Pius XII, Kutner helped free Jozsef Cardinal Mindszenty, who had been imprisoned in Hungary on charges of treason. The Catholic clergyman opposed both fascism and communism in Hungary for more than 50 years of the 20th Century.

When ordained as a priest in 1915, Cardinal Mindszenty became politically active and was arrested as an enemy of the totalitarian governments twice in 1919 and 1944, the same year he was consecrated bishop of Veszprem. Two years later, he was made a cardinal. After he refused to let the Roman Catholic schools of Hungary be secularized, Cardinal Mindszenty was arrested in 1948 and convicted a year later on charges of treason and sentenced to life imprisonment. However, the Cardinal was freed during the Hungarian uprising of 1956 and after the communist government regained control, he took asylum in the U.S. Embassy in Budapest. There, he rejected requests from the Vatican to leave Hungary. Kutner negotiated improved prison conditions for Cardinal Mindszenty and ultimately helped his departure from house arrest at the American embassy in Budapest.

A native Chicagoan, born to Russian-Jewish immigrant parents, Kutner entered the University of Chicago at the age of 15 and established himself as a poet, author and musician. While at the law school, Kutner was a clerk for Clarence Darrow.[6] In 1949, Kutner gained national prominence when he won freedom for a black mechanic from Waukegan, Illinois, who had served nearly 26 years of a life term in the rape of an itinerant who later died in a mental hospital. A federal judge called a "sham" the defendant's 1924 trial where a prosecutor withheld crucial evidence, principally a doctor's evidence that the woman had not been raped.

Kutner, who co-founded Amnesty International in London along with Peter Benenson, campaigned for a worldwide habeas corpus code so that any arrested person would be properly charged and, at the court's discretion, released on bail.

With such a public profile, Kutner seemed the right choice to handle the lawsuit. Makinen telephoned Kutner, who expressed interest, leading to a year-long round of talks.

"Kutner had a good idea, the right idea, and he had the right motivation," Makinen said. Most importantly, "He wasn't afraid to try and see it through."

This case was bold and probably unworkable, which attracted Makinen as a scientist. "Because something doesn't seem to work is not a reason not to consider this. A lot of good science comes because they find some other route."

Von Dardel traveled to Chicago, where he and Makinen went to Kutner's office. The pair of scientists found it difficult to judge the noted lawyer's success. "He had a one-man office, and it was hard to see what he could accomplish," Makinen recalled. The trio had a "rather amicable discussion," Makinen said. "I think sensibly that we knew this would begin an enormous effort."

Makinen checked Kutner's references, including a lukewarm response from Arthur Goldberg, former Supreme Court Justice and Ambassador to the United Nations. That was good enough to keep discussions alive, but raw doubts kept irritating Makinen.

Kutner, a bon vivant and self-promoter, claimed many successes, and Makinen believed he played some role in Cardinal Mindszenty's release. But Makinen, always the scientist, needed more empirical proof.

Twelve years later, Makinen verbalized the scientific questions he had in the early 1980s about Kutner's accomplishments. "How do you evaluate these successes? How far along was the process intact when he entered? Is it something he initiated or does he step in and take all the credit? That was his style."

Despite these doubts, Makinen, von Dardel and his sister, Nina Lagergren, visited Kutner several times in Chicago. During these meetings, Kutner mentally shaped the lawsuit. "It is clear . . . Kutner should have full credit for conceiving the idea," von Dardel said.

Kutner also told Makinen, von Dardel and Lagergren about a recent U.S. law that they could use as a key to open Raoul Wallenberg's prison cell. This international legal key was called the Foreign Sovereign Immunities Act, passed by Congress in 1976. A few years later a federal judge in Washington agreed with Kutner.

Initially, Makinen, von Dardel and Lagergren considered re-taining Kutner in the most unusual law case, suing the Soviet Union to free Wallenberg, the Swedish diplomat who had saved 100,000 Jews in World War II Budapest. Kutner loved the idea, ready to pursue this noble quest.

With the gift of hindsight, Makinen felt Kutner was the man for the job.

"Kutner was willing to fight everyone. The other team (that eventually took the case) wasn't. Kutner's approach was to tie them (Soviets) up financially."

Kutner correctly reasoned that the U.S. State Department would intervene on the Soviets' side. No problem. Kutner would then "write to the White House and ask the President to defend the rights of this person (Wallenberg) through the Constitution," for Wallenberg had become an honorary American citizen in 1981, Makinen said.

"Kutner would have tried every possible avenue," Makinen added with regret clouding his voice.

But social and financial reasons erased Kutner, the first of many setbacks that ultimately doomed the lawsuit.

"He was a loose cannon," Makinen explained. "He was impossible to work with. He would just shout at you."

Besides that, Kutner knew nothing about the many Raoul Wallenberg organizations around the world and their motivation to keep Wallenberg's name alive. "He drove them up the wall. They stopped taking his calls. He would screech at them, 'What are you doing sitting on your asses?'" Makinen added, "That's not a direct quote," but close.

Also, Kutner, who began helping veterans dealing with Agent Orange, tried to mix commerce and academia. "He wanted me to set up a toxicology laboratory at the University of Chicago," Makinen said incredulously. "I really felt he was not sensible."

Additionally, Kutner proposed a fee of one million dollars for Wallenberg's defense. "That was just to start," Makinen said.

Von Dardel and Lagergren, who did not have access to the

Wallenberg family's money, could never pay that fee. Makinen, a brilliant, but then poorly-paid faculty member, had no money to contribute. But Kutner, who saw the case as a way to make both more money and fame for himself, tried to dampen von Dardel's flickering anxiety.

"I want every survivor of the Holocaust to spend $10 for Wallenberg's defense," Kutner explained.

At ten bucks each, Kutner would only need 100,000 Holocaust survivors to reach one million dollars. With the first million, Kutner intended to launch a giant public relations and advertising campaign to raise further funds. This new money, most likely a large sum, would pay for Kutner's legal fees and expenses. However, von Dardel and Makinen wondered if Kutner were only interested in finding Wallenberg or making a lot of money and creating a lot of publicity amid a campaign to find Wallenberg.

Ultimately, Davis Polk & Wardwell, the large New York law firm that took the case for nothing, spent about one million dollars. Davis Polk took no money from any Holocaust survivors, but the in-kind return was probably three times as much. For years, Davis Polk could say, "We are the Raoul Wallenberg law firm." That was a magnet attracting the best young associates.

Von Dardel, a quiet man, said years later, "I don't recall we discussed the actual fees with Kutner. We had to be very careful not to personally get the family involved in our big lawsuit against the Soviet Union. We couldn't afford it ourselves."

But von Dardel could afford an unyielding effort, which meant pursuing every opportunity to free his half-brother.

"We were very close growing up," said von Dardel, who is seven years younger than his half-brother. Curiously, both were born in August—Raoul on the fourth day of the month in 1912 and Guy on the 26th day in 1919. Before his trip to Budapest, Raoul and Guy spent many years apart. "Raoul was away in the States," said von Dardel, referring to his half-brother's college education at the University of Michigan. Later, they were both in the military, which involved an overall three-year-tour in primary training and the neutrality guard, but the half-brothers were in separate places.

"Raoul was in the home guard in Stockholm, and I was up around the Arctic Circle," von Dardel said. He spent about 18 months in a tiny town called Boden, just below the Arctic Circle and near the Gulf of Bothnia, which separates Sweden from Finland. When asked if Boden had been brutally cold, von Dardel replied with the Scandinavian tolerance for nature, "It wasn't so bad."

While the Wallenberg family was rich, the von Dardels led a middle class existence. Guy taught physics during the winter at Lund University in Southern Sweden and during the summer worked as a physicist at the Centre des Etudes de Recherche Nucleare (CERN) near Geneva, Switzerland. He retired in 1984 and spends most of his time at Satigny, just outside Geneva.

Despite Wallenberg's achievements, no one was willing to give any money to try to gain his freedom via the lawsuit, and Kutner refused to handle the case without this large sum. Makinen, von Dardel and Lagergren decided to drop Kutner and his unorthodox methods, seeking different legal representation.

"I could see (the lawsuit) really couldn't go any place with Kutner," Makinen said.

"When it came to actually preparing a lawsuit, it became clear that we needed a lot more support than Kutner could offer or was likely to be able to mobilize," von Dardel recalled.

But which avenue to take next? Toward the end of the Kutner period, a group of refuseniks in Moscow supplied the answer. While listening to a television newscast, Makinen heard about a unique lawsuit filed against the Soviet Union to free a man kept in Russia. The lawyer involved, a university law professor and someone who worked with Kutner on human rights cases, won a stunning legal victory against the Soviet Union. His name was Anthony D'Amato.

That led Makinen and von Dardel to Room 311 of the Northwestern University School of Law. There D'Amato looked at his potential new client, whose half-brother, Raoul Wallenberg, had already been imprisoned in the Soviet gulag for more than 35 years. Now von Dardel and Makinen were proposing a variation on D'Amato's unique, legal way to free the heroic diplomat.

"We want to sue the Soviet Union to force Raoul's release," von Dardel told D'Amato, who specialized in human rights' cases.

Sitting in straight-backed chairs inside D'Amato's high-ceilinged office lined with books, von Dardel and Makinen explained to the lawyer-professor what they wanted. Both clients and lawyer knew their chances of winning such a suit were as good as walking outside the law school, which was on the downtown Chicago lakefront, and swimming across Lake Michigan. But the two men were determined.

D'Amato seemed the right man. Slight, dark-haired with a full beard and a full academic background, D'Amato had graduated Phi Beta Kappa from Cornell University in 1957 and magna cum laude from Harvard Law School in 1961. At Harvard, two of his classmates—Arthur M. Kennedy and Antonin Scalia—had become U.S. Supreme Court Justices while another, Bernard Nussbaum, served as President Bill Clinton's attorney, and a fourth, Janet Reno, was Clinton's attorney general. When D'Amato taught political science at Wellesley College in 1965, Hillary Rodham Clinton was one of his students.

"Hillary was the best student in class, and she worked as my research assistant. I was just starting out in teaching then and the students were the best there," D'Amato recalled. "Now students are only motivated to find out what's on the exam," he complained.

At the time D'Amato became involved with von Dardel, in the early 1980s, no one knew Hillary would become First Lady, but von Dardel and Makinen did know D'Amato had just won— de facto—a startling case against the Soviet Union that provided parallels to Wallenberg's problem. This, too, involved someone incarcerated in the Soviet Union and wishing to leave.

In the spring of 1982, Susan Keegan, a former student of D'Amato and then a practicing lawyer in Chicago, called him at home, seeking advice for her friend, Lois Becker Frolova, who had to handle a press conference the next morning.[7] Frolova had just begun a hunger strike in sympathy with the one of her husband, Andrei V. Frolov, who began starving himself in Moscow and vowed to continue "to the death if necessary."

Frolov—a Russian free-lance journalist, photographer and script writer—met Lois Becker, an American student from Stanford University who was doing research in Moscow for her dissertation on 19th Century Soviet liberalism. They fell in love and married in May 1981 in the Palace of Marriages despite Soviet displeasure over marriages between Soviet citizens and foreigners. She became Lois Frolova because in Russian, to indicate the feminine gender, the woman's surname sometimes changes.

A month later Frolova's visa expired and she was forced to leave the Soviet Union without her husband. The Soviets refused to allow Frolov to emigrate to Chicago, where his wife lived with her parents. A year later she saw her husband during a 19-day tourist visa, but again left without him. Frolov, then 51, started a hunger strike in his apartment. After a campaign of letters and appeals to Soviet officials failed to reunite Frolov with his family in the West, Lois Frolova, 27, started her own hunger strike in protest.[8] The night Keegan called D'Amato spoke with her and then with Lois Frolova. Although the Soviets were restraining Russian Jews from emigrating, this did not apply in the Frolova case. Lois was Jewish, but Andrei was not. When D'Amato questioned Frolova about why the Soviets kept her husband inside Russia, she offered several reasons—the cold war, Soviet bureaucracy or jealousy of minor Soviet officials who themselves wanted to leave. Perhaps, Frolova suggested, her husband's work as a photojournalist alarmed the Soviets. But Frolov's work was equivalent to taking pictures for the National Geographic.

Nevertheless, the Soviets had tricked Frolov into becoming unemployable. After he had requested permission to emigrate to the United States, "They suggested that he first resign from his union, the Committee of Literary Workers," Frolova told D'Amato over the telephone. Frolov resigned, but then discovered he could not find any work. "They denied him his exit permit, and he no longer was able to get his stories or photographs published. He was completely out of a job," Frolova said.

"Who is 'they'?" D'Amato asked.

"In Russia, 'they' is usually a man dressed in civilian clothes whom citizens can 'spot' just from the way he talks and carries himself," Frolova said. "The man tells you something authoritative, something that he probably would not know unless he were officially connected with the government. But he never produces any papers and never puts anything in writing. Yet Andrei can tell when it's the secret police or a government agent."

Frolova explained "they" once came to her husband's flat in Moscow and told him to go with them. Frolov refused.

"What happened?" asked D'Amato.

"Nothing. I guess he called their bluff. Or maybe they didn't want to officially arrest him," Frolova said.

Her husband learned of two men and two women who had begun a hunger strike to join their spouses in the United States and Western Europe, and he joined their effort, called the Divided Families Group. While eating breakfast, Lois Frolova learned about Frolov's decision to go on a hunger strike from the Chicago Tribune's Moscow reporter. Immediately her body decided to stop eating, and Lois Frolova began her parallel hunger strike.

But the two couldn't communicate. Frolov couldn't call his wife and telephoning Moscow was a laborious endeavor.

On the telephone in Chicago was D'Amato, who had a plan. "Of course, I'm only guessing, but I think that you can only help him by generating publicity here in Chicago. My guess is that there is a certain safety in a lot of publicity," he told Frolova.

She agreed, and they decided to hold the press conference at the Northwestern Law School. The next morning radio, television and newspaper reporters gathered, making Frolova an instant celebrity. The waves from Frolova's hunger strike spread throughout Chicago. D'Amato found himself losing weight and Frolova's friends were eating less while she ate nothing.

Frolova and D'Amato had achieved national publicity—and weight loss—but Frolov was still incarcerated in Moscow. "Frustrated and unable to sleep, an idea popped into my head about 3 a.m.: why not sue the Soviet Union?" said D'Amato.

That idea—conceptualized by Kutner and D'Amato and put into practice by D'Amato—became the cornerstone of the lawsuit that could have freed Raoul Wallenberg.

"No one had ever sued that nation in a United States court on a human rights matter, but why couldn't there be a first time?" D'Amato asked himself. Then he asked: Who would be the plaintiff?

In the morning, D'Amato concluded the plaintiff should be Lois Frolova, not Andrei Frolov. The Soviet Union, by preventing her from living with her husband, was directly harming her. D'Amato invited Frolova and Steven Lubet of the Northwestern Legal Clinic, a specialist in immigration law, to come to his office. Initially surprised at D'Amato's unusual plan, Frolova quickly became convinced. Already, she was writing letters to members of Congress, appearing on radio and television talk shows and bothering the Office of Human Rights of the State Department.

Lubet thought a lawsuit, whatever its legal groundwork, would probably help Frolov's safety as the publicity had done. D'Amato and Lubet immediately began drafting a complaint, agreeing that an action for monetary damages would present collection problems. That was unimportant. "Our main purpose was to pressure the Soviet Union to let Andrei Frolov emigrate to the United States. We were working under the shadow of Andrei's vow to fast to the death, and Lois had assured us that her husband was a most serious and stubborn Russian," D'Amato said.

First, D'Amato checked the Foreign Sovereign Immunities Act of 1976, the same law Kutner had mentioned to von Dardel.[9] With that act, the U.S. Congress attempted "to remove the defense of sovereign immunity when foreign governments or their instrumentalities were sued in American courts with respect to their commercial activities," said D'Amato, who then asked if Frolova's human rights problem was a "commercial activity"?

"Steve Lubet and I pondered that question seriously and thoughtfully for approximately five seconds, and simultaneously concluded that there was no way to construe Lois' case as 'commercial,'" D'Amato said.

However, another provision in the Act involved torts related to problems of diplomatic immunity. Legally, torts are wrongful acts, like trespass or assault, that result in injury, loss or damages for which the injured party can bring civil action. Under international law, the host country can't subject foreign diplomats personally to court jurisdiction. But if they commit a tort, "their own countries ought to be liable for the actual damage caused," D'Amato learned.

To D'Amato, the Soviet Union's act of refusing to let Frolov leave the country directly harmed his wife, Lois Frolova. Still, he wondered if Congress intended to cover such a case. "There was no evidence that Congress did not so intend," D'Amato concluded. "Congress never thought of the possibility."

Since Frolova's case seemed to fit within the statute, that was not "inconsistent with its purpose, and after all the very process of legislation is to enact general rules that may encompass specific cases that were not specifically foreseen by the legislators," D'Amato reasoned.

Next, D'Amato reviewed the Helsinki Accords of 1975, which in Part 1, Section IV, provides that the participating states "will deal in a positive and humanitarian spirit with the applications of persons who wish to be reunited with members of their family." Though the Helsinki Accords are said to have no legal effect, the United States and Soviet Union took them seriously.

Also, the Soviet Union's repeated denials to Frolov's requests for permission to leave his country violated an international treaty, the International Covenant on Civil and Political Rights, which went into effect in 1976. The treaty provided that "everyone shall be free to leave any country, including his own."

Therefore, in D'Amato's legal opinion, the Soviet Union

committed an international tort by unlawfully denying Frolov his right to leave the Soviet Union and join his wife.

While drafting the complaint and working out a strategy, D'Amato received two important suggestions. The first came from Kutner, who suggested D'Amato sue the United States as well as the Soviet Union. Since the State Department refused to help Lois Frolova, that established a base for her to sue the United States for failing to protect her human rights in relation to the Soviet Union.

D'Amato thought "the idea fuses the classical with the modern conception of international law." The classical does not give the individual "standing" to sue a foreign government. The individual's government may act for the individual. The modern concept of human rights loosens that "standing" requirement, promoting the idea that an individual may sue his own government as well as a foreign government. In fact, the suggestion is that no government, including one's own government, should be immune.

Moving from theory to reality, D'Amato knew that suing the United States would be the fastest way to bring Frolova's case to the top officials in the Soviet Union. That was essential, for Frolov—fasting in his Moscow flat—was rapidly losing weight.

The second suggestion came from Susan Keegan and her senior partner, Michael Coffield, who advised D'Amato to file for an injunction as well as trying for damages. Thus, D'Amato contended the Frolova case came under the terms of the Foreign Sovereign Immunities Act and an injunction should be implied in the case of a continuing tort where the threat of money damages may be ineffective.

Within two days, on May 20, 1982, D'Amato filed a complaint in U.S. District Court in Chicago, suing the Soviet Union and seeking reunification of the family. D'Amato asked the judge to bar the Soviet Union from doing business in northern Illinois, a major grain and commodity center, until Frolov was released. The suit, which accused the Soviet Union of violating international law in denying Frolov's requests for emigration, would have affected millions of dollars in wheat purchases and gold sales on the Chicago

Board of Trade. D'Amato also sought fifty million dollars in punitive damages for Lois Frolova's forced separation from her husband.

This became the template for the Wallenberg lawsuit.

In his haste, D'Amato made some errors in the lawsuit. His colleagues pointed out the mistakes, which D'Amato fixed a few days later in an amended filing.

The day of the original filing Lois Frolova, still involved in her hunger strike, held another press conference. By now, in the eleventh day of her hunger strike, her weight had dropped to 98 pounds from 112 and a Chicago Tribune reporter described her as looking "weak and wan."

Then D'Amato notified the Soviet Embassy in Washington via telegram—in both English and Russian, translated by Frolova and her friends—and sent the embassy copies of the complaint and motion by express mail. Five days later, the Soviet officials told Frolov to go to the passport office.

By now, Jim Gallagher, the Chicago Tribune reporter in Moscow, was maintaining regular checks on Frolov and related his findings to D'Amato and Frolova. Andrei Frolov's re-application was promptly processed, which brought an end to his 26-day hunger strike. In Chicago, his wife also began to eat while in Moscow Frolov granted Gallagher an interview, and The Chicago Tribune printed the story on the front page with this James Bond headline, "From Russia, with love—for a new life, new land."[10]

Since the Soviets did not want to lose the opportunity to purchase U.S. wheat, Frolov was released—one month after D'Amato filed his lawsuit—and put on a flight to Frankfurt, where he took another flight to Chicago, arriving at O'Hare International Airport on a Sunday afternoon, June 20, 1982.

D'Amato had filed a lawsuit in a United States court that had freed a man virtually imprisoned in Russia. Makinen admired D'Amato's finesse, which forced the Soviets into acquiescence. The Soviets couldn't do any business in Northern Illinois, the location of the grain exchanges. "It was subtle, but very deep."

Guy von Dardel reasoned the same method could be used to

free his half-brother. But Andrei Frolov was not Raoul Wallenberg.

During his discussions with von Dardel and Makinen, Kutner had mentioned the Wallenberg case to D'Amato and wanted to enlist his help. "As usual, I was quite wary of Luis Kutner and his propensity to enlist the help of other lawyers and then not sharing revenues or credit with them," D'Amato said. "So, I danced around the question with Luis for quite some time." Though D'Amato remained suspicious of "Luis' modus operandi . . . I genuinely liked him."

Makinen called D'Amato and met with him several times, including the one time accompanied by von Dardel. When the pair arrived at D'Amato's office, D'Amato remembers them saying how they were beginning to distrust Kutner, particularly about his willingness to follow through on the Wallenberg case. They outlined Kutner's plan on Wallenberg, much of which D'Amato had already heard from Kutner.

"The only difference was that Luis told me that, in order to do right by Wallenberg, we needed this (large) amount of money, and I tended to believe Luis on this point," D'Amato said.

After von Dardel and Makinen outlined the potential case to D'Amato, "in this very office," the lawyer-professor recalled years later, sitting in his office on the lakefront, D'Amato told them. "I don't think this approach is right for you."

"I believed they could bring a lawsuit in an American court against the Soviet Union, and if they won, decide from then on what to do," D'Amato said. That wouldn't cost a fortune, but another lawyer would have to do it. For D'Amato felt, "I had the case, but not the clout."

"I felt I didn't have the support, the backup in Chicago," D'Amato remembered. Irwin Cotler, a Canadian lawyer involved in Soviet human rights issues, later said, "'Jeez, Tony, you had the Wallenberg case, and you didn't run with it,'" D'Amato recalled.

D'Amato replied, "Well, there weren't any law firms in Chicago that were interested in helping."

Cotler, who eventually became involved in the Wallenberg case, told D'Amato that in Montreal he could have had five law firms.

"Maybe you're a more international community, but in Chicago there just wasn't any interest."

Therefore, D'Amato told von Dardel, "Look, it's fine that you want to hire me to do it, but if I don't have the resources to do a full court press for you, it won't serve you well and what you really need are some law firms that understand the publicity value of this thing and the value to their young associates and the prestige value of the case."

Alas, that couldn't happen in the Heartland. "You would think that was true in Chicago, but we're pretty much a hick town," D'Amato mused. "It took Morris (Wolff) and Davis Polk to really understand what was going on."

Instead of taking the case, D'Amato recommended two lawyers. The first was Morris Wolff of Philadelphia, whom D'Amato had met during an international law seminar in Washington about a year earlier. D'Amato figured Wolff could help the helpless. "If I had a client with no defense, I'd give him to Morris. He'd come up with something."

D'Amato remembered his first meeting with Wolff, a nearly bald, bespectacled man five feet, nine inches tall. During the dinner at the law conference, the two were at the same table. Though strangers, Wolff affixed himself to D'Amato, acting like classmates at a 25-year reunion. He was "ingratiating to me, calling me 'Tony.' He's my friend. I just met the guy and already we were engaged in conversation. I asked myself: 'Where did this guy come from?'"

D'Amato used a barnyard colloquialism to describe Wolff's chief characteristic. "He is such a good bull shit artist."

After their dinner at the Shoreham Hotel, the multitalented D'Amato, a professor with a penchant for theater, who knew as much about Broadway stage characters like Betty Rizzo and Danny Zuko as he did about the law, began playing the piano. He liked some tunes from "Grease!," a spirited look at High School USA, circa 1950s, that used the leather jacket as the de rigueur garment in the play. D'Amato had seen the original Chicago production of "Grease!" and thought it had great potential, but the play was floundering, so he helped co-produce and raise money, thinking a "live baby was better than nothing."

With D'Amato's aid, "Grease!" became a success on Broadway and later a hit movie with John Travolta and Olivia Newton-John. D'Amato, who has written musical comedies that were produced in Chicago and London, shared in the subsequent movie profits. When asked how much, D'Amato cryptically replied, "I did okay."

But he will say he likes the play more than the movie. The movie "annoyed" him. The play was a "parody of the Annette Funicello movies of the '50s, glorifying the goody-two-shoes teenagers. What I didn't understand about the movie was its enormous appeal to kids," D'Amato said.

While D'Amato threw the ball to Wolff, he still maintained an active interest in the case for the next seven years. In fact, when von Dardel felt the case could be handled differently, he again went to D'Amato, a man he learned to trust. D'Amato's involvement ended Luis Kutner's association with von Dardel or D'Amato.

A few days after D'Amato met with von Dardel and Makinen, Kutner called D'Amato, saying, "You betrayed me. I thought you were my son. You met with von Dardel behind my back and gave him advice that conflicts with mine."

D'Amato told Kutner, "They approached me, asking for my professional opinion in confidence." To which Kutner replied, "even so, you should have told me about it before you met with them."

The two lawyers never spoke again. Kutner, who died March 1, 1993, at the age of 84 from a heart attack, had felt, "I had stabbed him in the back," D'Amato said.

Similarly, later in the Wallenberg case, other lawyers fought over the prize of associating themselves with Raoul Wallenberg and their petty jealousies created friction and personal irritation that never ended.

Von Dardel didn't want Kutner, who was too expensive. D'Amato couldn't bear the expense, so that left Morris Wolff, whom D'Amato recommended for his initiative. "I told von Dardel Morris was a person who might be able to gather support in the New York-Philadelphia area. I was really trying to do what I could."

Von Dardel "called Morris straight away from D'Amato's office and asked him if he would be interested, which he was."

That was sometime in the spring of 1983. Wolff, a lawyer and law professor living in Philadelphia, had expected von Dardel's call after D'Amato had alerted him. Von Dardel knew this legal maneuver was a once in a lifetime opportunity. "For a lawyer, a lawsuit like this must be as for a physicist to discover a new particle."

Wolff had graduated from Yale Law School in 1963 and worked as a special assistant to Robert F. Kennedy, as a deputy prosecutor in Philadelphia and then an international lawyer for 14 years. In 1980, a friend lured him into teaching, which he loved, and when von Dardel called Wolff was a professor at the Delaware Law School of Widener University in Wilmington, Delaware. He knew the courtroom and the classroom.

This case was definitely for the courtroom and a world forum, but it was 5,012 miles from Washington, D.C., to Budapest. Still, Wolff failed to suppress his excitement. For him, this was "a unique opportunity to walk in the corridors of history, to make new law, and most importantly, free one of the heroes of the Twentieth Century." He was excited about the case from the first moment Tony D'Amato described Wallenberg's heroism.

Wolff agreed to represent the family as legal counsel in this effort to free Wallenberg. Wolff said he never took any fee, but Makinen said von Dardel paid Wolff $25,000 while von Dardel declined to discuss it. "I know for a fact Wolff got $25,000," Makinen asserted.

So, on the third try, von Dardel finally found a lawyer, Morris Wolff, who would take the case to free his half-brother, Raoul Wallenberg, but two years later von Dardel fired the same lawyer.

CHAPTER 10

Wolff said he immediately began to research the law and the case at the University of Pennsylvania law library. He had taught a class on international law and ethics as a special professor at the University's Law School in 1980 and still had library privileges. Over a period of weeks and with the help of other lawyers, Wolff said he tried to form the framework for the lawsuit.

The linchpin of the case remained the Foreign Sovereign Immunities Act of 1976, which D'Amato had used in the Frolova case and Kutner had recommended to von Dardel. The act limited the shield of governmental immunity for lawsuits, permitting foreign nations to be sued in U.S. courts. According to Wolff, he is the one who discovered the Foreign Sovereign Immunities Act in the Penn Library, wrote most of the lawsuit, "carefully prepared" it and brought it into existence while doing a first-rate job.

Makinen disagreed about Wolff's contributions. "There were many things that were inappropriate and unsatisfactory with Wolff," he said.

"I realized at one point he couldn't handle the lawsuit. His main source of information in this case was me," Makinen complained. "I thought that was limiting if he wants to take charge of the project."

Tony D'Amato also provided Wolff with some of the Wallenberg papers he had received from the family. In any event, Makinen wanted more legal discussions or counselors.

According to Wolff's rendition of events, he did solicit the help of other lawyers, including Tony D'Amato, while constantly researching the law, looking for a way to make the case work. Makinen helped on the lawsuit, providing D'Amato and Wolff with information. "I dug up information and looked up things. I was interested," Makinen explained. "I thought this had some potential."

Then Makinen blasted Wolff and his legal entourage. "They weren't coherent enough" to handle the case. "All I can say is I don't see how D'Amato got so much respect for Wolff."

Makinen's dissatisfaction with Wolff and his methods continued for more than 10 years. In a 1994 interview, Makinen lamented that "I brought Morris Wolff and Guy together. I feel badly about it."

Despite Wallenberg's fame, however, no other lawyer wanted to assume the legal burden to free him.

"This was the only person who would take the case," Makinen said. "I tried in many ways" to get a replacement.

That included talking to lawyers he knew like Chuck Levy in Los Angeles, who had an apparently lucrative practice. Levy is Jewish and interested in the Wallenberg case, which gave him additional motivation to take the lawsuit. Makinen talked with Levy in Los Angeles, but he had "no real interest," Makinen related. "He had no real insight who could pursue this. I felt totally stymied."

To Makinen, "other than Luis Kutner, who was persistently a, 'tenacious' is the applicable word here, fighter, Morris Wolff was the only person who gave any recognition this might just be the way to do it. I couldn't find anyone else."

At the root, the problem was money. Wallenberg was high profile, but not high profit. If someone—the Wallenberg family, the U.S. government, the survivors—had accumulated enough money, a muscular and singularly directed lawsuit might have overpowered the opposition, won the case and finally found out what happened to Raoul Wallenberg. But that never happened.

Instead, forced to use Wolff, Makinen kept helping him, but everyone realized more help was essential.

"I believe that Mr. Wolff very correctly soon realized that a lawsuit of this kind required the involvement of one or several major law firms," von Dardel said. "For one thing, the economic resources of Raoul's immediate family and myself did not allow any contributions for lawyer's fees or legal expenses on the American level. We are not part of the banking family Wallenberg," von Dardel explained. "It was with considerable misgivings and only on the condition that the lawsuit should not cost the family anything, therefore, that we allowed Morris to go ahead. I am glad to admit, that in fact, it has not ruined us."

To get support for the case, Wolff began recruiting friends and giving speeches. Other lawyers joining the legal effort were Alan K. Cotler, Erik N. Videlock and Martha A. Toll of Pepper, Hamilton & Scheetz, a Philadelphia law firm.

One of Wolff's speeches was at Villanova. Wolff's wife, Deborah, who has since divorced him, was then studying law at the Villanova University School of Law, where her professor was Joseph W. Dellapenna, who listened to Wolff's talk.

"I realized that he really didn't know much about the Foreign Sovereign Immunities Act," said Dellapenna, who wrote a book about the FSIA, titled "Suing Foreign Governments and Their Corporations," which was published in 1988.

"I was working on my book at the time, and I told him I would be willing to help. I felt somebody should be involved who knew about the law. Regrettably, the Wallenberg case was pushing the outer limits of the law."

Dellapenna felt whoever handled the case would have had a difficult time, but he didn't like Wolff's method. "Morris' whole approach to the case was to publicize Morris. He recognized the legal difficulties of making much headway in the case, so he used it as a means of generating publicity about Wallenberg. That was Tony D'Amato's strategy in Frolova."

Nevertheless, to help Wolff, Dellapenna sent Wolff copies of some articles he had written and Wolff sent him the case file, "which was fairly thin." When Dellapenna received the case file, "I rewrote the case."

Wolff contends he wrote most of the case while serving as the lead lawyer in what undoubtedly became a team effort. "The mission was to rescue Wallenberg," Wolff said. "It was not a glory trip for myself. I was to be merely an instrument for this accomplishment." In any event, the Foreign Sovereign Immunities Act remained the linchpin.

Normally, foreign nationals have immunity in a host country. For example, if an Irish diplomat gets a speeding ticket in Chevy Chase, Maryland, he can be immune to prosecution. But more serious offenses create more serious consequences. Hence, the Foreign Sovereign Immunities Act of 1976.

Under the Foreign Sovereign Immunities Act, a foreign state that engages in acts that violate international law should not be entitled to immunity when sued in U.S. federal courts. For example, if the Soviet Union kidnaps a Swedish diplomat, who is an honorary American citizen, the Soviets can be sued in U.S. federal court. At least, that is how the American legal team saw the case.

The American lawyers wanted an exception for an exceptional diplomat. The FSIA grants immunity in most cases to foreign nations, but a heinous crime strips the foreign sovereign of that immunity. Therefore, the Soviet Union could not use the shield of sovereign immunity in the Wallenberg case, argued the American lawyers.

To buttress the FSIA, the legal team asserted jurisdiction under the Alien Tort Claims Act of 1789. The American lawyers argued the U.S. court had jurisdiction in the Wallenberg case because the defendant Soviet Union had committed a tortious, or wrongful, act, denying Wallenberg his rights as a citizen of the United States.

One right of citizenship, the lawyers argued in one of their filings, "is to be free to reside in one's nation of citizenship, particularly when that nation is a sanctuary where full civil and human rights—including the right to free speech and the right to travel are guaranteed and protected." Since the Soviets had incarcerated Wallenberg, they had obviously denied him these rights, according to the lawyers.

Wallenberg, a U.S. citizen since October 5, 1981, "has been

denied and deprived of his right to enjoy and to exercise his United States citizenship rights." To the lawyers, this constituted "personal injury" to Wallenberg's basic constitutional rights because of the "tortious acts of the Soviet government and by Soviet officials who have continued to restrain Raoul Wallenberg illegally in a series of Soviet labor camps and prisons."

In order to give the lawsuit punch, the legal team decided to ask for thirty-nine million dollars, or one million for each year of Wallenberg's imprisonment up to the time the lawsuit was filed. Thirty-nine million is a lot to individuals, not much to a country like the United States, but might make the Kremlin blink.

All of this came together during a slow, collective process. As his research continued, Wolff said he soon developed a work regimen. He taught international law at the Delaware School of Law (now Widener Law School) in Wilmington during the week, where his law students helped with the case. He commuted one hour each way between Philadelphia and Wilmington— home and school—and returned at 6:30 p.m. Then he went into his study, glass-enclosed on three sides, where he worked on the case from 7 p.m. until 10:30 p.m. or until his eyes couldn't see. Saturdays, he went to the Penn Library, but not before he played tennis to have enough strength to keep himself in the library chair all day. He stayed at the library from 9:30 a.m. until 5 p.m., he said. Most Sundays were family days. That way he said he put in 30 to 40 hours weekly on the case. During the summer when he didn't teach, he said he put in eight to ten hours daily on the lawsuit.

Wolff said he had help from the legal team, which, as part of its research, keep looking for legal and diplomatic precedent. They found two cases—one old and one new.

The old one involved Eighteenth Century Philadelphia and a caneing incident while the Twentieth Century example was far more barbarous, involving the assassination of a Chilean diplomat in downtown Washington.

On May 17, 1784, Charles Julian De Longchamps, commonly

know as the Chevalier De Longchamps, went to the Philadelphia home of the Francis Barbe Marbois, secretary of the French legation and consul general to the United States.[1] According to court documents, De Longchamps spoke to Marbois in a loud and menacing tone, saying in French, "I will dishonor you." Two days later De Longchamps and Marbois met on Market Street near a coffee house and engaged in a long conversation.

Marbois said he would complain to the civil authority about De Longchamps, who told Marbois, "you are a blackguard." Then, according to witnesses, De Longchamps struck the cane of Marbois "before that gentleman used any violent gestures or even appeared incensed. As soon as that stroke was given, Monsieur Marbois employed his stick with great severity, till the spectators interfered and separated the parties."

De Longchamps, charged with both menacing and assault, was taken before a U.S. court in Philadelphia. At the trial, evidence showed the defendant De Longchamps had served with honor in the French army and had a commission of sub-Brigadier. Apparently, De Longchamps called upon Marbois to get authentication of his military service as well as other papers regarding his family, his rank in France and his military promotions. De Longchamps wanted these papers to refute newspaper stories attacking his character. Marbois refused because of De Longchamps' threatening attitude.

The attorney general of Pennsylvania supported the prosecution. He cited the "necessity of sustaining the law of nations, of protecting and securing the persons and privileges of ambassadors; the connections between the law of nations and the municipal law, and the effect which the decision of this case must have upon . . . citizens abroad."

Initially, the jury found De Longchamps guilt of only the assault, but the court told the jury to reconsider and the jury found the defendant also guilty of menacing the diplomat. The sentence was suspended pending arguments in open court July 10th and 12th. After that, the prisoner was brought before the court October 7, 1784, for sentencing. Then the court said the assault against Marbois "is an infraction of the law of nations. This law, in its full extent, is part of the law of this state . . . The person of a public minister is sacred and inviolable. Whoever offers any violence to him, not only affronts the sovereign he represents, but also hurts the common safety and well-being of nations—he is guilty of a crime against the whole world."

The court added that "[t]he independence and inviolability of the person of a minister, apply likewise to secure the immunity of his house. It is to be defended from all outrage. It is under a peculiar protection of the laws; to invade its freedom is a crime against the state and all other nations."

Finally, the court pronounced its sentence. De Longchamps was forced to pay a fine of one hundred French crowns to the commonwealth of Pennsylvania and be imprisoned for two years—until July 4, 1786. De Longchamps also had to pay one thousand pounds and two securities of five hundred pounds each as a deposit for the next seven years to insure he acted properly in the Commonwealth.

A U.S. court had ruled the "person of a public minister is sacred and inviolable" even if he were a foreigner. Under U.S. law, a diplomat had protection.

A more recent case involved Orlando Letelier, who served as the Chilean ambassador to the United States, Chile's Minister of Foreign Relations, Minister of the Interior and Minister of Defense after Salvador Allende was elected president of Chile in 1970. When the military junta led by General Augusto Pinochet killed Allende and seized the government in September 1973, Letelier was imprisoned until February 1974. The Pinochet government expelled Letelier from Chile, and he stayed in Venezuela before coming to the United States in January 1975.

While in the United States, Letelier worked as director of the Transnational Program at the Institute for Policy Studies, a left wing organization in Washington, D.C., that lobbied foreign governments against the existing Chilean government. Letelier also taught at a local university and remained active in politics, speaking and writing against the Pinochet regime.

Ronni and Michael Moffitt, a married couple who also worked at the Institute, had trouble with their car September 21, 1976, so they rode with their boss, Letelier, who drove while Ronni was in the front seat and Michael in the back. As Letelier's Chevrolet Malibu rounded Sheridan Circle, N.W., in Washington at about 9:50 a.m., an explosive device went off underneath the driver's seat, hurling the vehicle into the air.

When the car came to rest, Michael Moffitt managed to escape from the rear end of the wrecked car by crawling out the back window. He saw his wife stagger away from the car and thought she had survived whereupon he went to help Letelier. The former diplomat was still in the driver's seat with much of his lower torso blown off and his head rolling back and forth while he made unintelligible utterings. Moffitt unsuccessfully tried to remove Letelier from the car. Then, as the police arrived, he noticed his wife had disappeared, so he went across the street where he found her lying on the ground, bleeding heavily from the mouth, for the bomb had pierced her carotid artery. Ronni Moffitt, 25, and Letelier were taken to a hospital, but they both died of their injuries.

Isabel Letelier, the widow, and her sons, Christian, José, Francisco and Juan Pablo, as well as Michael Maggio, Orlando Letelier's personal representative, along with Michael Moffitt, Ronni's widower, and her parents sued the government of Chile in a civil action to recover for the bombing deaths. They contended six men acted at the direction of the Republic of Chile's intelligence agency, Centro Nacional de Inteligencia. On March 11, 1980, U.S. District Judge Joyce Hens Green ruled even if the acts allegedly undertaken directly by Chile to result in Letelier's death had occurred in that country, "that circumstance alone will not allow it to absolve itself under the act of state doctrine if the actions of its alleged agents resulted in tortious injury in this country."

Or, if you planned it elsewhere, but did it here, you're liable. Judge Green added, "To hold otherwise would totally emasculate the purpose and effectiveness of the Foreign Sovereign Immunities Act by permitting a foreign state to reimpose the so recently supplanted framework of sovereign immunity as defined prior to the Act 'through the back door under the guise of state doctrine.'"

Or, Chile was liable, not immune.

The court served Chile with copies of the complaint, but the country never responded, so a default was entered against Chile.

On November 5, 1980, the federal judge awarded $4.9 million to the families of Letelier and his aide, Ronni Moffitt. The judge said Chile should pay $2.9 million of the damage award because the Chilean Secret Police carried out the attack. The remaining $2 million was to be paid by the six defendants.

After the judgment, Chile appealed, sending a diplomatic note and memorandum to the Clerk of the Court via the State Department. These correspondences contended the court lacked jurisdiction over Chile under the Foreign Sovereign Immunities Act of 1976. "After thorough analysis of the language and history of the FSIA, Chile was found amenable to jurisdiction under" the FSIA, a U.S. District Court in New York ruled. The act allowed the exercise of jurisdiction in any case, according to the FSIA "in which money damages are sought against a foreign state for personal injury or death . . . occurring in the United States and caused by the tortious act or omission of that foreign state."

To get the money from Chile, the New York District Court on December 20, 1983, approved the appointment of a receiver of the property interest of Chile's National Airline, Linea Aerea Nacional-Chile, known as LAN-Chile.[2]

The civil action had been undertaken, providing precedent. Besides precedent, Wolff felt he needed publicity. During his work, Wolff read about Tom Lantos and his links to Wallenberg. He said he spoke with Lantos, who invited Wolff to appear at a Congressional hearing August 3, 1983, one day before Wallenberg's 71st birthday. Wolff thought the Wallenberg affair would be a political lawsuit, and public opinion was vital, so a Congressional hearing would serve as an excellent forum.

Congressman Lantos, now with a receding hairline battling his gray hair for prominence on his skull, had been the prime force in establishing this hearing—the second such effort—of the House Subcommittee on Human Rights and International Organizations of the Committee on Foreign Affairs. The hearing, which began at 10:20 a.m. in room 2172 at the Rayburn House Office Building in Washington, became a daylong inquiry about Raoul Wallenberg.[3]

Politicians from both parties, activists and survivors asked, reasoned and pleaded with committee members to help free Wallenberg. The witnesses spoke of promises made in the Rose Garden, but unkept at the State Department. They told of ex-prisoners who swore they saw Wallenberg alive long after his supposed death in 1947. They told of how the Soviet jailers wouldn't let the prisoners die until they had completed their sentence. Ultimately, they created a resonance that spoke of Wallenberg's heroism.

Lantos, the first to testify, went to the witness table and mentioned all the high schools, libraries, museums, parks and major boulevards named after Wallenberg. "In a sense, one of our two objectives, to prevent the Soviet Union from making Raoul Wallenberg a nonperson, has been achieved. Raoul Wallenberg has penetrated the conscience of mankind and, as such, will live forever as one of the handful of giants who have stood up for human freedom at enormous risk to themselves."

The Congressman had succeeded with the first goal but failed with the second—to free Wallenberg or determine what had happened to him. Then Lantos praised the opposition party, saying Republican Secretaries of State Haig and Shultz had raised the Wallenberg issue at every international forum and many private meetings between the United States and the Soviet Union. Next, he castigated the Swedish government for doing nothing. Finally, he blasted the Soviet Union.

"First, Mr. Chairman, I think it is clear that the continuing insistence on the part of the Soviet Union that Wallenberg died in 1947 is a blatant and unvarnished lie. Wallenberg lived through the forties; he lived through the fifties; he lived through the sixties, and he lived well into the seventies. The evidence of that is unquestioned.

"I cannot tell you today, Mr. Chairman, whether Raoul Wallenberg is alive. I think it is clear that with every passing day the chances of his being alive diminish. But I think the Soviet Union will not be able to clear the slate until minimally it provides the world with an accounting of what happened to Wallenberg in all those decades."

Annette Lantos was next and told of her efforts to have her children know about the Holocaust, "this black hole of history."[4] She formed Concerned Citizens Committees and invited Nina Lagergren, Wallenberg's half-sister, to come to Washington "to stir American public opinion and Government to action."

Gus Yatron, the chairman and a Pennsylvania Congressman, invited Lantos back to the committee panel and Senator Claiborne Pell to the witness table. The senator's father, Herbert C. Pell, was the last U.S. minister in Hungary before the war and was interned there. Young Claiborne Pell had lived in Hungary and as a young man had followed that country's wartime tragedy.

In his testimony, Senator Pell complained that "the American government could have done even more.[5] I can remember pressing a series of our Ambassadors in Moscow to raise this matter. I am not sure it was raised with the vigor with which I would have liked." That aside, Pell wanted to "keep the spotlight of public concern on the problem . . . making sure the name Wallenberg is not only not forgotten but continuously emblazoned further on the conscience of the world . . ."

Next to testify were two Republicans—Congressman Hamilton Fish of New York and Millicent Fenwick, a former congresswoman from New Jersey, who has since died.

"We had the spectrum of government there," remarked Makinen, who attended the hearing, but didn't like some remarks.

"Fenwick said something totally symbolic and not very substantive." After Fenwick, the next witness was Joshua Eilberg, a former representative from Pennsylvania and member of the Wallenberg Committee of Greater Philadelphia.[6] Eilberg discussed other Wallenberg sightings. He said that on June 14, 1979, an anonymous Soviet Jewish immigrant told the U.S. Embassy that on May 1, 1978, at a party of a friend whose father was a senior KGB official the official said when drunk that he had a Swede in his charge at Lubyanka Prison who had been a prisoner for more than 30 years.

In 1980, Victor Herman, jailed as a spy and returned to the United States in 1976, claimed he had contacted a former co-prisoner who said prison guards told him in 1976 that Wallenberg was in special block of Gorky Central Prison. He said the other prisoner told him Wallenberg was later transferred to prison in Kirov. In March 1980, British spy Greville Wynne claims while in Lubyanka Prison in early 1963 he overheard conversation between a guard and a prisoner identifying himself as Swedish.

In 1981, Cronid Lubarsky, a Soviet dissident, living in Munich, claims a Moscow source saw an old Swede in bad physical condition in Blagoveshchensk special psychiatric hospital near the Soviet-Manchurian border. Prisoners speculated this was Wallenberg. In 1981, dissidents smuggled a bulletin out of Russia that said the Swede was "on his last legs."

Eilberg also repeated Makinen's account of imprisonment as well as a Russian lawyer identified only as "Ivanov," who said in 1973 a client formerly in a prison camp in Mordovia in the Mordovian Republic needed his help, so he spoke with the camp commandant. When drunk, the camp commandant mentioned "very important foreigners" in camp, including a Swede imprisoned more than 20 years.

In 1981, the Associated Press quoted "Estonian exile sources" concerning Estonian dissident Veljo Kalep who claims to have new evidence about Wallenberg, Eilberg reported.

Two years earlier during the initial hearing on Wallenberg,

several people who had met Wallenberg in the Soviet gulag testified about their experiences. At that hearing, the committee recommended the President take immediate action to secure Wallenberg's release and to threaten suspension of trade agreements and cultural exchanges if necessary. The Congress directed the State Department to carry out its wishes. Some members of Congress were disturbed that nothing had happened and that the Soviets had supplied no new information on Wallenberg.

Edward J. Derwinski, a former Republican Congressman from Illinois and then a counselor to the State Department, testified next.[7] Derwinski, once a Republican leader on the House Foreign Affairs Committee, had served in the House for 24 years, but he had lost his Congressional seat in the primary after a reapportionment. President Reagan had then appointed the Republican veteran as counselor to the State Department, a prosaic reward for a losing candidate of the party in power.

The committee asked Derwinski if Wallenberg's name arose during negotiations between the U.S. government and the Soviets. Derwinski demurred. "This isn't something where we would want to be swapping let's say the grain agreement for some information on Wallenberg." But Derwinski said the U.S. government wanted to know "the truth. What happened?"

Guy von Dardel, who had planned to attend the hearing, had fallen and broken his hip on the day he was to leave Geneva for Washington. Instead of testifying, he spent the time in a Swiss hospital.

But Sonja Sonnenfeld, executive director of the International Raoul Wallenberg Committee in Stockholm, testified and titillated the audience.[8] "I am more convinced than ever and have more reasons than ever to believe that Raoul is still alive. I am very sorry I cannot go deeper into this. However, tomorrow, on his 71st birthday, he still suffers somewhere in the Soviet Union, waiting for us to come for him. His only hope lies with the United States, a country he loved and lived in for quite a few years and whose mission he was so eager to take on."

Then she said something remarkable. "It sounds very cynical

that you can survive 39 years in a Russian prison. My experts, who are all dissidents, experts on the Soviet prison system—we have one with us today, but he will not testify—all assure me that you are not even allowed to die until you have served your sentence."

Maybe there was still hope. The Soviets would not even let Wallenberg die until he had completed his prison term.

Ms. Sonnenfeld continued, "Since they most probably have sentenced Raoul for spying, that would mean a lot of years. Then they can give him any amount of years for just nothing. They don't need any reason, as you know."

She reminded the panel, "Raoul isn't just a symbol. He is a human being who needs your help, our help, everybody's help. You and your government must be prepared to take some risks if you ever intend to live up to your promises."

For 50 years, the United States did neither.

The next witness, Rachel Oestreicher Haspel, president of the Raoul Wallenberg Committee of the United States, asked that a U.S. postal stamp be issued to honor the War Refugee Board bearing Raoul Wallenberg's picture because he is alive and a memorial stamp would be inappropriate.[9]

In her prepared statement entered into the Congressional Record, she, too, felt Wallenberg might still be alive. "Based on very concrete information, it is my opinion that Mr. Wallenberg has been given preferential treatment by his Soviet jailers. Never in all the thousands of pages of testimony released by the Swedish government has hard labor ever been mentioned."

She then repeated the story about Dr. Nanna Svartz and Dr. Alexander Myasnikov, who had examined Wallenberg. "What is staggering," said Ms. Haspel, "is that . . . Myasnikov was the personal physician of Nikita Khrushchev. How often, in any country, does the personal physician of a President or a Prime Minister examine an ordinary prisoner?" Many ex-prisoners had lived a long time in the Soviet gulag. Again, there was hope that Wallenberg was still alive.

Most definitely alive was Agnes Adachi, who worked with

Wallenberg in Budapest during the war, and at the time of the hearing was vice president of the Raoul Wallenberg Committee of the United States and president of the Queens Chapter of the Wallenberg Committee.[10] She talked about the Raoul Wallenberg public school in Brooklyn, the Wallenberg humanitarian award, the Queens Wallenberg Square, a park at the foot of Forest Park and other living legacies.

Then she made a plea. "When I worked with Raoul, I never, never heard him say it cannot be done or it is impossible or it is dangerous. In his spirit, it is our hope that through the recommendation of your subcommittee and the Congress and all our committees together, because we are one body, we will find the truth about Raoul. He is alive. I know that. His spirit must be still high. He is waiting for our help. Please, the Congress and all the Wallenberg committees, please work together."

After Adachi, Wolff testified, saying he had decided to challenge the Soviet Union in court after the family retained him.[11] He came before Congress not to ask for permission to file the lawsuit but to gather more public support. Wolff felt the U.S. Congress needed to get behind the effort to rescue Wallenberg. "The United States has an obligation. We had put him in motion."

Wolff told the panel "even if Raoul Wallenberg is a Swedish citizen, and only an honorary American citizen, even if the offense began in Hungary by his abduction, in protective custody into the Russian prison system, we may assert jurisdiction under the law as presently written. We will argue that the alleged offender is not only the three or four people who took him and abducted him from his diplomatic post in Hungary but that the offender is the Soviet Union, which put him into their prison system and has admitted that they had him in prison."

Wolff asked the State Department to help the lawsuit by filing an amicus curiae brief supporting the position on the violations of international law involved. Instead, the State Department ultimately worked against the lawsuit.

CHAPTER 11

Though he broke their legal relationship, Von Dardel remained grateful to Wolff for one accomplishment. "Wolff realized we needed a big law firm and could not go it alone. He convinced Guy Struve to take the case. That was Mr. Wolff's big contribution. This is somewhat ironic since in the later conflict between powerful law firms and the individualistic, academic Wolff, the latter was squeezed out of the project," von Dardel said.

Wolff met Struve, a partner with the prestigious New York law firm of Davis Polk & Wardwell, during a late 1983 meeting at New York University Law School. Each man gives a different account of how they met. Wolff said he gave a speech at NYU and then Struve followed him to the NYU library, introduced himself and offered his services. Struve said he gave a talk at NYU, Wolff introduced himself and suggested Davis Polk join the lawsuit.

However they met, Struve—a cleancut, slender and careful man who tells all reporters before granting interviews that only indirect quotations are permissible—became involved because he felt the Wallenberg lawsuit was a worthwhile effort. D'Amato, who had philosophical disagreements with Struve, explained the New York lawyer's cautious demeanor. "He's the kind of guy who if you ask him if it's raining, he'll look outside and say 'hmmm.'"

Indeed, Struve weighs every word given to a reporter as though a misplaced verb could become a dagger in the writer's hand, but Struve does give interviews and answer questions. Part of Struve's hesitancy may relate to a congenital hearing problem that forces him to wear a hearing aid in each ear. During conversations, Struve sometimes presses the hearing aid inward with his finger to grasp the speaker's sounds. Despite his hearing deficiency, Struve graduated summa cum laude from Yale in 1963 and magna cum laude from Harvard Law School in 1966. He became an influential lawyer at an influential law firm, Davis Polk.

The federal government liked to choose Davis Polk lawyers for special assignments like Whitewater and Iran-contra. For example, on January 19, 1994, U.S. Attorney General Janet Reno named Robert B. Fiske Jr., a partner with Davis Polk, as special counsel to investigate the investments of then-President Clinton in the Whitewater Development Co., an Arkansas real estate venture. Eventually, the investigation—without Fiske—led to the impeachment of President Clinton, whom the Senate acquitted February 12, 1999.

Reno chose Fiske because of his excellent record and moderate Republican background. President Gerald Ford, a Republican, appointed Fiske as U.S. Attorney in Manhattan and President Jimmy Carter, a Democrat, retained Fiske. After Fiske investigated Whitewater for about seven months, a federal appeals panel on August 5, 1994, replaced Fiske with Kenneth W. Starr, a federal appeals court judge and a Solicitor General under President George Bush. Starr zealously pursued the impeachment investigation against President Clinton. William H. Rehnquist, Chief Justice of the Supreme Court, had appointed the three-member panel of judges that replaced Fiske. Reno wanted to reappoint him, but the panel said that it would be inconsistent with the independent-counsel law for the Clinton Administration to be involved in selecting the individual to run the investigation. The three judge panel said the change did not reflect any unhappiness with Fiske's performance on Whitewater, which many saw as the crowning point to his career.

Lawrence E. Walsh, the independent prosecutor for the Iran-contra affair, had retired from Davis Polk before embarking on his six-year-long investigative task of Iran-contra, the scheme that involved selling weapons to Iran and using the money to help the contras in Nicaragua. Struve, who served as an associate counsel on Iran-contra, spent a great deal of time on the case, helping Walsh during the life of the inquiry, from December 1986 to February 1993. With men like Walsh, Fiske and Struve, Davis Polk had money, power and prestige.

When Struve agreed to join Wolff in late 1983, he also brought along the name and resources of Davis Polk. Since the legal team was doing this case pro bono publico, the lawyers needed funds to continue. With Davis Polk aboard, that cured the financial problem.

Four other Davis Polk lawyers joined the case, Jerome G. Snider of Davis Polk's Washington office along with Jo Backer, John G. Rich and Whitney L. Schmidt, all of the New York office.

To Struve, what Wallenberg did was inspiring, so the least Davis Polk could do was get involved. Struve learned the complaint was nearly done, but it lacked one key element: Translation into Russian, a language and ethos linked to Struve all the way back to author Leo Tolstoy. At Yale, Struve studied Russian and reads that language, though he can't speak it well. Additionally, the fraternal grandmother of Struve's first wife was a Tolstoy, and one of Struve's children from his first marriage, which ended in divorce, is named Catherine Tolstoy.

The lawyers needed five copies of the complaint, in Russian, to be sent by diplomatic pouch to the defendant, the Soviet government, in Moscow. To have the complaint translated independently would have involved a huge expense, but Davis Polk eliminated that problem. Gregory Kopchinsk, then an associate at Davis Polk and someone from the Soviet Union, volunteered to handle the Russian translation of the Wallenberg lawsuit while Struve read the final translation. Occasionally on weekends, Wolff came up from Philadelphia and worked with Struve. They also sent documents back and forth via Federal Express.

While Struve and Wolff began as associates, the relationship deteriorated into competitive hostility with Struve the victor, ultimately replacing Wolff as lead lawyer. For that, Wolff resents Struve, feeling he stole the case—and the glory—from him. In Struve's view, Wolff overemphasized publicity, which Struve thought would make the court regard the whole affair as a publicity stunt.

Makinen thought Dellapenna was better suited as lead lawyer than either Struve or Wolff. "He looked like the best of them all to handle the case."

Understandably, Dellapenna agreed. "This could be lawyerly self confidence, but I could have done a better job than Struve or Wolff. Those two got into a shoving match over who would be the lead attorney."

Unlike Struve, Dellapenna specialized in the Foreign Sovereign Immunities Act. "I've been studying it for 15 years," Dellapenna reminded a listener.

Wolff did well arousing interest, and enlisting people like Dellapenna to help write the original complaint, but Davis Polk, led by Struve, then did most of the work. In fact, Struve gradually took over the Wallenberg case. Only a giant firm like Davis Polk, which had huge resources, could handle the increasing demands of the law suit, further convincing D'Amato he could never have done the case alone. "This was prior to the days when I had word processing, so I would have had to type everything and then run it off on a Xerox machine and try to make copies and then submit it to some court. It would have driven me crazy."

However, D'Amato explained, "At the Davis Polk law firm, they can put chicken scratches on a piece of paper, send it out to their print shop and it comes back nicely bound with a paralegal checking all the citations and everything. It's so much easier for a law firm to crank some of these things out then it would be for someone like myself who's trying to teach classes at the same time, so it's really a resource problem."

When the clients met Struve, they were impressed by him and by his giant law firm. With the economic might of Davis Polk, Struve could bring in plenty of lawyers seated around a conference table. He could do instant research on the case. As D'Amato said, "It's a major law firm taking the case on a pro bono basis. Most clients would be dazzled by that."

Davis Polk may have spent $1 million on the von Dardel case, but derived three times as much in benefits. "I think they got a lot more out of this then they spent because for many years it was the biggest attraction they had when they went around to law schools to get the best students out of all the best classes," D'Amato said.

After taking the case, Davis Polk could say, "We're the Wallenberg law firm." With that altruistic lure, they hooked "really excellent people," D'Amato explained. "Law firms can spend three or four million dollars trying to get their next group of associates, so this was peanuts compared to that. It was a heck of a bang for the buck."

While admitting the Wallenberg name provided cachet for Davis Polk, Struve said he was only interested in doing a first-class job and didn't care who received credit. He thought Wallenberg was still alive and since Wallenberg had done so much to help others, even if there were only a wafer-thin hope of winning the lawsuit, Struve said he had to try.

By early February 1984, or about three years after Makinen developed the idea, the lawsuit was ready to be filed at the U.S. District Court in Washington, D.C. Von Dardel, a research physicist, would come from Europe. Von Dardel was to walk up the steps of the Court House and file the papers, providing television pictures around the world of Wallenberg's half-brother trying to free the famous diplomat. The legal team also wanted von Dardel at the subsequent press conference on Capitol Hill, for he knew more about his brother's plight than anyone, had credibility and would serve as a good addition to Lantos and Wolff.

Thus, the latest attempt in a never-ending quest to free Raoul Wallenberg, this time via American law and an American court, was set to begin.

CHAPTER 12

Bryant Gumbel—slick, confident and in control—moved verbally and unctuously from one topic to the next even at this early hour. How else could he be host of the "Today" show, seen every morning by millions?

As Lantos and Wolff sat in the Washington studio and via monitor watched Gumbel perform in New York, they anticipated their own showtime. Since Lantos and Wolff were about to discuss suing the Soviet Union and invoking the holy name of Raoul Wallenberg, the national networks were interested. Von Dardel, Wallenberg's half-brother, wasn't scheduled for the television show and almost didn't make it to Washington. Amazingly, a problem in his passport delayed von Dardel when he arrived at Dulles International Airport. There, von Dardel realized his passport had expired.

"But I had a California driver's license for which I paid $15," von Dardell recalled 10 years later.

He had needed that license during his two-year stay at Stanford University, and that document convinced the authorities to let von Dardel into the country. When he later told his American companions about his passport difficulties, they jokingly suggested he should have had a Schutz-pass. Unlike the Jews of Budapest, von Dardel did not need an ersatz Swedish document to save his life, requiring only the ubiquitous identity card of every American, a driver's license, to let him enter this country.

Von Dardel had not been involved in the nuts and bolts of the lawsuit. After convincing Wolff and Struve to take the case, "I did not participate much in the further activity, which led up to the filing of the lawsuit," von Dardel explained. Marvin Makinen also came to Washington, which provided bittersweet memories. Makinen's doubts about Wolff kept growing. "There seemed lots of promises made that never materialized."

For example, Makinen explained, he helped Wolff, unearthing information and sending him books. "I sent him a personally autographed copy of Elenore Lester's book about Wallenberg. He never returned it, and she has since died," Makinen said. "I felt badly."

Wolff asked Makinen to come to Washington for the filing of the case. "At that time, I was a struggling young faculty member without too much salary. Anything I'd done was from my own personal funds."

According to Makinen, Wolff told him once the lawsuit "gets into place" and Wolff got money from the Wallenberg family, he would reimburse the professor. "He never has. I asked him privately about it, but he did nothing," Makinen reported.

Wolff said he did the case pro bono publico and never expected to make any money; altruism was his motivation. But Makinen complained that Wolff insisted on everyone spending the night at the Hay-Adams Hotel, whose rooms have a view of the White House, but cost $600. Wolff brought his wife, further angering Makinen. "This was no social occasion."

Instead, this was an opportunity for international publicity about the Wallenberg case.

An NBC limousine picked Wolff up at 6 a.m. at the hotel and drove him to the studios. On arrival, he was ushered into the studio room, where first they put something on his face and then let him put something in his mouth. The makeup people applied some pancake makeup so Wolff would look good on the tube. Tom Lantos and his wife, Annette, were already there, so everyone chatted and then were taken into the TV room. After years of just watching Bryant Gumbel interview people, Lantos and Wolff could be interviewed by him on national television. Exciting. Even more exciting was the thought that millions of viewers would hear about the Wallenberg lawsuit and the efforts to free him.

Next came the NBC breakfast, including kiwi fruit, strawberries and honeydew. Shortly thereafter, Lantos and Wolff went out to the studio floor and sat down. At 8:08 a.m., Willard Scott threw it back to Bryant, who was about to throw it to Lantos and Wolff.

First, Gumbel gave some background. "During the holocaust, Swedish diplomat Raoul Wallenberg reportedly saved the lives of tens of thousands of Hungarian Jews.[1] After World War II, he disappeared, believed imprisoned by the Soviet Union. But today in federal court Congressman Tom Lantos, who was saved by Wallenberg, and lawyer Morris Wolff will file a suit against the Soviet Union, a suit designed to free Wallenberg and get damages from his captors."

Gumbel asked, "What's the basis of your suit? What specifically do you seek?"

Wolff answered, "We're filing this suit against the Soviet Union, seeking the release of Raoul Wallenberg from 39 years of Soviet custody." He explained that the Soviets were violating international law since Wallenberg was a Swedish diplomat when abducted. "We will file a suit this morning in federal court to obtain his release."

Gumbel, playing the naysayer, asked, "Realistically, what can you hope to get? I mean our courts have no jurisdiction over the Soviets, and who's going to enforce it, anyway?"[2]

Indeed that was the case's Gordian knot, so Wolff tried to unravel it by telling Gumbel and millions of other people, "Our courts do have jurisdiction, fortunately. During recent years, there are new laws, which provide that when foreign governments violate international law, the federal courts of the United States may hear the case and determine liability. Our case focuses on two aspects of violation of sovereign immunity, which are important to our case."

To get Lantos involved, Gumbel switched his questions to the Congressman. "The Soviets have claimed on numerous occasions that Wallenberg is dead. What makes you think that he is alive?"[3]

Lantos talked about the Soviets' variety of claims—first that they never had Wallenberg and then, in 1957, that he had died ten years earlier. "Yet the reports we have had through the '60s and the '70s, from utterly impeccable sources, was that Raoul Wallenberg was still alive. I think it's important to realize, Bryant, that this lawsuit that we are filing this morning is part of an ongoing effort by individuals and by our government to obtain the release of Raoul Wallenberg, or, should he be dead, to finally find out the truth about him."

Lantos then talked about his wife's efforts and Wallenberg's honorary U.S. citizenship. Gumbel asked if Wallenberg had worked against Nazi Germany, "What would be the Soviet Union's motivation for continuing to hold him . . . ?"

A good question, and Lantos had a good answer. The inquiry "assumes that all Soviet actions are rational actions . . . There are lots of irrational Soviet actions. Our hope is that the filing of this suit, which hopefully will make the Soviet Union respond in a responsible fashion, might be a step towards relaxing tensions between the Soviet Union and ourselves, because it is our judgment, Bryant, that there is nothing the Soviet Union could do, which would be more effective in relaxing tensions than to release Raoul Wallenberg."

Gumbel switched back to Wolff, asking if the uneasy relations between the United States and the Soviet Union would hurt the case.

The guest told Gumbel the Cold War confrontation would work to the United States' benefit "because the entire American public supports our action. We have the support in Congress of such men as Tom Lantos and Senator Pell and a broad range of congressmen." Then Wolff mentioned President Reagan's apparent support, demonstrated when he signed the law making Wallenberg an honorary citizen. "So with that momentum, I think America has come to realize that he was on our mission. It was at our request, in 1944, that the Swedes found a human being with the courage to go to Hungary and do this work. Now it's time for America to respond and to bring him home."

Gumbel, again the naysayer, responded, "I'm not trying to put an unnecessary damper on all of this, but what do you do if the Soviets just ignore your effort altogether?"[4]

Reasonable question, so Wolff gave a reasonable answer. "That will be up to the courts. We have the power of asking the court to enter a default judgment, and to assist our effort we are delighted that the step we are taking today will have the majesty of federal law and the good hearing of a federal court."[5]

Gumbel thanked Lantos and Wolff; they thanked him and, like Andy Warhol said, they had had their 15 minutes of fame. Actually, it was four minutes and 50 seconds. After the 290 seconds of fame had ended, the lawyers had to actually file the lawsuit. Three days before the filing date the legal team, aided by the Washington office of Davis Polk, had done a dry run. They went through all the formalities, so they would not bungle some last second detail like filing fees or necessary copies of the complaint or the accurate identification of defendants. The lawyers were determined to avoid embarrassment in front of the world press and, more specifically, the world's television cameras.

After the "Today" show, the lawyers, von Dardel and Makinen gathered at the federal District Court of Columbia, Third Street and Constitution Avenue, at the eastern end of The Mall and a few blocks from the steps of the U.S. Capitol. When assembled, the legal entourage and about 200 supporters went up the 13 low rise steps from Constitution Avenue—with television cameras recording every step—and swept past the circular statue of Major General George Gordon Meade, commander of the Union forces at Gettysburg, and on into Room 1825 of the courthouse to file the civil case.

"I walked up the steps with a whole bunch of lawyers," von Dardel said. That included Wolff and was the first time von Dardel had met him "in the flesh."

The lawsuit, which had taken about three years from conception to completion, listed Guy von Dardel and Sven Hagstromer, Wallenberg's legal guardian, as the plaintiffs and the Union of Soviet Socialist Republics as the defendant. Two Swedes, aided by American lawyers, were suing the Soviet Union for the release of one hero. When filed, the lawsuit asked for five things:

A. A judgment declaring the Soviets' seizure and detention of Raoul Wallenberg and his concealment "violate the law of nations, the laws and treaties of the USSR and the laws of the United States . . ."

B. An order making the Soviets produce in the district court Wallenberg "or his remains if he is dead."

C. An order requiring the Soviets to furnish to the plaintiffs all information it holds about Wallenberg.

D. A judgment for the plaintiffs of thirty-nine million dollars, or one million dollars for every year Wallenberg was incarcerated, as compensatory damages.

E. A judgment giving the plaintiffs "reasonable attorney's fees and costs."

Then the court clerks stamped the official papers February 2, 1984, United States District Court for the District of Columbia. "Civil Action No. 84-0353." The legal team had done it.[6]

When the entourage left the courthouse, survivors from Hungary, heads of committees to save Wallenberg from all over the world, supporters and sympathizers joined them to comprise an exalted army. Arms linked, von Dardel and his supporters walked two blocks amid cold, but clear weather down Pennsylvania Avenue toward the Capitol, one monumental symbol of U.S. government. The scene in Washington felt reminiscent of so many freedom marches for so many causes, but this one was only for one heroic man, Raoul Wallenberg.

After the short walk to the Capitol, the entourage went to a Committee room in the nearby Rayburn Building for a press conference arranged by Lantos. Already television lights were there along with about 85 reporters from 38 countries, including the United States, Israel, the Soviet Union, Hungary, Argentina, Germany, Canada and Australia.

Reporters buzzed around and made the lawyers feel like

celebrities. Before the press conference, Struve and Wolff argued about the press kits. Dellapenna, who also attended, said, "Morris' whole approach to the case was to publicize Morris. At the press conference when the complaint was filed, it was embarrassing. He handed out a dossier of himself, his picture, his resume and what a great job he was doing with only a little bit about Wallenberg."

Struve and Wolff began arguing if they should pass out the press kits. Wolff had "a stack of them," Dellapenna recalled, but "Struve pointed out that this was not the way to handle the case. That set Struve off in trying to push Wolff out."

Wolff recognized the legal difficulties of making much headway in the case, so he used it as a means of generating publicity about Wallenberg, Dellapenna said. "That was Tony D'Amato's strategy in Frolova." But what Wolff did, said Dellapenna, was to "generate publicity for himself."

Wolff saw things differently, saying he intended to glorify Wallenberg, not himself, at the press conference. "It was an excellent opportunity to educate the public about the plight of Wallenberg. Many people still had not heard about him. The law suit was to be a vehicle of publicity" to drive world opinion, and thus pressure "the Soviet Union for his release."

To show the new and the old, the press kits contained pictures of Wallenberg and Wolff, the "old warrior and the young lion," Wolff said.

During the press conference, Lantos, von Dardel and Wolff sat at a table to field the inquiries. In Wolff's version of the events, he answered reporters' questions well about the lawsuit while Lantos talked about his early days in Hungary and how he had run for Congress, partly on a promise to try to free Raoul Wallenberg. Reporters asked if Wallenberg were still alive and Lantos was hopeful.

Makinen saw the press conference in another way. "Morris did not answer well the several questions from reporters. He essentially clammed up. I forgot the questions, but he got flustered."

That performance further eroded Makinen's limited confidence in Wolff. "On many occasions, I could see that this person could not do the job."

But at the same press conference, Makinen saw and heard Dellapenna for the first time, which led to his belief that he indeed would have been the best man for the job. Too late, though, and the press conference continued.

In his soft but intelligent voice, von Dardel thanked Davis Polk and generally talked about human rights and what it meant to search for his half-brother. The American law team explained its motivation: They simply wanted one of the heroes of the Twentieth Century released so he could enjoy what remained of his life.

When the press conference ended, the legal team had a luncheon celebrating the new initiative and then von Dardel and Makinen took a two-hour walk.

"I remember that walk with Guy von Dardel," Makinen recalled a decade later. "It was probably the time at which Guy and I got to know each other. We became good friends."

Though the pair—both professorial looking—had met twice before, once in Chicago and another time in Stockholm, "We sort of started a deeper level kind of communication during that walk," Makinen said. "Somehow we saw in the other someone capable of being able of giving real support."

It was a chilly, but beautiful day in Washington during the late afternoon. Makinen, the former prisoner and now a brilliant scientist who had helped conceive the idea of the lawsuit, walked west along the National Mall with von Dardel, the living link to Raoul Wallenberg. In one of those fascinating ironies, the pair walked down Independence Avenue to 15th Street, the future site of the United States Holocaust Memorial Museum that would open nine years later with a special corner for Raoul Wallenberg.

At 15th Street, which was later renamed Raoul Wallenberg Place, the two men turned south and walked along the Tidal Basin and through West Potomac Park, which in a month would bloom with cherry blossoms. They continued their pleasant walk, with the Tidal Basin on the right side and the park on the left, to the

Jefferson Memorial, a 19-foot high bronze statue of America's third president.

Later, in recalling that walk, Makinen explained why he had become involved in the Wallenberg lawsuit. "This was not an ardent desire to lead on my part. My whole motivation related to my prison experience."

The painful memories forced Makinen's voice to drop. "If you've ever been in prison and know what those conditions are and you have a chance to help someone who's there, how can you say 'no'?"

Von Dardel and Makinen—the two scientists, now strangely linked by the Soviet gulag—kept walking through the American capital.

"We talked about everything from science, the research experiments we were each doing. Even though we were in different fields we could appreciate what the other was doing." Makinen's voice rose, buoyed by the memory.

They talked about further pursuing the lawsuit and trying to get Wallenberg committees to help. "We covered everything," Makinen remembered.

"I knew him after that," said Makinen, who called von Dardel "one of the most cultured persons I have ever met. He is a prince of a man. If I had a brother, I would want him to be like Guy."

The legal team was exhausted from the ordeal, which began with the Today show. Von Dardel was ready to fly back to Stockholm via Copenhagen and tell his family about the case's progress.

The first part of the work was done. The lawyers had constructed this legal edifice on behalf of Raoul Wallenberg, but now could it withstand the coming international attacks—from both the Soviet Union and the United States?

CHAPTER 13

After living at the peak—a television appearance, publicity, the filing of an historic lawsuit, a march to the Capitol and a press conference involving Raoul Wallenberg's half-brother—the legal team resided in the valley of waiting. All the hoopla had ended. The legal team had translated the complaint into Russian in Struve's New York law office, using an IBM word processor with Cyrillic letters. Once the State Department delivered the complaint in a diplomatic pouch, as required by the Foreign Sovereign Immunities Act, the Soviets had sixty days to reply.

Five days after filing the case, the plaintiffs telephoned and wrote to Paul H. Bator, deputy solicitor general and counsel to the Solicitor General, telling the Justice Department about the lawsuit and enclosing a copy of the court papers. The letter said, "We would be very pleased if the United States Government found it possible to support our effort, as *amicus curiae* or otherwise." The plaintiffs also requested an "opportunity to discuss" any intervention in opposition that the U.S. government might consider.

The federal government ignored the letter. Four months later a similar letter was sent and received the same lack of recognition.

That aside, the plaintiffs awaited the judicial assignment. The District Court clerk takes the cases in the order filed and assigns them to a specific judge. The lawyers understandably hoped the case would go to a seemingly sympathetic judge, feeling some judges would have no desire or appetite to deal with a case of this political complexity.

The case's ties to the United States remained tenuous. Even though the U.S. government had selected Wallenberg to do his merciful work, this was insufficient to establish jurisdiction. The entire matter was shrouded in foreign relations and complex issues normally handled by the State Department, both behind the scenes and through quiet diplomacy. Therefore, chances remained remote that the von Dardel lawyers would get a judge who would listen to the case, and no one expected to see a thirty-nine million dollar damages claim awarded by the court.

"We were afraid of putting pressure on the Soviet Union," von Dardel explained. "We had to go carefully there."

Ten days after filing the suit, on Lincoln's birthday, February 12, 1984, the legal team won its first victory; the case was assigned to Judge Barrington D. Parker, whom the American lawyers felt would at least listen.

Judge Parker, who had been appointed to the Federal District Court in Washington by President Richard M. Nixon on December 19, 1969, was 68 when assigned the Wallenberg case. By 1984, he had presided over notable cases, including the trial of John Hinckley, the would-be presidential assassin.[1] Hinckley had shot and wounded President Reagan and three other men, including James Brady, the White House press secretary. During the 1982 trial of Hinckley, the jury found Hinckley not guilty by reason of insanity of attempting to kill President Reagan. Judge Parker had told the jury they had to be convinced beyond a reasonable doubt the prosecution had proved the gunman could comprehend the wrongfulness of his act. After the acquittal, Judge Parker ordered Hinckley committed to a mental hospital.

Judge Parker also presided in the case involving Richard Helms, the former director of the CIA, who was accused of coloring the truth in testifying to Congress about CIA operations in Chile. The judge also handled the criminal part of the Letelier case, and he was the judge in the trial of veteran Louisiana congressman Otto Passman, who was charged with accepting a bribe from a South Korean businessman.

A brief inspection of some other high profile cases provides a glance into Judge Parker's judicial soul. In 1973, Judge Parker barred the Nixon Administration's attempts to impose certain price controls, labeling them "arbitrary and capricious." Also, Judge Parker ruled against a National Guard attempt to stop its men with long hair from donning short-cropped wigs while on duty. He ruled in 1978 that federal securities regulations did not require lawyers to disclose fraud by their clients, which arose in connection with a merger between the National Student Marketing Company and an insurance holding company.

Judge Parker also handled far less famous cases, but just as important to the individuals. For instance, he presided over the case of Clifford Beebe, a mentally disabled man whom the federal government denied a job to as a photocopy machine operator. He also handled the case of James McKelvey, a veteran the Veterans Administration denied benefits to because the agency found his alcoholism was due to "willful misconduct." The judge also was involved with the Western Poverty Law Center, one of many legal services organizations that the Reagan Administration stripped of funding as it tried to deny legal services to people who could not afford to hire lawyers. Judge Parker ruled the rights of these people and organizations were violated, forcing the government to comply with the law.

"Few judges possess his commitment and passion for deciding cases in a way that is fair and just," said Binny Miller, who was one of the judge's former law clerks and who became a law professor at American University in Washington.[2]

Parker was born in Rosslyn, Virginia, the only child of George A. Parker and Maude Daniels Parker. The judge's father, a self-taught lawyer, founded the Robert H. Terrell School of Law in Washington, which produced some of the city's leading black lawyers and judges. Judge Parker once taught at the school, which has since closed. Parker also practiced law as a partner in the firm of Parker & Parker.

In 1936, Judge Parker graduated from Lincoln University in Pennsylvania with a bachelor's degree in economics, and two years later he received a master of arts degree from the University of Pennsylvania. In 1947, he earned his law degree from the University of Chicago. But the judge had a major health problem. While crossing a Washington street in October 1975, a car hit him and his left leg had to be amputated. After that, Judge Parker wore a prosthesis but had great difficulty moving around.

What people liked about Judge Parker and what made him perfect for the Wallenberg case was his humanity. Robert L. Carter, an old friend and fellow federal judge, had said, "He has no hesitancy in coming forth with unpopular decisions."

A Republican, Parker refused to support Barry Goldwater's presidential bid in 1964.

Miller said the judge "brought a zeal to find the right answers to the question raised. He once told me that he would rather read a well-written brief than a good novel"—a worthwhile compliment because the judge enjoyed historical fiction, including James Michener.

Miller added that Judge Parker also "shared with me a vision of law that is different from that taught in many law schools."

That was exactly what the legal team wanted. As Miller explained, the judge liked the legal doctrine's intellectual challenge, but "he cared most about the people represented by the cases. He believed that the rights of individuals mattered a great deal when threatened by a majority that could not be trusted to protect the rights of minorities."

Others described him as "the most cantankerous federal judge in Washington." Indeed, Judge Parker was a stern disciplinarian who jumped on the smallest informality as a sign of disrespect, but off the bench he treated his law clerks like an extension of the family. The judge wanted respect not for himself, but for the law.

The Parker's legal gene pool extended into the third generation. In May 1994, President Clinton nominated one of Judge Parker's sons, Barrington D. Parker Jr., for a judgeship in the Southern District of New York State, based in Manhattan, and later in the year the Senate confirmed him. Barrington Parker Jr. was a partner at the New York law firm of Morrison & Foerster and vice chairman of the NAACP Legal Defense and Education Fund Inc. [3]

While the Wallenberg legal team liked the judge, it disliked the Soviet Union's response to the complaint. In its delivery of the documents, the State Department included a diplomatic note dated April 2, 1984, addressed to the Soviet Minister of Foreign Affairs. This said "under United States law, neither the embassy nor the Department of State was in a position to comment on the present suit that any jurisdictional or other defenses, including claims of sovereign immunity must be addressed to the court by the foreign state."

The diplomatic note also referred to the possibility of a default judgment entered against a defendant that does not respond to a complaint. For the purpose of asserting jurisdictional and other defenses, the State Department advised the Soviets to consult a private attorney in the United States. This used the Foreign Sovereign Immunities Act to make a foreign government accountable in the U.S. court for illegal behavior. The correspondence attached to the complaint told the Soviets the only way to plead their defense, such as jurisdictional, was to come into the U.S. District Court and not to stay out and expect the State Department to carry its brief, which had occurred in the past.

The Soviets ignored the lawsuit. On April 19, 1984, the Soviet Ministry of Foreign Affairs returned all of the documents to the U.S. Embassy in Moscow, along with a note asserting absolute sovereign immunity from the suit in non-Soviet courts.

Since the Foreign Sovereign Immunities Act became law, the Soviet Union had been a defendant in U.S. federal court cases, appearing via U.S. counsel to contest jurisdiction without waiving any of its rights. The Soviets knew the necessary actions, but they avoided them.

The aforementioned cases involved tourist claims or commercial contracts with little or no political risk. But the Wallenberg case was a dumdum bullet, ready to hit and expand in every direction. The other cases were valuable as precedent, showing the Soviets' normal practice of responding and defending cases with local U.S. counsel, but they were not embarrassing like the Wallenberg matter.

The Soviets' decision contradicted its prior practice, creating a new strategy for the Wallenberg case. They ignored the lawsuit, sat on their sovereign immunity and waited for foreign policy considerations to help them.

Meanwhile, Wolff moved west and became dean of the new law school at the University of Nevada at Reno while trying to remain lead counsel on the Wallenberg case. Struve stayed on the law case, handling more and more of the duties. The lawyer and the dean communicated at least once a week during the first 60 days. Struve sent Wolff papers; he marked them up in Nevada and returned them to Struve in New York.

While the plaintiffs' lawyers worked, the defendants did nothing. During the 60 days allotted them, which meant by June 1, 1984, the Soviets failed to do anything while the legal team pressed for a default judgment and were granted a hearing in federal district court. Judge Parker agreed to hear oral arguments, the centerpiece of the lawsuit, August 10, 1984, in Washington.

Dellapenna, who sat at the counsel table during the argument, met with Struve two hours before the oral argument to prepare him. Struve may not have been the ultimate expert on the Foreign Sovereign Immunities Act, but he knew how to argue a case. He is "an accomplished litigator," Dellapenna said.

While sitting in the courtroom, Dellapenna felt the judge's manner indicated he didn't take the case seriously. "Judge Parker came in at 11:30 a.m., and he had lunch scheduled for noon."

That changed after Struve started arguing the case. As expected, the Soviet Union failed to appear, prompting the judge to tell the plaintiff's lawyers, "You should have an easy task this morning. You don't have any opposition."[4]

Struve swiftly outlined Wallenberg's accomplishments for the United States, Sweden, Hungary and humanity. Judge Parker then pressed Struve for "hard information" that Wallenberg was still alive. In response, Struve discussed accounts during the 1970s and into the early 1980s that Wallenberg was still alive in the gulag.

Then the litigator turned that into justification for the hearing. Struve told the judge that despite the Soviets' claims Wallenberg died of a heart attack in 1947, dozens of accounts dispute this contention. Therefore, "We have a situation where either we must assume he is alive, in which case the statute of limitations has not begun to run or we must assume that he died under circumstances that we don't know, the plaintiffs don't know, and the court doesn't know, in which case again both under the doctrine of fraudulent concealment and under the discovery rule the statute of limitations has not yet begun to run."

Either way—dead or alive—Struve concluded, and the judge agreed, the litigator had something to argue.

Next, Struve proceeded to prove a crime existed. "Under both international law, Soviet law and United States law the seizure of a diplomat—the detention of a diplomat is per se illegal. This is perhaps the clearest proposition of international law."[5]

For specifics, Struve cited Blackstone's Commentaries, which said this is part of the common law of England, which the United States received in the 18th Century. This is also part of the 1961 Vienna Convention, which both the United States and the Soviet Union signed. Besides that, the safety of a diplomat is reaffirmed in the 1973 Convention on Internationally Protected Persons.

"This is that unusual case against a foreign sovereign in which there is no question about the illegality of what was done. That illegality has been admitted by the defendants," Struve told the court.

Judge Parker wanted to know how a U.S. court could possibly have jurisdiction.

Struve explained that the family had "four possible venues theoretically to bring an action in this matter." First was Hungary, where Wallenberg was initially seized; next the Soviet Union, where he was held after the Soviets took him from Hungary; then Sweden, the country that accredited Wallenberg to go to Hungary and where he is a citizen and finally the United States, which sent Wallenberg to Budapest and in 1981 made him an honorary citizen.

Since Hungary and the Soviet Union then were part of the Soviet monolith, neither judicial system "can be expected to find the Soviet Government violated international law," Struve said.

The family chose the United States as the legal forum partly because of Wallenberg's honorary citizenship. In the resolution granting citizenship, Congress requested the president to take every diplomatic means to find out about Wallenberg's detention and secure his release. But Struve explained to the court, these were more "moral" than legal grounds, a "background fact."

Under U.S. law, "intended offenses against internationally protected persons (like diplomats can be) redressed wherever in the world they were committed and by whatever nationality they were committed."

Therefore, Struve told the court, "there clearly is subject matter jurisdiction in the United States to deal with the abduction or killing of a diplomat wherever this occurs and Congress . . . has specifically said that it wants that jurisdiction exercised."

After that, the litigator said the Soviet Union had claimed absolute sovereign immunity, "not even a duty to come in and show this court why sovereign immunity applies, which is the position that Congress rejected in the Foreign Sovereign Immunities Act." The Soviet Union elected to default, "knowing what the proper procedure was," Struve told the judge.

Struve explained that previous disputes involved property left to people in the Soviet Union or contract disputes or the Frolova case. "So the suits in which they have been sued embrace a wide variety of both more or less ordinary commercial and tort matters and others which they might view as having more of a political significance," Struve added.

Judge Parker asked Struve if this case had "political significance"? He felt it did because what Wallenberg achieved "obviously engaged the attention of a lot of people . . ."

Next, the judge wanted to know what was the point in proceeding if Struve discovered Wallenberg in fact were dead? "Then our prayer for injunctive relief would be addressed only to his remains and there would remain only a claim for damages, which I will be frank with Your Honor, was not the primary reason why the family brought the action."

Instead, Struve explained, the main purpose was to "establish the illegality of the detention, to have a court declare that for what effect it would have on the defendant and hopefully to obtain his release, assuming that he is still alive."

Judge Parker then asked a question asked by many. If the court found for the plaintiffs and awarded them the requested 39 million dollars, or one million for each year of Wallenberg's imprisonment up to the date of the filing, "How would I enforce the order?"[6]

Struve suggested the judge impose criminal contempt and follow execution procedures outlined in the Foreign Sovereign Immunities Act. "It is no longer the case that the property of a foreign sovereign or its instrumentalities is absolutely immune from execution if it comes to that," Struve told the court. The FSIA provides a carefully graduated procedure, including ample notice to the defendant.

When the court asked what cases the litigator used as precedent, Struve mentioned Letelier, who, like Wallenberg, was an internationally protected person. He said Chile, though it also failed to appear, went further than the Soviet Union because the South American country prepared a memorandum of law arguing the lack of jurisdiction in the U.S. courts.

To emphasize his contentions about the Soviet Union, Struve talked about that nation's renegade actions. Soviet history is "unfortunately not free of violations of international law, but as written by themselves it is free of any admitted violations of international law . . . They are not the kind of country that would brazenly admit they were holding a diplomat like Wallenberg and continue to hold him."

The Soviets, Struve said, had to "continue the illegal detention" of Wallenberg and tried to deceive the rest of the world about it, particularly Sweden and the United States. That led Struve to the Gromyko note of 1957 and the underlying "detention and concealment." In the note, the Soviets admitted they had imprisoned Wallenberg and then lied about it. Hence, that constituted criminal activity by the Soviet Union.

Though the Soviet Union and Chile failed to appear in these cases, this was unusual Struve explained. "In almost every such case the foreign sovereign appears and either moves to dismiss or defend because that is what Congress expressly said should be done."

Struve contended the tortious, or wrongful, act occurred both inside and outside the United States. When the judge asked what, Struve responded, "The misrepresentations, Your Honor, and concealments . . . because throughout the years and most recently since the grant of citizenship in 1981 there have been repeated inquiries to the Soviets," which they failed to answer honestly.

Toward the end of the hearing, Judge Parker again asked Struve how his court could enforce anything against the Soviet Union? "What troubles me is when we get really to the position where . . . you get on the mat with the opponent, what relief can we give?"

If the judge found against the defendant, the Soviet Union, Struve again said the judge had the power under the Foreign Sovereign Immunities Act to grant criminal contempt penalties as though it were a domestic case. Specifically, that meant attaching property of foreign nations.

Finally, Judge Parker asked Struve to submit "proposed findings and conclusions of law" to him within two weeks. At the end of the one hour and seventeen minute hearing, the judge felt different about the case. "This matter certainly is topical, and it is a very serious matter."

Ten years later, someone reading the oral argument, which created the initial victory, finds it prosaic instead of preeminent. Struve explained Judge Parker tolerated no nonsense, so the litigator stuck to the basics and effectively made his points. Dellapenna both praises and criticizes Struve's arguments.

"Struve got Judge Parker's interest. He won over Parker, and he won the case," Dellapenna said.

But Struve's winning argument carried the seeds of its own destruction, according to Dellapenna. As he saw it, Struve's arguments had worked along several paths, "but I thought they were weak grounds."

He argued that the Soviets by not filing an answer waived their immunity, which Dellapenna said is not substantiated by the law. Still, the argument worked with Judge Parker.

"I don't think he understood the relevant law," Dellapenna said. "Struve had a good sense of how to persuade Judge Parker when there was no one to raise troublesome questions. This was a misguided argument. When the Soviets entered an appearance, the argument quickly fell."

Instead, Dellapenna would have argued a tort occurred because Wallenberg's guardian was frequently in the United States, and Wallenberg had relatives here. "By keeping Wallenberg a prisoner, the (Soviets) were depriving his relatives, who lived in the United States, of his companionship."

Dellapenna admitted, "This was also an iffy argument."

Although this was "pushing it, at least it was what lawyers call a 'colorable argument' under the statute. There is some justification with this argument. With the other argument, I wasn't the least bit surprised when the decision was overturned," Dellapenna said.

Struve and Dellapenna clashed over different aspects of the case. One was an experienced litigator and the other an academic.

"I was too academic, Struve told me, and he said that it wouldn't work in the courtroom," Dellapenna remembered. "But other lawyers call on my services."

Their arguments, though never heated, continued. "We had clear disagreements about how to handle the case," Dellapenna said. "After a while, I didn't argue with Struve anymore. Wallenberg is one of the very few heroes of this century. I never disassociated myself from the case. Even if it were something small, I wanted to help because it involved Wallenberg."

At some point after the hearing, control of the case shifted from Wolff to Struve. Sonja Sonnenfeld, director of the Swedish Wallenberg Committee, said Wolff was originally hired for a fee but then dismissed. She declined to specify the fee or the reason for the dismissal. Wolff contends he couldn't be dismissed, and that he remained the lead lawyer for the case, de jure if not de facto. In fact, von Dardel eventually fired Wolff from the case. Nevertheless, for at least the next 10 years, Wolff has insisted he is Raoul Wallenberg's lawyer and introduces himself that way.

"He is not Wallenberg's lawyer and never has been," Sonnenfeld said.

Wolff persists in that self-endowed characterization.

"He was freed from this case. He has nothing to do with this case," Sonnenfeld said. "He was paid a fee. Do you know a lawyer who isn't?"

"We sent him a letter saying we did not want to pursue it with him. Personal reasons," Sonnenfeld said. "Wolff went in to it with body and soul, too much. It became too big a thing. Listen, he is such a nice fellow, not for us. We don't want to have anything to do with it."

Whatever his link to Wallenberg, Wolff has a bitter bond with Guy Struve. Wolff feels Struve, whom he calls "an intimidating son of a bitch," stole the case from him.

Initially, Struve said he let Wolff remain the spokesperson, but Struve wanted everyone to keep quiet while Judge Parker deliberated. In Struve's judgment, Wolff publicized the Wallenberg case too much. The coup de grace came in June 1985. The Jewish Community Center of Margate, New Jersey, which gave their Man-of-the Year Award to Raoul Wallenberg, asked Wolff to make a few remarks about Wallenberg and the efforts to free him. Wolff, who was back in Philadelphia after an unhappy experience in Nevada, drove down to Margate, about an hour's trip, on a warm Friday afternoon. He was out of a job, out of the case and out of a marriage.

Wolff said the law school had failed to get enough students in Reno, ran out of money and had to close, so he left Reno in January 1985 to return to Philadelphia and the school closed the following

May. Back home, Wolff said he continued to work on the case, but his wife divorced him and locked him out of his house. Eventually, he affiliated with another Philadelphia law firm, Sprague, Albert & Thall.

While things went badly in Nevada, Wolff felt Struve was scheming on the East Coast to usurp Wolff's authority in the case. In Wolff's view, Struve clandestinely formed an unethical relationship with Sven Hagstromer, Wallenberg's legal guardian and a man to whom Wolff said he had introduced him. Wolff insisted he was chief counsel, and that Struve began to trash him behind his back.

By that June evening, Wolff still felt the magnetic pull of the Wallenberg case, and looked ahead to the dinner in the hero's honor and prayer service in the synagogue for Wallenberg. During his remarks, Wolff told the rabbi he would focus his talk on Wallenberg's life, the efforts to rescue him and would not comment on any specific legal issues in the case itself, such as jurisdiction of the court since these were still pending before Judge Parker.

One of the people in the audience asked Wolff if there had been opportunities to rescue Wallenberg. He mentioned the visit of Dr. Nanna Svartz to Moscow in 1961. Another opportunity came in 1979 when the Swedish government convicted Stig Bergling, a former Swedish Defense Ministry employee, as a KGB agent and sentenced him to life imprisonment.[7] Apparently, the Swedes offered Bergling in an exchange for Wallenberg.

In his book, "Angel of Rescue," which is a biography of Wallenberg, author Harvey Rosenfeld wrote that the Soviets were not interested in the swap. Wolff said he opened the Rosenfeld book to page 181 and read the passage about Bergling and then told the congregation. "It is my understanding from what Mr. Rosenfeld had reported that Bergling was offered to the Soviets for Wallenberg on a one-for-one swap. Apparently, the Soviets asked for more—that one more Soviet spy in Swedish custody had to be included in the swap."

But Rosenfeld only said, "The Bergling affair was the biggest Swedish spy scandal in recent times.[8] Bergling was offered to the

Soviets for Wallenberg, but the Russians were not interested."
Rosenfeld mentioned nothing about a two-for-one deal, but that
certainly was a possibility. In any event, the deal collapsed.

Wolff said he told the congregation, "The Swedes could have
(used) this opportunity to accomplish the long-awaited goal of
Wallenberg's freedom. The Russians refused, and the deal fell
through. That failure to swap . . . was a tragedy. Sweden should
now reopen those diplomatic negotiations and bring Wallenberg
home. I hope all of you will support this effort."

Since these events had occurred six years earlier and had been
written about, to Wolff this was background, not news. The two-
for-one aspect would qualify as news, but Wolff had qualified that
assumption. He merely said the Swedes had missed an opportunity to reclaim Wallenberg. Unbeknown to him and the members
of the congregation since the talk was off the record, a news reporter was in the audience. Specifically, Wolff contended he had
not discussed any aspect of the case or issues pending before Judge
Parker. He felt his criticisms of the Swedish government's handling of the Bergling affair was a subject of fair comment in the
theater of international politics.

All this was hardly news, in Wolff's view, but it was news to
someone who lacked the appropriate background in the case. The
next morning a story appeared in a New Jersey newspaper about
Wolff's remarks and the Bergling affair. An international news
service picked up the story on a slow news Saturday and sent it
all over the world. Now it was news even if it hadn't been news
before.

In the 1980s, probably until the Soviet Union broke up, the
Swedish government lived in fear of Soviet reaction, intimidation
and possible military retaliation. Russia, Sweden's ancient antago-
nist, had nuclear arms while Sweden was basically armed only
with its neutrality.

The week after L'Affaire Margate Wolff contended the Swedish
government maintained the pressure on the Wallenberg family to
dismiss the case and terminate the lawsuit, but no one else confirms

that. When von Dardel was asked if he ever discussed the case with the Wallenberg family, he had a defiant one word answer, "never."

Soon after the Margate incident, Wolff said Struve called and asked him to resign from the case because of the uproar over the Bergling story. Wolff explained the circumstances, but that failed to mollify Struve, according to Wolff. On September 20, 1985, Struve filed a notice with the court dismissing Wolff as co-counsel.[9] Struve, von Dardel, Hagstromer and Jerome G. Snider, an attorney in Davis Polk's Washington office, all signed the document.

"There were difficulties between Morris Wolff and Guy (Struve). I didn't go into that," von Dardel said. "I had very little contact with Morris during the whole lawsuit. I realized that he had problems, left his university, divorced and got a post in Nevada, but that he was still interested in Raoul's fate. I am not familiar with the exact reasons for the controversy between Morris and mainly Guy Struve in New York, who quickly evolved to the chief lawyer on the case."

Makinen, who was on sabbatical in the Netherlands but still interested in the Wallenberg case, returned to the United States occasionally. One of these times he stopped in New York City at a Wallenberg dinner and gave a seminar at Columbia University. Then he had dinner with Guy von Dardel, where they discussed the lawyer problems.

Von Dardel brought the entire case and told Makinen how the endeavor could not continue with Morris Wolff. "This was doom for the case. You lose a lot of momentum when you switch," Makinen said.

Specifically, Makinen didn't know all the reasons for terminating Wolff. "His actions and the way he was proceeding were very inappropriate," Makinen recalled.

Naturally, Wolff disagreed, saying he was the lead lawyer, did everything properly and Struve stole the case from him. In fact, Wolff said he told Struve, "You have no right and no authority to remove me from the case or even suggest my removal."

Within that framework, though, there wasn't "much to decide

about switching lawyers," Makinen reported. Guy von Dardel, who conferred with his sister, decided on Guy Struve.

D'Amato tried to walk the line of neutrality between the two lawyers. When asked if Struve poached on Wolff while he was in Nevada, D'Amato carefully replied, "I think that is Morris' interpretation of the events. You're dealing with a bunch of people, everyone of whom really felt that it was a noble cause and everyone of whom wanted to work on it. The interpersonal irritants that came up from time to time shouldn't obscure us from the larger picture, which is we won a hell of a decision the first time around against the Soviet Union."

CHAPTER 14

After 14 months of deliberating—20 months after the lawsuit's filing and four years after its inception—Judge Barrington Parker on October 15, 1985, ruled for the plaintiffs, an unqualified—and unexpected victory—for the Wallenberg lawyers. Struve's oral argument had delayed the judge's lunch, but swayed his opinion.

Thus, after more than a forty-year odyssey to free his half-brother, Guy von Dardel—through his American surrogates—had won a major battle. Seemingly, von Dardel had the power of the American courts to force the Soviets finally to release Wallenberg or tell what had happened to him. Judge Parker, a thoughtful jurist, used the 14 months after the oral argument to consider the complex legal issues and to have them fully researched so that the decision would be sustained. A thoughtful move, but other, unrelated factors reversed the decision four years later.

Unlike the splashy courtroom events on "Perry Mason," civil decisions are quietly handed down by the judge to his clerk, who files the decision and gives copies to the press. In clear language, Judge Parker explained his decision. Basically, he employed the Foreign Sovereign Immunities Act to justify his decision. For further support, Judge Parker also used the Letelier, De Longchamps and Frolova cases.

The judge, in his 40-page opinion, held that the U.S. District Court had jurisdiction under the Foreign Sovereign Immunities Act, the very law researched by D'Amato during the Frolova case.[1] Parker also held the statue of limitations had not run out on the plaintiffs' claims, and the Soviet Union's seizure and detention of Raoul Wallenberg violated the law of nations, international treaties and conventions to which the Soviet Union was bound as well as the domestic laws of the United States and the Soviet Union relating to diplomatic immunity.

He entered a default judgment against the Soviet Union.

Specifically, Judge Parker ruled the Foreign Sovereign Immunities Act failed to extend immunity to a foreign nation's "clear violation of diplomatic immunity arising from arrest, imprisonment and possible death of (the) Swedish diplomat." Since the Soviet Union agreed to be bound by the international human rights agreements and of treaties discussing the fundamental principle of diplomatic immunity, the Soviet Union "implicitly waived its sovereign immunity" by seizing Wallenberg.

The judge also mentioned, the Alien Tort Claims Act. This act provided that district courts shall have original jurisdiction of any civil action by an alien for a tort committed in violation of the law of nations or a treaty of the United States. Though old, this law remained valid. The system worked.

Judge Parker also said the statue of limitations remained in effect because the "unlawful detention of the diplomat was (a) continuing violation of (the) laws of the United States, laws and treaties of the Soviet Union and the law of nations." The judge also ruled the Soviet Union's 1945 seizure and subsequent detention of Wallenberg "violated the law of nations as well as a number of international treaties and conventions relating to human rights, all of which have been signed by the Soviet Union."

The judge said "personal jurisdiction is present when the defendant may be found in the United States, through its agents and instrumentalities . . ." He ruled the case was a civil action arising under the laws and treaties of the United States, making the Foreign Sovereign Immunities Act appropriate. Then, for precedent, Judge Parker cited Letelier v. Republic of Chile.[2]

"Under the Act, a foreign state is generally immune from the jurisdiction of federal courts," the judge wrote.[3] However, the act gives the district courts jurisdiction over civil cases against foreign governments where immunity is inappropriate. Furthermore, Judge Parker ruled the act creates personal jurisdiction over the foreign government. Without immunity, that establishes both subject matter and personal jurisdiction against a foreign government.

In 1976, Congress had a twofold purpose for enacting the Foreign Sovereign Immunities Act:[4] To liberalize the immunity law by adopting and codifying the doctrine of restrictive immunity. Second, this was to assure consistent application of the law by eliminating the executive branch's participation. That would assure litigants that decisions are made on purely legal grounds, the judge said.

To accomplish these goals, Judge Parker said, the act set up legal standards governing claims of immunity in civil actions against foreign states, "According to the drafters of the FSIA, 'sovereign immunity is an affirmative defense which must be specially pleaded [and] the burden will remain on the foreign state to produce evidence in support of its claim of immunity.'" Thus, Judge Parker said, "the burden of demonstrating that immunity exists rests upon the foreign state."

Judge Parker liked four of the five independent reasons the legal team cited why the Soviets should not enjoy immunity. First, by default, the Soviets "failed to raise the defense of sovereign immunity." Second, the FSIA incorporates pre-existing standards of international law under which a government is not immune for certain acts in clear violation of the universally accepted law of nations. Third, the FSIA is limited by treaties to which the United States is a party. The Soviets could not claim immunity under the FSIA for acts that constitute violations of some treaties involving the Soviets. Fourth, the Soviets waived immunity in this action and are therefore, not entitled to raise it as a defense.

The judge did not accept the last argument—the actions of the Soviets constitute noncommercial torts; immunity for committing such is thus inappropriate under the FSIA.

To Judge Parker, "Congress explicitly intended that sovereign immunity remain an 'affirmative defense which must be specially pleaded, the burden [remaining] on the foreign state to produce evidence in support of its claim of immunity.'" He added, "In the present case, defendant has not only failed to plead immunity as an affirmative defense, but has chosen to raise immunity in a manner explicitly precluded by the act." Before passing the act, the immunity defense could be raised by going to the U.S. State Department.

The FSIA expressly wanted to remove the executive branch from determining such issues, the judge reminded everyone in his opinion. By raising the sovereign immunity issue in a diplomatic note, the USSR has "knowingly chosen a procedure that is no longer available under United States law." Thus, it cannot be recognized as an adequate pleading of the defense of immunity.

Moreover, the judge wrote, sovereign immunity is "inherently limited and appropriately disallowed where the foreign state defendant has acted in clear violation of international law." Another clear violation involved the diplomatic immunity of Raoul Wallenberg. "The ancient and universal consensus on diplomatic immunity places it squarely within even the most restrictive interpretation of the coverage of the Alien Tort Claims Act . . . As such, the Congress in 1789 opened the district courts of the United States to suits by aliens claiming tortious violations of diplomatic immunity." Also, Congress has passed laws to protect internationally people, like diplomats.

Then Judge Parker quoted Frolova v. Union of Soviet Socialist Republics and De Longchamps. The Supreme Court held that De Longchamps committed "an atrocious violation of the law of nations," when, having first insulted the Consul General of France to the United States, he struck the cane of the diplomat. The court described De Longchamps' actions as gross insults and diplomats as the "peculiar objects" of the law of nations.

To some, Judge Parker's words making the Soviets liable for violating Wallenberg's rights as a human being were the most satisfying.

When kidnapped, Wallenberg was an accredited Swedish diplomat, thus an "internationally protected person . . . His kidnapping was therefore a violation," the judge ruled. Even if

Wallenberg had died, the judge said the Soviets had still committed a violation. In Letelier, the jurisdiction was upheld in a suit brought by the surviving spouses of the late diplomat and his co-worker against those responsible for their murder. "The same rationale should apply . . . Under both, plaintiffs are entitled to immediate declaratory relief."

The Soviet Union's treatment of Raoul Wallenberg is unlawful even under its own statutes, the judge said. The statute on Diplomatic and Consular Representations of Foreign States on the Territory of the USSR confirmed by edict of the Presidium of the USSR Supreme Soviet on May 23, 1966, "affirms the privileges and immunities due to diplomats." Article 18 specifically insures the "inviolability" while traveling in the "territory of the USSR," Judge Parker wrote. "The detention of Wallenberg plainly violates the diplomatic immunity guaranteed by the statute."

Article 178 specifies an arrest or detention known to be illegal, the judge continued. "Wallenberg's arrest and detention were and continue to be illegal under principles of international law and international agreements, which were in force in 1945 and to which the USSR was a party. Moreover, the 1957 Gromyko Note acknowledged the illegality of Wallenberg's detention and of the misinformation that made it possible."

Therefore, Judge Parker ruled, "The Soviet Union's treatment of Raoul Wallenberg is unlawful under any standard of applicable law." The Soviet Union never argued otherwise; it had "denied and disclaimed its actions, but it has never defended them."

The judge realized his ruling was unprecedented regarding foreign sovereigns, but the Soviet Union has already admitted its actions were unlawful. This involves a "gross violation of the personal immunity of a diplomat, one of the oldest and most universally recognized principles of international law. Furthermore, this action involves a deliberate default by a defendant which had repeatedly demonstrated its familiarity with the proper means for raising a defense of sovereign immunity under the Foreign Sovereign Immunities Act."

The Soviet Union's sovereign immunity is subject to international agreements on which the United States was a party when the FSIA was enacted in 1976. That "prohibits defendant's actions regarding Mr. Wallenberg," the judge ruled.

For all those reasons, Judge Parker entered a default judgment against the defendant.

When Guy von Dardel heard from Guy Struve via telephone that Judge Parker had ruled in his favor, von Dardel felt relief. Not relief that he had won the lawsuit, but financial relief. "I was always aware of the consequences that we had to pay $1 million in lawyers' fees. I was relieved that nobody asked us to pay the lawyers. The result would have been the same if we had lost the case," von Dardel said.

To him, the lawsuit was a "great success for a few individuals to successfully sue the Soviet Union."

The Washington Post asked a Soviet Embassy spokesman for a comment, but he only said, "I think that the case of Raoul Wallenberg was closed in 1957 when it was stated that Mr. Wallenberg died of a heart attack." When asked about reports that Wallenberg was still alive, the spokesman said, "There is no evidence except rumors."

What had started more four years earlier with an unusual idea had progressed from only a dream into reality. To von Dardel and the lawyers, victory was theirs; defeat was the Soviets'.

Three weeks later, on November 7, 1985, Judge Parker enhanced the victory by handing down an order giving the U.S. lawyers everything they needed. He ordered the defendant, the Soviet government, to:

1. Within 60 days after the serving of the default judgment to produce in court "the person of Raoul Wallenberg or his remains if he is dead."

2. Within 30 days after receiving the judgment to produce in court all information documents in their custody or control relating to Raoul Wallenberg.

3. "Defendant is liable to plaintiff for compensatory damages in the amount of $39 million with interest and costs."

A diplomatic courier was sent to Moscow from the State Department to deliver these papers. A diplomatic note of transmittal accompanied the papers and another copy of the Foreign Sovereign Immunities Act translated into Russian, prepared by the American lawyers. The Soviets couldn't argue for reversal on the basis of ignorance of the law or language.

The legal team now had the legal authority to "ascertain the whereabouts of Raoul Wallenberg and to secure his freedom."

CHAPTER 15

The Americans won, but then they started to lose. Instead of requesting an order from the judge to attach Russian assets, Struve felt the ruling was unenforceable, so he chose to file for contempt penalties. Some of his colleagues sharply disagreed.

"I'll tell you my consistent opinion . . . on the case," D'Amato said. "The judge found in favor of us against the Soviet Union. My view was to say, 'Fine, let's sue on the judgment, let's go out and attach Soviet property in the United States to the satisfaction of the thirty-nine million dollars. That certainly would bring the Soviet Union out of the woods."

The legal team had identified 120 Russian asset bases in the United States, both tangible and intangible. That meant assets in banks or property around the country. The Soviets had assets in every part of the United States, so, "We would do a blitz all over the country; we'd have a lot of commotion. We'd start a hundred brush fires, and some might catch on," D'Amato explained.

Specifically, "We'd find an asset and swear out a lien," D'Amato said. "We'd go to the court and show the judgment, a certified copy, and want to have a sheriff's sale of the asset. We had the presumption on our side. We had the decision. That's good enough."

Once the lawyers started selling Soviet assets, D'Amato is sure the Soviet Union would have done something—either release Wallenberg or show positive evidence of his death. Marvin Makinen agreed. "Why didn't Struve try to get the assets after he won the case? That always puzzled me. That was the time to do it." Then Makinen speculated that "there was so much loss of momentum when they switched from Wolff to Struve, they (the legal team) were disorganized."

Struve felt the legal team would have a difficult time seizing assets, which had to be tied to the underlying violation. Soviet embassies, consulates and official residences were immune, so Struve felt contempt penalties were a better legal avenue.

Dellapenna added, "It is more difficult to execute a judgment than to get one under the Foreign Sovereign Immunities Act." To him, the judgment was "uncollectible." The FSIA could be used only against property that had been used for the wrong connected with the judgment. "No property associated with the Wallenberg imprisonment was in the United States," according to Dellapenna.

"If we had been lucky enough to find something, could we collect? We could have taken the order to some other country where execution might have been easier and do it there," but that country would have had to decide if the judgment were valid, Dellapenna explained.

In the Letelier case, the court did not let the plaintiffs seize the airplanes of LAN-Chile. Judge Green never signed the order, and when a judge in New York tried to do so he was quickly reversed by the Second Circuit Court of Appeals.

Von Dardel took a different approach. "I never expected much to come out of the suit. I never thought it was enough. Combined with other forms of pressure, it could work."

This meant the United States pressuring the Soviet Union. Instead, the American government pressured von Dardel, trying to make him drop the lawsuit. Von Dardel has a hazy recollection about a federal government official named "Anderson," whom he met in the courthouse after visiting Judge Parker. Von Dardel remembers this Mr. Anderson telling him that "if we did press for payment of the thirty-nine million due, probably the U.S. Treasury, not the Soviet government would have to pay, which certainly was not the intention."

The only Anderson associated with the case was David J. Anderson, an attorney for the Justice Department, who aided the defendant—the Soviet Union—via the American government's subsequent response to the lawsuit. When asked if he had made the previously mentioned statement to von Dardel, Anderson replied, "I can't conceive of my saying that."

Whoever said it, von Dardel feared the American taxpayer might ultimately pay the thirty-nine million dollars in damages. "I just assumed that if the Soviets did not pay, the Americans would have to take up the bill, and that it would eventually wind up with the American taxpayer. Of course, there could be a number of ways of doing it which would make the end result less visible."

Then von Dardel had another potential problem: What if the Soviets did pay the thirty-nine million dollars? The lawyers would have wanted a chunk of that money, "and they probably would have deserved it. But what if Raoul had come back and claimed the money?" The lawyers supposedly had never intended the thirty-nine million dollars to better themselves, preferring instead to use the money as a lever to free Wallenberg. If the legal team actually collected some of the money, the lawyers said they would have used it to establish a Wallenberg Foundation or Scholarship Fund, something humanitarian to honor Raoul Wallenberg.

To von Dardel, the money was secondary. "All the time our position [was] that we did not want the money; we wanted Raoul. Our fear was that the Soviet Union would seize the opportunity to get rid of an embarrassing affair, simply by paying us off. We hoped that they would find it cheaper to release Raoul, but we could not be sure."

Von Dardel was certain that, "The outcome of the case put the U.S. government in a very difficult position when it was trying to give support to Gorbachev and improve relations." He thought the United States was "interested in negotiating with Gorbachev to give up our gains from the lawsuit."

During the mid-1980s, rumblings of major changes moved through the Soviet Union, and the U.S. government wanted rapprochement, not more cold war. Mikhail Gorbachev had taken over Russia in 1985 and made seismic changes. To the State Department, this lawsuit seemed as welcome as a nasty paper cut.

Others outside government, like Sonja Sonnenfeld, were equally critical of the lawsuit. "What good does it do if (an American judge) rules in our favor? The Soviet Union was not willing to follow. The Soviets didn't care what the judge ruled in America. They couldn't care less. If (the lawyers started) seizing their assets, so what do you think would happen? They'd start a third World War for that?" she said in an incredulous tone that shot into the telephone line all the way from Stockholm. Sonnenfeld had only scorn for the money. "What did we need those millions for? There were people there to get him free. That was not done. It's not reality at all," she continued, her exasperation with the questioner only slightly reduced. Some discussion centered on seizing Soviet airplanes, which Sonnenfeld found equally preposterous. "Aeroflot would fly to America, and we'd seize the planes. So what? What this was was something alone in theory."

D'Amato disagreed. When asked if the Russians would have ignored any asset seizures, he leaned back in his office chair in Chicago until his head was almost parallel to the ceiling and thoughtfully uttered, "Oh, no."

The dozens of brushfires would have turned into a conflagration that the Soviets would have had to confront, according to D'Amato. That would have led to some action, either Raoul Wallenberg's release or definitive proof about his death. D'Amato's arguments carry more validity today, for we now know the Soviet Union, weakened by numerous problems, during the 1980s was an inept giant.

But D'Amato's plan remained theoretical since Struve chose a different legal maneuver. Instead of seizing assets, related D'Amato, "Struve said, 'No, no, let's go for a contempt order.'"

"If somebody doesn't pay you a judgment, you sue. Guy Struve didn't want to do it," D'Amato said. Instead, Struve sued on the judgment, trying to get a contempt order against the Soviet Union as a whole, which was faulty strategy to D'Amato. "That was like using a penknife against a castle."

In D'Amato's opinion, this strategy could only fail. "If it did win, you wouldn't be in any better position than you already were. We had quite a lot of discussions between Guy Struve (and other lawyers) about that, and he said, 'I appreciate your point of view and everything.'"

His appreciation failed to extend to action. So, for the next four years Struve filed an elaborate series of contempt penalties while the case deteriorated. Specifically, Struve wanted the court to impose a fine on the Soviet Union of fifty-thousand dollars a day for each day it failed to pay the judgment. This would require a delay in enforcing the judgment itself, making the maneuver questionable to many of his associates.

Struve had an elaborate formula to increase the penalty for noncompliance. He proposed multiplying the daily fifty-thousand dollar fine by a factor of two every fourteen days after the defendant remained in contempt of the amended judgment, but totaling no more than one million a day.[1] The lawyers argued with Struve about his mathematical maneuver. "Go for the attachment now. Ask the judge for a court order. We don't know how long he will be on the bench."

Judge Parker was 70 then and still in poor health due to his amputated left leg. "If he gets replaced, our case will be in trouble," the lawyers said. The judge had taken 20 months to decide the case, including 14 months after the oral argument, because, in D'Amato's opinion, he was "sending us a signal. 'You guys got more than you expected; don't force me to go back and do more.'"

The legal team could get no more, so they had to attack with the available weapons. But they chose to leave the weapons unused, the judgment untouched. Some felt the delay doomed Wallenberg—if he were still alive—to remain in the gulag.

The contempt order meant "re-litigating the case in front of different judges, and you're taking the awful chance that a group of judges might see it differently," D'Amato warned. "The case was always a bit fragile. You can't win an innovative case and expect it to be sound law."

For example, D'Amato ultimately lost the Frolova case in court, but it failed to matter. Stanley J. Roszkowski, U.S. District Judge for the Northern District of Illinois, dismissed the action and Lois Frolova appealed.[2] The U.S. Court of Appeals for the Seventh Circuit decided on May 1, 1985, that the Soviet Union did not waive its sovereign immunity by signing the United Nations Charter of Helsinki Accords. Plus, the failure of the Soviet Union to defend the action did not constitute a waiver of its sovereign immunity and finally the tortious act did not provide a basis for jurisdiction, "where neither injury nor tortious omission or act occurred in the United States," the court ruled.

Perhaps legally sound, but totally irrelevant. Andrei Frolov had escaped the Soviet Union to be with his wife, Lois Becker Frolova, in the United States. D'Amato saw the same possibility with the Wallenberg case. He feared the case might be overturned, but he wanted to see if the initial victory could free Wallenberg. "Hey, he might still have been alive," D'Amato said.

Therefore, D'Amato wanted to push ahead.

"If you hired me to do something, and I got the job done, you wouldn't care what the aftermath would be if some court reversed it five years from now on some technicality."

Had Wallenberg been a traditional private client with a thirty-nine million-dollar judgment, he would have insisted that the lawyers immediately file for attachment of assets, but this client, if alive, was in the Gulag Archipelago.

Unlike Struve, D'Amato wanted to use publicity in the von Dardel case. "With Lois (Frolova), I certainly decided to go public, and I did it. There are times when you don't do it, but it seemed to me in the Wallenberg case that was exactly the time to do it because we had credibility. We had a judicial opinion. What did we do with that opinion?"

To answer himself, D'Amato said, "Guy Struve convinced the clients that a low profile is what you needed. I took the opposite side of that and at one point after nothing had happened for about a year and a half, the clients and I had a little meeting."

Then, the clients told D'Amato in his Northwestern School of Law office, "Maybe you're right; maybe we should turn on the publicity thing. Nothing's happening." D'Amato told the clients to "reexamine" the effort and discuss it with Struve. "But apparently he must have talked them out of it again."

Makinen agreed with D'Amato. "They could have made more of the lawsuit. I don't know in the end if it would have worked." Oddly enough, Makinen felt the irascible Luis Kutner could have ultimately achieved victory. "I think if we had a guy like Kutner fighting with the jurisdiction, he would have found some way to make it work. We needed someone to make it work and unwilling to give up for any reason," Makinen said wistfully.

The legal team needed money, the necessary fuel in modern America, as well as a tireless legal combatant, ready to fight two governments—the United States and the Soviet Union. Someone ready to sue anything that moved or crawled in order to free Raoul Wallenberg. Or they needed a secular saint, someone willing to sacrifice everything in order to save a life. The American lawyers needed another Raoul Wallenberg.

Makinen, who knew the KGB's modus operandi, warned of darker consequences.

Unlike American lawyers who theorize in courtrooms or classrooms, the KGB uses the terror of the street—"murder. If it were serious enough, why not frighten someone?" asks Makinen. "They would threaten you or your daughter."

Makinen's empirical knowledge of the KGB's terror came from the prison camps. "I saw people in prison in labor camps with me. They were stolen. One was stolen from Paris and the other from West Berlin."

The man stolen from West Berlin, Gerd Pinkus, was a fellow prisoner in the Mordovian labor camp. Pinkus was later released, but he has since died. "He was a young German Jew working for the OSS and CIA. He was stolen with five passports on himself,"

Makinen said. After a pause to deal with the bitter memories, Makinen continued, "If I could have allowed someone to be a close friend with me in the labor camp, he would have been one."

He told D'Amato and Wolff how the KGB might employ extraordinary measures if the Soviets lost the case and had to pay the 39 million dollars, which certainly must have given the lawyers' some restless nights.

D'Amato, though, remained involved with the case until the last day while always pushing his strategy of asset seizure. But Wolff, separated from the lawsuit, moved to Florida in 1986 and became a businessman and unsuccessful politician. During the Democratic primary, he ran as lieutenant governor on the ticket headed by Mark K. Goldstein, former mayor of Gainesville. The Goldstein-Wolff ticket won 55,630 votes, or six percent of the vote, and finished fourth out of main five candidates in the Democratic governor's primary.[3] That ended Wolff's political ambitions. He later moved to New York and joined a small law firm.

While Struve pushed his contempt penalties, a notice of default judgment, with a Russian translation, was served on the defendant January 22, 1986, giving the Soviet Union thirty days to respond. The defendant had another thirty days to produce Wallenberg or his remains.

On March 6, six weeks after the notice of judgment, the Soviet Union at last responded, returning all the papers served upon it to the U.S. Embassy in Moscow along with a note, which made it clear the Soviets did not intent to comply with the court's judgment.[4] They would not produce Raoul Wallenberg; they would not produce his remains, and they would not pay thirty-nine million dollars in damages ordered by Judge Parker. To first insult and then threaten the United States, the Soviet Union included a nasty note that said, "It is quite obvious that the American court, in rendering its decision, was not guided at all by legal rules, but [by] other motives."

Then the Soviet Union asked the U.S. State Department to

"take appropriate measures in guaranteeing the jurisdictional immunity of the Soviet state" while warning that "otherwise the American side will bear the full responsibility for the consequences of failing to take such measures."

A provocative response. At that time, the United States and Soviet Union remained the Cold War's prime antagonists, each aware the other could destroy the world. The dissolution of the Soviet Union was a few years away and Reagan's hawklike pronouncements about Russia hardly aided relations.

When the Soviets rejected the judgment, Struve pushed his contempt penalties and ignored asset seizure. While the Wallenberg lawyers employed that maneuver, the Soviets and the State Department were practicing Realpolitik. The Soviets did not respect the American courts, but expected the American State Department to help it eliminate this bothersome lawsuit.

Thus, the six-week window when the default judgment was issued and before the Soviets responded was the time to strike, said one faction of the law team. Seize assets. Push the Soviet Union. Do something. This was the time to attack and win, not a time to divert resources to weird efforts to collect additional civil contempt penalties beyond the thirty-nine million. Then thirty-nine million in Soviet assets around the world was precious to the Soviets, a nation with a weak currency and limited foreign reserves.

Instead of advancing, the legal team retreated. Instead of seizing and selling assets to get the thirty-nine million and free Raoul Wallenberg, the legal team filed tedious motions that kept him in the Soviet prison system. Instead of consolidating the victory, the U.S. lawyers delayed until they lost.

"I'm wondering what the hell was Guy Struve's motivation?" Makinen asked. "I really don't know."

Struve, the man who won the case, insisted the assets would be difficult to seize and the legal team was better off getting the order for the monetary fine. The court ignored Struve's formula for contempt penalties. The only people who received contempt were the lawyers remaining on the case. The contempt citation was never heard, and the Soviets were never penalized, the thirty-nine million dollars never collected.

The interminable delays created a second opportunity for the State Department to abandon Wallenberg while opposing U.S. federal court actions to seek his release. Like Sweden, the United States had adopted a passive attitude toward the Wallenberg affair. Neither government wanted to do anything. After the Soviet Union failed to comply with the judgment and returned the notice of default and support papers, the plaintiffs moved to hold the Soviet Union in civil contempt and to start imposing fines. The von Dardel lawyers filed a motion to that effect on April 28, 1986.[5] The court, realizing this involved important foreign policy issues, said on October 29, 1986, it wanted a second opinion. "Because the entry of an order of the type that plaintiffs contemplate would involve issues of foreign policy, the Court deems it appropriate to have the views of the United States before proceeding further in this matter."[6]

CHAPTER 16

Across from the FBI building in downtown Washington, David J. Anderson sat in his 10th floor office looking tense one October afternoon in 1994. "You're asking me to recall events that happened six to eight years ago," he politely told a visitor questioning him about his participation in the Wallenberg lawsuit.

Anderson wore a blue shirt and yellowish tie decorated with triangles. His glasses and receding hairline spoke of middle age while his desk and office spoke of moderate governmental power. Anderson is the Justice Department's Federal Programs Branch director and ninety lawyers report to him. Years earlier Anderson had carried the water for the Justice Department when the government, at the judge's request, entered the Wallenberg case. Now Anderson wanted the visitor, who had requested the interview, to know the precise terms and motivation of the government's entry.

"The United States generally does not have a role in these cases," Anderson explained. "The last thing the U.S. government wants to do is appear as a surrogate for the foreign sovereign."

Some of the plaintiff's lawyers charged that the government entered the Wallenberg case on the side of the Soviet Union, a contention Anderson vigorously tried to refute.

The State Department attempted to convince the Soviet Union to defend itself in this case. Philosophically, the government interpreted the Foreign Sovereign Immunities Act differently from the plaintiffs, thinking the FSIA involved commercial areas, such as dealing with situations where foreign states had trading companies. Anderson and the U.S. government felt if the Wallenberg lawsuit had succeeded, that would have sparked future lawsuits against foreign sovereigns in the United States, and the Soviet Union "might take reciprocal action."

To the U.S. government, "We thought this was an improper application" of the FSIA, Anderson said. Nevertheless, Anderson again told his visitor, "We were not supporting the Soviet Union. We did not want to be misunderstood in the public arena."

Instead, the federal government's objective was to convince the Soviets to "retain counsel and assert their immunity. They needed an American law firm, skilled in litigation."

Congress' intent under the FSIA, Anderson said, was not to "scare off foreign sovereigns from court," but the Wallenberg lawsuit might have achieved that effect.

Anderson also doubted Struve could have executed an order to get thirty-nine million dollars in damages from the Soviet Union's assets in the United States. "We believe that would not have been allowed by the Foreign Sovereign Immunities Act."

When a visitor asked Anderson how the Soviets would have replied to any attempted seizure of their U.S. property, he replied, "Your guess is as good as mine. I don't think the Soviets would have let it go unresponded."

In return, how would the American government have responded to any Soviet actions?

"I don't know what the U.S. government would have done."

Could this possibly have gone to the unthinkable consequence of armed conflict?

"We didn't go to its logical extreme."

But could something terrible have happened between the two superpowers over this lawsuit?

"We didn't want to paint ugly scenarios."

Anderson said that the "Soviets saw this as a political case. If a foreign state's acts become the basis of a case, that would displace the diplomatic process."

However, the case fell into "unfortunate circumstances. We abhor the Soviet's treatment vis à vis Wallenberg," Anderson said.

Did Wallenberg's humanitarian accomplishments on behalf of the United States influence Anderson in his legal dealings?

"My role—I was the lawyer for the State Department . . . I did not get into grand issues."

Rather, Anderson said he accepted the State Department's word on trying to free Wallenberg. He went to Moscow with the State Department officials to present the U.S. view, but State handled the diplomatic maneuvers to try to free Wallenberg while Anderson handled the legal case.

Anderson's counterpart at the State Department was a pragmatic and legally astute man named Abraham D. Sofaer.

Sofaer, a former federal judge, was the State Department's legal adviser from 1985-1990, where he turned that job into a position of power. Some of the plaintiff's lawyers felt he used that authority to oppose the Wallenberg law suit on practical grounds, a charge the federal government disputes. A feisty five feet, four inches, Sofaer was deeply rooted in minorities—a Jew, raised in Bombay, India, by parents of Iraqi descent. Because of Sofaer's distinguished career as a law professor at Columbia University, President Carter appointed him a New York judge, which led to his State Department position in June 1985. Since the Democrat Carter appointed Sofaer, conservatives intensely questioned him, so Sofaer made sure that in conversations he supported the Republican administration and the Republican President.

A Wall Street Journal profile described Sofaer as an aggressive man who had a "strong influence on many foreign policy issues."[1] In his job, Sofaer had a dual role as the Secretary of State's lawyer and the senior U.S. official who had to make sure foreign policy conforms to international law. Sofaer too frequently was "perceived as being out in front of the parade rather than keeping an eye on the procession."

Carl Levin, a member of the Senate Armed Services Committee, said, "I think he's smart, but I also feel he's applying his talents in directions that are not necessarily consistent with what the State Department should be doing." Levin, a Michigan Democrat, added, "I don't view the State Department's position as undermining treaties."[2]

While most of his predecessors cautiously gave advice in the background, Sofaer's brains and energy made him a foreign policy player and provided direct access to Secretary of State George Shultz. Due to his enthusiasm, Sofaer brought prominence to the small legal adviser's office. The bureau known as "L" in the department's bureaucratic speak, was put in charge when Secretary Shultz established a task force to provide information to the various agencies and committees investigating the Iran-contra affair. "It's the first time I can remember us heading anything up," said Michael Kozak, who had been with the State Department for 16 years.[3]

Four days after his appointment as legal adviser, hijackers seized a Trans World Airlines jet in the Middle East and executed an American passenger. Sofaer saw a way to satisfy the terrorists' demand that some Shiite prisoners in Israel be released. Some years before, the United States had said the prisoners were held illegally and should be freed. Thus, the administration had only to restate its position, Sofaer thought. He took the idea right to Secretary Shultz, who agreed.

That gave Sofaer cachet at State. "There is a sense of energy and competence in the bureau now," Elliott Abrams, Assistant Secretary of State for Inter-American Affairs, said in 1987.[4] "People very much want the legal adviser's views and care what he thinks."

Sofaer—short and fiery—and Anderson—taller and quieter—were the government's team opposing the Wallenberg lawyers. The legal adviser's office was subcutaneous, on the surface expressing support for the noble aims of freeing Raoul Wallenberg, while below view trying to help the Soviets respond properly to the lawsuit. But Sofaer said he acted properly on every level.

"I never met them (the Soviets) when I didn't raise the issue of Wallenberg," said Sofaer in a November 1994 telephone interview from California.

Sofaer left the State Department in 1990, working as a lawyer in Washington[5] until the fall of 1994 when he was appointed a

senior fellow at the Hoover Institution at Stanford University in
Palo Alto, California.[6] Sofaer also won the first George P. Shultz
Distinguished Scholarship in Foreign Policy and National Security
Affairs. The three million dollar fellowship, named in honor of
former U.S. Secretary of State Shultz, who is a Hoover Distinguished
Fellow and Sofaer's former boss at the State Department, is funded
by gifts from Shultz, corporations, foundations and individual
donors.

While in California, Sofaer told his questioner over the telephone that when he asked the Soviets about Wallenberg, "They
would listen and never say much. They played it like professional
diplomats."

Sofaer said the Soviets opened some files and said they would
do what they could, but, "They didn't tell me he was dead nor did
they tell me he was alive." And Sofaer doesn't believe Wallenberg is
alive, but the U.S. government wanted to know "where he is and
what happened to him." Thus, Sofaer would constantly raise the
issue with the Soviets. "I considered it an important question."

He felt the Russians should be more "forthcoming" and the
appropriate diplomatic maneuver was to continually pressure the
Russians, said the former legal adviser. Like Anderson, Sofaer did
what he was "instructed to do. These issues are worked up with
the cooperation with a variety of units in the State Department,
the European bureau, the legal bureau, a number of people were
consulted as what ought to be said." He brushed aside any discussion of this issue resulting in armed conflict. "No one ever said
anything like that."

Sofaer also couldn't fathom the Wallenberg lawsuit. "I don't
know what they were trying to do. Why should we get involved in
a judgment of thirty-nine million dollars from the Soviet Union?"
To him, "The lawsuit was clearly inconsistent with the Foreign
Sovereign Immunities Act." Then, tired of the questions, Sofaer
said, "I've got to go back to my family. Read my statement and
quote from that," and he abruptly concluded the short interview.

When one inspects and "quotes" from the documents, the facts show the U.S. government supported the Soviet Union and tried to undermine the Wallenberg lawsuit. The State Department met with Soviet officials four times in Washington or Moscow and constantly advised them on how to deal with the lawsuit. The two countries signed a memorandum on aiding each other legally, which the State Department embraced, acting almost as an on site defense attorney for the Soviet Union. Except for the 40-year-old platitudes, the American government did not represent the interests of its honorary citizen, Raoul Wallenberg.

For example, on December 8, 1986, the State Department filed with the court its statement of interest, headed by Sofaer's name. At the heart of the 29-page-statement came a familiar refrain: "The United States abhors the Soviet Union's unjust imprisonment of Wallenberg and continues, through Governmental channels, to seek a full and satisfactory accounting for his fate. The proper forum for such matters, however, is the diplomatic arena and not the courts of the United States."[7]

For decades, U.S. diplomats complained about Soviet imprisonment of Wallenberg while U.S. diplomacy had failed to free him. Now, the State Department objected when outside forces tried to assume its role.

Rather, Sofaer and the State Department said, the federal government "must also consider the current proceedings in terms of their potential impact on broader foreign policy interests." For example, "Imposing contempt sanctions in this case would set a precedent which could affect our legal and political relationships with all foreign nations potentially subject to the jurisdiction of United States courts."

Amid the foundry of words emerges this steel-hard fact: The U.S. government still didn't care about Raoul Wallenberg.

Two weeks after the State Department filed its statement of interest Anderson and Struve faced Judge Parker in a hearing to discuss the State Department's involvement. Anderson's verbal presentation contained twin goals: Disavow linkage with the Russians and destroy the case.

Initially, Anderson told the judge, "I do not represent or speak for the Soviet Union."[8]

When Judge Parker asked Anderson why the U.S. government hadn't entered the case sooner, he said the federal government did not routinely appear in such cases even though they involved foreign sovereigns. After the judge pressed him, Anderson admitted the government had expressed its views in some cases and then the federal government tried to get the foreign sovereign to appear via counsel and present its defense.

Next, Anderson tried to demolish the case. "Are you saying that the Court has no jurisdiction in this matter under the FSIA?" Judge Parker asked Anderson.

"That would be our view, yes."

The judge told Anderson to proceed. "First of all, the FSIA was an attempt by Congress to balance the interests of foreign states against those of private individuals who might have legal controversies with them . . . any interpretation of the FSIA or the Alien Tort Act that goes beyond what we think Congress had in mind would have the Courts involved in what are essentially political disputes which should be for resolution by diplomatic means by the governments involved."[9]

In rebuttal, Struve hurled a verbal barb into the State Department's pinstripe pants, repeating Anderson's statement about how this matter should be left to "statecraft and diplomacy. Now the Wallenberg family left this issue to statecraft and diplomacy for 39 years . . . but the answer that the Soviet Union now consistently gives to diplomatic approaches on the subject of Raoul Wallenberg is that they said all there was to be said in 1957 when they said he died of a heart attack in 1947 and that the matter is closed."[10]

Next, Anderson distanced his country from its biggest foe and concentrated his attack on the FSIA. "We are not here because of any pressure by the Soviet Union," Anderson told the judge. Instead, the government responded to the dual calls of the judicial request and the country's foreign policy interests.

To Anderson and the federal government, Congress had intended the FSIA to deal with commercial transactions, not rescuing famous diplomats. "Congress did not intend violations of international law to be a basis for waiving sovereign immunity . . . even violations as serious as this one . . ." Anderson told the judge, who interrupted him, asking for the authority.

"The act itself," Anderson replied.

Thus, the government feared if the von Dardel case were successful, the U.S. courts would be flooded with every alleged violation of international law by any plaintiff.

Anderson also told the judge the government felt the Alien Tort Claims Act "does not provide jurisdiction against foreign states" because Congress probably had in mind offenses like piracy, possibly violations of diplomatic safe conduct, but those done by individuals.

In his response, Struve specified the government's reluctance to enter similar cases until now. "This is the first case in the ten years since the enactment of the Foreign Sovereign Immunities Act in which the government, without the foreign government itself coming into the case in any form, has interceded to present the jurisdictional arguments that . . . should be presented by the foreign government itself."

Struve also interpreted the FSIA differently. "Clearly, Congress intended that injunctions could be rendered against foreign sovereigns under the FSIA." Then Struve addressed the question cleaving his own legal team: "Why have we not taken that thirty-nine million dollar damage judgment . . . and gone out and executed on Soviet assets..?"

The judge agreed. "That's a good question. Why not?"

To reply, Struve said the money was "not unimportant," but collecting the judgment would put the focus on the money and not on the issue of freeing Wallenberg or finding out what had happened to him. That was the entire purpose of the lawsuit.

However, when Judge Parker later pressed Struve for where he could seize assets, Struve said the Soviet Union had diplomatic representation in three U.S. cities—Washington, New York and San Francisco. There the Soviet Union owned real estate and had bank accounts, ready for seizure, but Struve never touched them.

In his own rebuttal, Anderson admonished the Soviets and the plaintiffs. "The Soviet Union has flouted world opinion on the Wallenberg case for four decades now, and it's a little bit hard to believe that as a result of a Court Judgment in the United States they are going to turn around and suddenly own up to what they've done."

He was right.

After the one hour and twenty minute hearing ended, Judge Parker told Struve he could file a "post-hearing memorandum," but the judge never took any action.

While the State Department told the court why it couldn't rescue Wallenberg, the same people in 1986 engineered spy swaps to free three prominent men—Anatoly Shcharansky and Yuri L. Orlov, both Soviet citizens, and Nicholas Daniloff, an American—from the Soviet Union.

Instead of arranging a spy swap for Wallenberg, the State Department filed motions—matched page for page by the von Dardel lawyers—as the case remained mired in endless court proceedings. Many trees died to create the mountain of legal pleadings piled high on Judge Parker's desk. The one most instructive about the U.S. government's action helping the Soviets came from Sofaer, the one he told a writer to "quote." On July 28, 1989, Sofaer filed a 14-page statement, based on his "personal knowledge and recollections and on information provided to me in my official capacity."[11]

First, Sofaer stated the obvious: "Many foreign governments simply do not understand the United States legal system. Many are intimidated by the expense and complexity of litigation in United States courts."

Then he told about the four U.S.-Soviet tête-à-têtes. Officials from the State Department "have met with Soviet representatives both in Washington and in Moscow on numerous occasions to explain United States requirements regarding litigation and to urge the Soviet Union to seek advice of private counsel concerning participation in or other means of resolving these and other lawsuits against it."[12]

After the default judgment on October 15, 1985, Sofaer reveals, people from State, "including members of my staff," told the Soviets about the default judgment in this case. The people of State explained "requirements and procedures under United States law" about attachment and encouraged the Soviets to seek private legal counsel.

"These judgments were entered at a time of extreme sensitivity (and opportunity) in U.S.-Soviet relations," Sofaer wrote.

The legal adviser himself went to Moscow March 3, 1987, heading a delegation of State and Justice Department officials that met with a high-level Soviet delegation, which included representatives from several agencies of the Soviet government. The topic: Sovereign Immunity.

In Moscow, Sofaer and the Soviets discussed "issues of principle, as well as specific cases against the Soviet Government and its agencies or instrumentalities in United States courts, including this case." During the discussions, Sofaer said the U.S. delegation explained U.S. law concerning foreign sovereign immunity.

"We advised the Soviet Union that it could appear in United States courts to assert its immunity without either conceding its principled adherence to the absolute theory of sovereign immunity or waiving its claim to such immunity," said Sofaer, who advised the Soviets to hire counsel and appear in the several cases filed against that country, including the Wallenberg case.

The U.S. delegation told the Soviets that the American government "has filed statements of interest in appropriate cases brought under the FSIA in which a foreign state has moved to have a default judgment against it set aside." So, the Americans told the Soviets, in effect, you have a friend in the State Department. The Americans told the Soviets to show up in the U.S. court if only to "assert immunity."

Once again, almost as an afterthought, Sofaer said, "We urged the Soviet Union to provide a full and satisfactory accounting of the fate of Mr. Wallenberg."

But that met with the Soviet stonewall. The Soviet officials "repeated their view that this was a very special, political case, unlike the other cases in which the Soviet Union had recently appeared, all of which involved commercial considerations . . ."

After signing the memorandum, the State Department continued to discuss the Wallenberg litigation with the Soviets. "In particular, Department personnel, including members of my staff from the Office of the Legal Adviser, informed Soviet Embassy representatives in December 1988 and March 1989, of the plaintiffs' filing of additional pleadings in this case" while urging the Soviets to hire a U.S. lawyer to fight the lawsuit, Sofaer wrote in a subsequent filing to the court.

To some on the legal team, the U.S. State Department should have done the opposite, immediately supporting Judge Parker's decision and confronting the Soviet Union. But those were the Reagan years when the administration regarded the Soviet Union as the "Evil Empire" but still sought rapprochement because of the changes sweeping through the country. However, the goals were not mutually exclusive. Why not seek closer ties with the Soviets but tell them "enough already, we want to know about Wallenberg"?

Instead, the State Department retained the party line though the administration had changed from Reagan to his vice president, George Bush. After at least four pleadings, the Soviets in June 1989 retained an American law firm, Baker & McKenzie of Washington, which directed two of its attorneys, Eugene Theroux and Thomas Peele, to handle the case.

In his declaration, Sofaer sounded relieved that the Soviets had hired an American law firm. "The Soviet Union has now engaged counsel and has appeared to assert appropriate defenses to set aside the default judgment in this case. This action represents the completion of the U.S. diplomatic objective of convincing the

Soviet Union to litigate its immunity claims in U.S. courts in all cases."[13]

Sofaer's joy was mitigated by the plaintiff's statement in opposition to the Soviet Union's motion, saying that the U.S. statement of interest "'neglects to mention any specific, concrete foreign policy concerns involving this particular case.'" Sofaer then spins 180 degrees. "To the contrary, this particular case involves very substantial specific foreign policy concerns."

He thought this was only the second time the Soviet Union had appeared in a U.S. court in a proceeding brought just against the Soviet government and not one of its agencies. By then, the Wallenberg case had become a cause célèbre at State.

"This case has become a significant issue in bilateral United States-Soviet relations. The United States Government has expended considerable effort to urge the Soviet Government to appear in this case and raise its defenses, including the contention that it is absolutely immune, before the court instead of through diplomatic channels," Sofaer wrote.

Casting any subtlety aside, Sofaer added that the State Department believed Judge Parker's judgment was "void for lack of jurisdiction on the face of the complaint." Allowing discovery would be "inconsistent with the sovereign immunity extended to the Soviet Union by U.S. and international law and could significantly complicate the relations between the Soviet Union and the United States."

On July 31, 1989, Russia's newly hired American lawyers replied in opposition to the plaintiffs' motion on the lawsuit. As expected, lawyers Theroux and Peele from Baker & McKenzie asked for dismissal "on the grounds of sovereign immunity of the USSR."[14]

In concluding their 19-page attack on behalf of their client, the two lawyers contended "'no legal claim'" has been pleaded by the plaintiffs. Consequently, "the default judgment in this case should be vacated, and the complaint dismissed."

Attached to the filing is a three-page letter from Anderson, the Justice Department attorney. This letter went to U.S. District Court

Judge U.W. Clemon in Birmingham, Alabama, asking him to uphold Communist China's foreign sovereign immunity. For its American lawyer, the Peoples Republic had selected Eugene Theroux.

By now, Judge Parker's desk and bookcase groaned under the weight of all these legal filings, but the judge neither did or said anything else about the case. During these legal maneuverings, Judge Parker never mentioned any pressure regarding the Wallenberg case or his reasoning to support his decision for the plaintiffs. One of his sons, Barrington D. Parker Jr., himself now a judge, said in a telephone conversation a thorough search of his father's papers failed to uncover any written thoughts about the decision, which he didn't discuss with his son. All anyone can interpret is the actual written document; everything else is supposition.

By 1989, Judge Parker had suffered a heart attack and a stroke, necessitating his resignation from the bench. Complications from these attacks ended Judge Parker's life June 2, 1993. He was 77.

CHAPTER 17

Immediately after Judge Parker resigned from the court, the Wallenberg case went to Chief Judge Aubrey E. Robinson Jr., a man who held a different view about international law and human rights issues against a foreign government. For example, Judge Robinson had dismissed on August 1, 1985, a suit claiming damages against the Soviet Union, whose fighter plane two years earlier had shot down a Korean Air Lines jetliner, KAL 007, which had gone off course into Soviet territory. Two hundred and sixty-nine people died in the incident. Several plaintiffs, who were heirs of passengers killed on the flight, brought financial claims in a U.S. court against the Soviet Union.[1] The plaintiffs cited the Foreign Sovereign Immunities Act and as an alternative, the Alien Tort Claims Act, the same legal precedents the Wallenberg lawyers employed.

Judge Robinson cast both arguments aside, saying, "It is not for the courts to make inquiry into the legality, validity or propriety of the actions taken by foreign governments." He ruled, "the general presumption of immunity, restricted under the FSIA, is not overcome." The judge also said the Alien Tort Claims Act lacked validity in this case. In conclusion, Judge Robinson ruled, "Resolution of such political issues is better left to the political branches," and he dismissed all claims against the Union of Soviet Socialist Republics.[2]

Judge Robinson, whom President Lyndon B. Johnson appointed a U.S. District Court judge for life on November 16, 1966, made other high profile rulings, some moderate, some liberal. In 1980, he sentenced Church of Scientology officials, Jane Kember and Morris Budlong, each to six years for a series of document thefts from government officials. A year later Judge Robinson ordered the Drug Enforcement Administration to reinstate an official who had been demoted in retaliation for testifying in a discrimination suit by black employees.

Also, Judge Robinson overturned a U.S. Air Force order barring Rabbi Captain Simcha Goldman from wearing a yarmulke while in uniform in 1981. The judge in 1982 held Bernard C. Welch Jr. liable for $5.7 million for the 1980 murder of Dr. Michael Halberstam, brother of author David Halberstam. In another 1982 case, Judge Robinson awarded more than 3,000 women flight attendants of Northwest Airlines $52.4 million in a job discrimination lawsuit.[3]

When he received the Wallenberg case, Judge Robinson acted quickly. Without a hearing, he dismissed the von Dardel complaint on March 9, 1990, and vacated the default judgment, effectively killing the case. The von Dardel family chose not to appeal, and Wallenberg, if he were still alive, remained in the gulag.

In reversing Judge Parker's decision, Judge Robinson ruled that no separate matter of jurisdiction under the Foreign Sovereign Immunities Act existed and that the Soviets could raise jurisdictional arguments at any time. Judge Robinson said that the Soviet Union did not waive sovereign immunity under the Foreign Sovereign Immunities Act by failing to appear. He added that, "The Soviet Union was entitled to wait to see if the contempt motion was decided against them and enforced . . . No such action has occurred here . . ."[4]

In conclusion, the judge found "none of the grounds upon which jurisdiction was asserted in 1985 currently withstand scrutiny. The FSIA provides for quite limited exceptions to the bar posed by sovereign immunity in cases against foreign states." Judge Robinson also ruled an exception to the FSIA would conflict with international agreements and did not apply in the Wallenberg case. When the Soviet Union agreed to human rights and diplomatic immunity treaties, that failed to apply to the Soviets for the "allegedly unlawful seizure and subsequent imprisonment and possible death of [a] Swedish diplomat," according to Judge Robinson.

To support his ruling, Judge Robinson—who died in the year 2000—had principally relied on the U.S. Supreme Court decision involving the Argentine Republic and Amerada Hess Shipping Corp., decided January 23, 1989.

In that case, the Hercules, a crude oil tanker chartered by Amerada Hess, had unloaded its cargo at the Hess refinery in the U.S. Virgin Islands and was returning to Valdez, Alaska, the terminus of the Trans-Alaskan pipeline.[5] The Hercules' planned route around Cape Horn in South America would have taken it past Argentina, then engaged in a war with Britain over the Falklands Islands. On June 8, 1982, the Hercules was in international waters about 600 nautical miles from Argentina and 500 miles from the Falklands. Without provocation, Argentine planes bombed the Hercules in three separate attacks, including an air-to-surface rocket. Disabled, but not destroyed, the Hercules reversed course and sailed to Rio de Janeiro, the nearest safe port. The ship had suffered extensive deck and hull damage and an undetonated bomb remained lodged in her No. 2 tank. United Carriers Inc., a Liberian corporation that chartered the oil tanker to Amerada Hess, determined it would be too dangerous to remove the undetonated bomb. The Hercules was scuttled 250 miles off the Brazilian Coast.

Amerada Hess tried unsuccessfully to get damages from the Argentine government. When that failed, the American company sued, using the Alien Tort laws as the Wallenberg law team had in its case. United Carriers sought ten million dollars for the loss of the ship and Amerada Hess sought $1.9 million in damages for the fuel that went down with the ship.

Amerada Hess said the District Court had jurisdiction under the Alien Tort Statute. This confers original jurisdiction on district courts over civil actions by an alien for a tort committed in violation of the law of nations or a treaty of the United States as the lawyers had successfully argued before Judge Parker.

Amerada Hess also brought suit under the general admiralty

and maritime jurisdiction of federal courts. The District Court dismissed the complaints for lack of subject-matter jurisdiction, ruling that their actions were barred by the Foreign Sovereign Immunities Act. The Court of Appeals reversed, holding that the District Court had jurisdiction over the action under the Alien Tort Statute.

The Supreme Court, in an opinion written by Chief Justice William Rehnquist, reversed the Appeals Court and upheld the District Court. The District Court had dismissed the action because the FSIA provides the sole basis for obtaining jurisdiction over a foreign state in the courts of this country and that none of the enumerated exceptions to the Act apply to the facts of this case.[6]

In the Amerada Hess case, the District Court addressed the plaintiffs' arguments in detail "only because similar arguments have been accepted—incorrectly, we feel—in Von [sic] Dardel v. U.S.S.R . . ." Next the District Court said Judge Parker had ruled against the Soviets because the FSIA should not be read to "extend immunity to clear violations of universally recognized principles of international law." The Parker court based this on language in the FSIA's legislative history, which said the statute incorporated standards of international law.

"With all respect," said the District Court, "nothing in the FSIA or its legislative history supports that interpretation."[7]

The Chief Justice of the Supreme Court upheld the District Court's view and thus yanked out the linchpin of the Wallenberg case, immobilizing the lawsuit.

Rehnquist said the FSIA "must be applied by the district courts in every action against a foreign sovereign, since subject-matter jurisdiction in any such action depends on the existence of one of the specified exceptions to foreign sovereign immunity." To Chief Justice Rehnquist, "We draw the plain implication that immunity is granted in those cases involving alleged violations of international law that do not come within one of the FSIA's exceptions."

Since the Supreme jurist in the country overturned the FSIA, any lower court judge would have to rule similarly.

Six other Supreme Court Justices agreed with Rehnquist on the Amerada Hess ruling while Harry Blackmun filed an opinion concurring partly and one in which Thurgood Marshall joined.

The United States entered the case as amicus curiae, urging reversal. One of those listed on the brief for the U.S. government was Abraham Sofaer.

Like Monday morning quarterbacks, analyzing their defeat, the Wallenberg lawyers showed both insight and regret. Tony D'Amato understood Judge Robinson's overturning of the case. "How can you ask for a contempt order against a foreign state? It's like asking for the moon."

In the course of reexamining the entire case, D'Amato said the judge reasoned, "Hey, this doesn't have any basis." To D'Amato, the law team should have looked at the first judgment and said, "We're lucky we won this. It was a good argument, and it was everything else, but it's possible to be overturned."

Most American judges avoid international law, said D'Amato, an expert in international law, because they don't know too much about that discipline. "They're a little scared of that field. They haven't studied it in law school, and they really don't know much about it."

Recently, there have been some human rights cases where American lawyers have made a partial breakthrough, but it remains an educative process. "You have to sort of show judges that horrible wrongs can be committed. That these things can be redressed through the courts and the fact that it's international law shouldn't be frightening." Still, to some judges, according to D'Amato, this aspect of the law remains alien.

"Back in the early days of the United States, in the early days of the Republic, they (judges) were statesmen; they were state department people; they were foreign service officers. They knew a lot about international law and if you look in the early decision of the Supreme Court, you'll find they were very comfortable with international law. It was used all the time, but we have gone away from that," D'Amato lamented.

"Now we are appointing judges from lower courts who have no international experience at all, and the subject matter is not taught very much in law school any more, so we're in a culture now where we're very insular. We're not looking at the rest of the world and judges, who are conservative by nature, find it very hard to apply that kind of law," D'Amato said.

However, as a law professor, he feels differently. "I think, personally, it's perfectly sound to apply (international law). There's a great deal of precedent in our history to apply it. But again if you come across some judges who don't see it and don't know about it; don't want to know about it; what can you do?"

The once victorious legal team had squabbled over tactics much of the time. D'Amato had preferred attaching assets, at least having some assets in hand when the Soviets came in and tried to "pry them loose before litigating again. Whereas if you go in as a plaintiff the second time around, you're again knocking on the door of the court and saying, 'Please give us this,' and the second court might say 'no, we don't want to give you that.'"

The von Dardels still had the right of appeal, but decided to do nothing.

Dellapenna, who remained active in the case, said, "We had a telephone conference call after Judge Robinson's decision, and we decided there was nothing to appeal." To Dellapenna, an "appeal was useless. You try what you can but sometimes you don't succeed. I don't regret being involved, but I don't know what else we could have done."

Of course, as he said earlier, Dellapenna felt Struve could have argued the case better, contending the tort occurred because the Soviets kept Wallenberg a prisoner and thus deprived his relatives, who lived in the United States, of his companionship. Struve had argued that the Soviets by not filing an answer waived their immunity, but that changed when the Soviets entered an appearance.

"Something might have happened if our government wanted to pick it up and run with it, but it didn't want to," Dellapenna said. President Ronald Reagan, for all his talk about the "Evil Empire," avoided confrontation. "If the U.S. government had taken action," Dellapenna continued, "that possibly could have freed Wallenberg. That's the dream."

In Dellapenna's opinion, if the U.S. government had given the lawsuit "a lot of publicity and made it a diplomatic issue, if our government had brought it up at Reykjavik (the summit in October 1986), the Soviets sooner or later would have had to do something. The Soviets nonetheless would have had to respond."

But they didn't, so they did nothing as they have for the last 50 years.

Struve, the lead lawyer, also advised against an appeal, explaining that various decisions by the Washington, D.C., District Circuit court went against the case, so he doubted any other judge would have ruled differently. Struve explained that it was hard to get relief for noncommercial cases under the Foreign Sovereign Immunities Act, then the State Department entered the case and the judge saw the law more restrictively, making it hard to rule in favor of von Dardel. Like a swift current, the law was moving against the legal team and von Dardel.

Since the trend went against these types of cases in the district court and the Soviet Union began to change, Struve recommended against filing an appeal. Von Dardel agreed.

"First, it seemed unlikely that we would be able to overcome the objections. Second, as the conditions in the Soviet Union were changing drastically," that provided hope, von Dardel said.

Third, von Dardel thought, "It seemed likely that even if we did win, it would be the American taxpayers, not the Soviets who would have to pay. We certainly, anyway, did not want to profit economically by Raoul's predicament. Also, as to myself, I had from the spring of 1989 gotten contacts with higher Soviet officials in the Human Rights field and was intent on organizing an International Commission to investigate the archive of one of the major Soviet prisons in Vladimir. As Guy Struve suggested that the time was ripe to call it a day, I, therefore, felt it was not a surrender, it was a shift to more direct methods of contact with the Soviets. However, we did not do it lightly. We had a special meeting with Struve, Irwin Cotler . . . and another well-known lawyer from Boston, whose name I do not recall, and only after this meeting did we in fact decided to drop the suit."

After nine years, the lawsuit—a microcosm of the then 45-year-effort to free Raoul Wallenberg—ended in failure. However, a few months earlier von Dardel had begun to pursue yet another path in the never-ending trail—direct contact with the Soviet Union.

CHAPTER 18

Along with glasnost came an invitation. On August 14, 1989, or 44 years after imprisoning Raoul Wallenberg, the Soviet Union finally invited his family to Moscow to search for him.

This came only one month after the death of Andrei Gromyko, who had preceded Mikhail S. Gorbachev as president of the Soviet Union. In 1957, while deputy foreign minister, Gromyko had declared that Wallenberg had died of a heart attack ten years earlier. That remained the Soviet position even under Gorbachev's glasnost, or openness, but the family hoped Gromyko's death and the Moscow invitation could provide the combination to unlock the Wallenberg mystery.

The Soviet ambassador gave the invitation to the Wallenberg Association in Stockholm, where Per Anger, the Swedish diplomat who had served with Wallenberg in Budapest, received it. Anger said he would travel to Moscow that October with Nina Lagergren, Guy von Dardel and Sonja Sonnenfeld, who all saw different opportunities for the journey.

"The trip to Russia was a beginning," von Dardel said five years ex post facto. "It coincided with human rights actions in Russia." Additionally, he was "intent on organizing an International Commission to investigate the archive of one of the major Soviet prisons," Vladimir.

To Sonnenfeld, "It was a breakthrough." She thought this was the first time anyone connected with Wallenberg had been invited to Russia, adding, "It appears that they wanted to talk with us, and we were told the meeting would be a high-level talk."

Nina Lagergren said she was going to Moscow to find out

about her brother. "Although [almost] 45 years have passed, I believe that he is alive."[1]

Von Dardel first met with the Soviets in 1989 in Geneva, talking to Anatoly Adamishen, the Deputy Minister of External Affairs for Human Rights, and then the Wallenberg party went to the Soviet Union. Anticipation aside, von Dardel spoke with people inside and outside prison, ending up with only a few pieces of paper, but without Raoul Wallenberg.

During von Dardel's trip to Moscow, the Soviets said the Wallenberg family would not receive any new information but would see the original 1947 document reporting that Wallenberg had died. This handwritten message, most likely a forgery, is the only trace the Soviets said they have ever found of the missing diplomat's death. When shown the much-discussed document, von Dardel said this did not seem authentic since it was not on official paper, lacked an official stamp and failed to give Wallenberg's first name.

Shortly thereafter, the Russians on October 17 gave the family Wallenberg's diplomatic passport, driver's license, an address book, a calendar he was carrying when seized, some cash and a few apologies.[2] Three days later the family received the card dated February 6, 1945, registering Wallenberg as a prisoner of war in Lubyanka. This was the first official evidence the Soviets had made public since the 1957 Gromyko letter saying Wallenberg had died. Valentin Mikhailovich Nikoforov, deputy foreign minister, handed over the documents, which Soviet officials said were found "by chance" at KGB headquarters during an investigation of Stalinist repression.[3]

"It was the first meeting there, and they handed back some of Raoul's personal belongings," von Dardel said in a 1994 telephone conversation from his home in Switzerland. "They found it in the cellars in Lubyanka. Seems almost a miracle after so many years, they could find it," said von Dardel, who freed his sarcasm to flow through the telephone line to America and engulf his listener.

"This was obviously prearranged. We had been able to force them. It was a beginning."

Independent experts told the family, according to archival rules, all the items could have been kept only in his dossier, which then must exist somewhere in Moscow. Apparently, the Russians took these items out of Wallenberg's dossier as a piecemeal offering to his family, telling them they found these bits of their half-brother only a month before in the KGB archives. The Russians would only give the family a few insignificant bits of paper, mementos emptied from the pockets of Raoul Wallenberg before his incarceration in Lubyanka. Poor substitutes for flesh and bone.

But the Soviets would not produce von Dardel's half-brother or an accounting of what happened to him. When the Wallenberg party asked for relevant information, they only received niceties and clichés. If the Soviets could find his driver's license, they could find his dental records, his record of transport from prison to prison and the autopsy report of his alleged death, which, according to the Soviets, happened to be a murder at the hands of a KGB official.

"It was terribly emotional to see Raoul's passport and photographs again," said Nina Lagergren.[4]

Per Anger said he found it "peculiar" that the Soviets should suddenly have discovered these items. "It gives us hope that they can find new things again."[5]

Mrs. Lagergren agreed, for to get anything was "quite an achievement. They must have much more. In that regard, something was achieved. There was hope."

A Russian documentary film, with English subtitles, chronicles the visit to Moscow. The film showed Nina Lagergren asking all Soviet citizens to help her with any information about Raoul Wallenberg and giving a phone number, which was put on a Moscow television station, of the Raoul Wallenberg society representative in Moscow. Then one sees von Dardel—with white thinning hair, glasses and angular features—first in Lubyanka Square amid journalists, then at the Soviet Foreign Ministry and finally at the KGB, which received the entire delegation. During his visits there, at the agency that had imprisoned and interrogated his half-brother, von Dardel gathered his new evidence.[6]

At the end of the visit, the Russians surprised von Dardel and allowed him and his sister to visit Vladimir Prison, so they extended their stay. The two elderly Swedes—von Dardel was then 70 and Nina Lagergren, then 68—wandered through the Russian prison, looking for their half-brother. Mostly they found convicts and curious stares, but the trip to Vladimir yielded conversations with several prisoners who said they saw Wallenberg after 1947, the date the Soviets insisted Wallenberg died.

"We were able to look at some prison files and talk to officials," von Dardel said. "We were not able to confirm the sightings we had there, and thus the visit was not conclusive. But we never expected that. Nevertheless, it points the way, and it's very exciting for me," von Dardel said, but he declined to discuss the new evidence gathered.

To counteract the staid proceedings, the film makers interviewed Ferdinand Arutyunian, a disheveled man, who said he came from Yerevan to try to meet the Wallenberg family, claiming he spent time in prison with Raoul Wallenberg. Wallenberg supposedly was happy after the death of Stalin, but suffered a stroke himself, according to Arutyunian. Wallenberg was then put in the central hospital, where Arutyunian stayed with him. "During the night, he started to feel worse. After 10 o'clock, he had another stroke and he calmed down. He didn't have a doctor or anything. Wallenberg died," said Arutyunian, who has no proof other than his words.

Even more ludicrous was V. Shaphorostov's contention he was Wallenberg's son. After an absurd story about how he was the offspring of Wallenberg and a Russian woman, Shaphorostov takes off his wool cap, revealing not the slightest resemblance to Wallenberg.[7]

While the Wallenberg delegation was in Moscow yet another story surfaced, this time a Hungarian magazine published an article contending that Wallenberg was killed by Soviet troops in

Hungary during February 1945.[8] Pont, a Defense Ministry journal, printed the account of two brothers named Molnar who said their father, now dead, saw two Soviet soldiers kill Wallenberg and his driver, Vilmos Langfelder on February 2, 1945. In the article, the brothers said they dug the grave about a month later and could still identify the place.

From the Swedish archives, the Russian documentary showed an interview with Abraham Kalinski, the man who claimed to have seen Wallenberg while both were in prison. Kalinski, who died in 1988, was well dressed with a coat, hat, leather gloves and tie showing through the top of his overcoat. He looked and sounded credible. For the film, Kalinski repeated the story about how he saw Wallenberg in 1952 through the prison window.

"The last time I saw him was two days before my release, October 27, 1959, in Vladimir Prison," said Kalinski.

He added, "It is the fault of the Swedish government (for not freeing Wallenberg). They never published anything. Many persons could have seen him and everything would have been sorted out a long time ago."

V. Kukin, a retired officer of the Soviet prison system, remembered Kalinski but not Wallenberg. Kukin explained that the number on the prisoner's door changed annually. "A person could be hidden behind a number or another name."[9]

The jailer's tale becomes the thread in the fabric of another story: Wallenberg may have become lost in the Russian prison system and even the jailers couldn't find the jailed. "Perhaps they haven't been able to trace him," Lagergren said in 1989. Even if the family had found Wallenberg, whom they had not seen in 44 years, would they have recognized him? Or, would Wallenberg even have known his own identity?

The Russians may have given Wallenberg a new name and a new identity. If the jailer tells his prisoner for 44 years, his name is Boris Godunov, what else could he believe? The Russians, in fact, could have taken a corpse in 1947 and given the cadaver the name Raoul Wallenberg. Then they could have told the real Raoul

Wallenberg, he was someone else. Isolated and helpless, Wallenberg's mental defenses could have crumbled along with his true identity. Thus, two Raoul Wallenbergs could exist—the ersatz one who died of a heart attack in 1947 and the real Wallenberg, who could be named anything and kept anywhere in the Gulag Archipelago.

Thus, Wallenberg could be alive, but not know himself. Makinen pondered the possibility. "Let's say a person has become sufficiently psychologically changed, so you can't pronounce him as sane. He's disoriented in respect to time, place or date. There is that possibility. More likely, he could be kept in a secluded, isolated part of Russia."

In the documentary film, another Russian named Pimenov said Wallenberg could have been hidden for decades. "It could have been possible, for ours is a miraculous country. You could do anything here."[10]

However, like many stories, the KGB could have planted that idea through its agents, who, in turn, repeat this to people in the West, letting them think Wallenberg was still alive in some desolate spot. But why would the authorities invent such an elaborate coverup, more intricate and successful than Watergate or Iran-contra?

"You expect logic from the Russians," snapped Sonja Sonnenfeld, lecturing to a Western writer.

If one generalizes, an answer emerges. The Germans were fascists, but logical. The Russians, untouched by the Renaissance and other monumental influences, are mentally impenetrable. Those in the West can never understand the Russians.

But in the late 1980s and early 1990s, thanks to glasnost and perestroika, economic restructuring, the Soviet Union was crumbling, maybe permitting some comprehension and candor to seep over the ruins.

During a press conference at the conclusion of the Moscow trip, Nina Lagergren said, "We have testimony from witnesses that Raoul Wallenberg is alive, and Mikhail Gorbachev when he was in New York promised me to do everything to cast light on the history of my brother." When she finishes, Nina starts to cry. She leaves with Raoul Wallenberg's diplomatic passport, his driver's license, notebook, silver cigarette case and Hungarian bank notes confiscated at the time of his arrest.[11]

The Russians refused to yield Wallenberg or his remains, but they did admit his imprisonment and "death" were crimes of the Stalin era. Gennadi Gerasimov, Soviet foreign ministry spokesman, said Wallenberg's treatment was a "tragic mistake that has never been corrected. He was caught up in a maelstrom of repression."

Von Dardel returned to Sweden, carrying back mostly regrets. Nevertheless, he remained upbeat. After returning home, von Dardel organized a special commission including Soviet and foreign specialists. They studied the archives of the Vladimir prison, and concluded the Wallenberg dossier exists. It is kept by the KGB in the Soviet Union, and the documentary film ends.

In an interview with the Los Angeles Times, von Dardel said his 10-day trip to the Soviet Union was "very exciting," adding he planned to return to pursue several leads. "I loved my brother very much. And I think it would be one of the great injustices if we left this alone, without trying to find out what happened."[12]

He believes his half-brother was held from 1950 to 1980 in a special section of Vladimir prison maintained for foreigners. The special section was then turned into a new wing of the prison hospital, and inmates kept there were sent to other locations.

His historic meeting with the Soviets "made me more convinced than ever that Raoul was alive after 1947," von Dardel said.

John Bierman, author of a book about Wallenberg, wrote a magazine piece about von Dardel's escapade in Moscow. "After their talks with foreign ministry and state security officials last week, the Wallenberg mystery remained . . ."[13]

In his magazine article, Bierman asks rhetorically why the Soviets invited the Wallenberg family to Moscow when they had no new evidence to give them? A report by an Amnesty International delegation the prior week said, "The human rights picture in the U.S.S.R. is deeply confusing."

Gerasimov, the Russian spokesman, insisted Wallenberg's death in 1947 was "an irrefutable fact." Gromyko was dead, but the Russians resolutely stuck to the Gromyko letter.

Hardly true, said many people. Andrei Sakharov, a leading Soviet human rights advocate, wrote in a 1989 article in the English-language weekly Moscow News, "The file of a foreign diplomat which could some day become crucial for the reputation of this country could not possibly be destroyed."[14]

Elie Wiesel, who won the Nobel Peace Prize in 1986 for his work as a human rights activist and chronicler of the Holocaust, has frequently spoken out on Wallenberg's behalf. He, too, doubts the Russian claims about what happened to Wallenberg. Wiesel felt, "There must be people who dealt with him in all kinds of ministries, in jails, in Siberia. They should bring them forward. Let's interview them. The man deserves to be remembered."[15]

Perhaps responding to pressure, in August 1990, the Soviets agreed for the first time to open prisons and archives to an international commission, called the Soviet-International Joint Commission on the Fate and Whereabouts of Raoul Wallenberg. Irwin Cotler, a Canadian lawyer long involved in Soviet human rights issues, was commission chairman and other members included two former political prisoners, Cronid Lubarsky, who ran a human rights information service in Munich, and Makinen, then chairman of the biochemistry and Molecular Biology department of the University of Chicago. Cotler, who was chairman of an earlier commission that operated with limited Soviet authority and closed in May 1990, said the new investigation followed an international commission that led to the official Soviet admission of the massacre of Polish soldiers in the Katyn forest in World War II.

Cotler added, "The Soviets have said they will not insist on their position that Raoul Wallenberg died in 1947, but will allow for an open-ended investigation. And they have promised to make all the evidence available. In our discussions, they acknowledged that their own previous inquiries had been superficial."[16]

The Soviet ministries cooperated with the commissioners, but unresolved inquiries and missing documents led to the KGB, which remained uncooperative. Cotler thought, "If there is a smoking gun, that's where it is." This commission filed a report that will be specified later.

A more permanent commission then arose, The Swedish-Russian Working Group on The Fate of Raoul Wallenberg. This commission is made up of the Ministries of State Security, Internal Affairs, Defense and Foreign Affairs of the Russian Federation and from the Swedish Ministry of Foreign Affairs. Von Dardel and Makinen, who relinquished the department chairmanship to become a professor of the Biochemistry and Molecular Biology department at the University of Chicago, are not formally affiliated with either government. Makinen serves as a permanent consultant. The permanent commission has a three-pronged goal:

1. If the commission finds Wallenberg, it wants to return him to Sweden.

2. If he has died, the commission wants his remains returned to Sweden.

3. The commission also wants to obtain all possible documentation about the reasons for his imprisonment and how he was incarcerated for the historical record.

Von Dardel and Makinen spent two weeks in Russia. For one week, Makinen went through the dusty archives at Vladimir Prison in a relentless search for hints of Raoul Wallenberg. The card catalogues at Vladimir contain the prisoner's name, his date of birth, official address, place of work, arrival date, his cell number and where the prisoner was placed. Also on the card was a chronology of the cells the prisoner occupied. Makinen checked the cards of the cell placement involving the prisoners who said they had heard about Wallenberg, and "There are very few errors. Ninety percent of the information is corroborated, which gives their stories some validity. That means such and such a prisoner was in such and such a prison at such and such a time."

At the conclusion of the two-week mission, the commission

made its biggest gain. Von Dardel and Makinen met with Vadim V. Bakatin, then the Soviet minister of foreign affairs, to thank him for his help on the fact-finding mission.

After the failed coup d'etat in August 1991, Gorbachev named Bakatin chief of the KGB, with a mandate to clean it up. When Makinen met Bakatin, he and his associates were impressed with his warmth and his tribute to von Dardel's efforts. "I understand what you are trying to do," Bakatin told them, for he had a similar problem. "I and my family would like to know where my grandfather is buried. We only know he was shot in 1930 in Tomsk."

To Makinen, that was "an amazing revelation." Circumstances may prevent Bakatin from opening all the files, "but his statement shows his qualities as a human being. And it makes me feel he's quite sincere in wanting to clear up this case."

A few weeks after Bakatin took over the KGB, he termed the Wallenberg case, "the most embarrassing matter against the Soviet government since World War II." He added that "It must be cleared up and all information released."

However, this became another misstep in the Wallenberg journey. Bakatin was ousted too soon, for, just like in the United States, a new regime fires the old appointees. Thus, when Boris N. Yeltsin rose politically and Gorbachev fell, Bakatin lost his job. Besides, the KGB disliked his recommendations.

During Bakatin's short tenure, though, the Russians released numerous documents, including some regarding Wallenberg. For instance, there were references in logbooks from Lubyanka to Wallenberg and Langfelder. These entries had been inked over and then restored following the coup when the KGB temporarily came under Bakatin's direction.

In the National Archives in Washington, the CIA documents have entries from Russian files showing transfers of Wallenberg and Langfelder in and out of the "internal prison," ostensibly for more interrogation. The final Wallenberg entry is on March 11, 1947, and for Langfelder on July 23, 1947. Experts said the entries were inked over most likely in 1947, supporting the Soviet contention that Wallenberg's case was covered up by Viktor S. Abakumov, the vicious and corrupt Stalinist who ran the Soviet wartime counterintelligence unit and then the Ministry of State Security, the predecessor of the KGB, until 1951. After Stalin's death, Abakumov was arrested and executed in 1954.

Other Russian entries recorded three interrogations of Wallenberg and five of Langfelder with the name of the interrogator and the time.[17] Daniel Grigorovich Kopalyansky was the most frequent interrogator of Wallenberg and a man Makinen interviewed five times.

Inside Room 359 of the Cummings Life Science Center at the University of Chicago campus on the city's south side, Makinen has positioned his plastic-enclosed molecular model to his right and the six gray metal cabinets of four drawers each, including two drawers with Wallenberg material, behind him. Makinen, a medium-sized man who wears glasses, is dressed in a red sweater and casual pants. He has lost most of his hair, but none of his zeal for the Wallenberg case, so he precisely tells a writer sitting across from him why Kopalyansky was the perfect choice to interrogate Wallenberg. An educated man, Kopalyansky worked in Smersh, interrogating German spies. "Kopalyansky spoke German and had a German nanny, but he was a Russian, trained as an architect," and Makinen paused, "he was Jewish."

Wallenberg, of course, spoke German well, had studied architecture at the University of Michigan and his links to Judaism were unbreakably tight.

"Kopalyansky's role was to be the nice guy in the good cop, bad cop routine. Maybe he was the one with the prisoner and talked with him, offered him some tea, bread and cheese," Makinen speculated.

Despite that role, "Kopalyansky was shifty, a trained interrogator. I went to his home, which is near the first McDonald's in Moscow," Makinen explained. "He said it was a mistake, that he never interrogated Wallenberg."

Makinen, the scientist, persisted with Kopalyansky, the

interrogator. Once when Makinen came to his home, only his wife
was there. She told Makinen her husband feared getting the blame
for Wallenberg's imprisonment and disappearance.

"Kopalyansky probably knows what happened to
Wallenberg, but if there is a person who has personal knowl-
edge about what happened to Wallenberg, he will not speak,"
Makinen explained.

Fear silences him and everyone else connected with the case.
After living in an oppressive society for so long, the Russians can
not mentally free themselves. "They want to cover their backsides,"
Makinen said.

Those involved in Wallenberg's incarceration don't want to
admit they took part, fearing they will become scapegoats. "These
people worked under conditions whereby they took an oath" that
insures obedience, Makinen said. Even when Makinen identified
himself as working on an official commission with the Russian
government, those involved will say nothing. The Russian commission members sent letters to these people, telling them they
can speak, but they still remain silent. Paranoia grows in the soil of
Mother Russia.

After five interviews, Kopalyansky reached the end of his tolerance for Makinen and his questions. In fact, during the last interview, the Russian became so anxious, he tried to hit von Dardel,
but Makinen intervened. That ended the inquiries. But the indefatigable Makinen continued his quest. When he was in Vladimir
prison in 1993, he reencountered Yelena Nikolayevna Butova, a
female physician, who oddly enough had treated Makinen while
he was a prisoner. After World War II, female doctors were common in the Soviet Union because so many men had died in the
conflict. When asked about Dr. Butova's talent, Makinen carefully
answered. "She did what was necessary to keep a person from dying. She supported the Soviet system," he said, but admitting,
"She may have saved me."

During his imprisonment, Makinen constantly suffered from
gastrointestinal problems. Sometimes the abdominal pain was so

bad, "I had to crouch to hold myself up." But Dr. Butova treated patients "when she had to."

Before Makinen left for labor camp in June 1963, the Soviets immunized him against smallpox, sterilizing the needles in boiling water. Later, Makinen, who went to medical school, learned this was insufficient. "You need a pressure cooker; otherwise, you can't achieve high enough temperatures to kill the germs."

Consequently, Makinen became jaundiced, but the Soviets insisted he leave, saying Dr. Butova permitted him to travel. They put him in the Russian equivalent of a paddy wagon and when Makinen arrived in Mordovia three and a half weeks later, he remained sick. In five to six months, the normal incubation period for hepatitis, Makinen developed that affliction, which eventually dissipated, but leaving Makinen with ill feelings about Dr. Butova.

When Makinen met Dr. Butova thirty years later, she was sick with congestive heart failure. Burdened with that illness, the heart works less efficiently as fluid builds in the lungs, and the patient can't sleep lying flat. One of the questions doctors ask is "How many pillows do you need to sleep?"

After Dr. Butova failed to remember Makinen, von Dardel told her she had treated him during his incarceration at Vladimir. Then von Dardel asked the elderly Russian doctor about Wallenberg and she replied, "I'd like to help you, but I have no information. We have no prisoner here by that name."

After that, Makinen pored over medical records for hours in a dusty closet in Vladimir. Just as he was ready to leave a woman named Polinina, the new chief physician at Vladimir, told him, "There's a person who's worked here since the 1940s."

The doctor introduced him to Varvara Ivanovna Larina, a pleasant woman in her 70s. Speaking to her in Russian, which he learned during his imprisonment, Makinen asked about her days working at Vladimir. After each question, Larina looked at Dr. Polinina, the chief physician, who indicated she could answer. Larina had worked in the Vladimir hospital since 1946 as a sanitary worker, cleaning cells, sterilizing equipment and distributing food to prisoners in their cells. When Makinen asked if Larina remembered any foreign prisoners, she immediately mentioned Powers, the U2 pilot, who attained celebrity status at Vladimir. Did she know of any other foreign prisoners kept alone in a cell? Though hazy about the times, Larina began to talk about one foreign prisoner. She thought it was in the 1940s-1950s, and he was in cell 49, isolation.

"I remember him," she told Makinen. "We weren't supposed to know the prisoners' names." Larina again looked at the prison doctor, who again indicated she could speak.

Larina said the foreign prisoner was opposite the cell of a woman who died. When Makinen checked, the name given didn't match the records, but it was possible Larina had become confused about that name. In any event, she described the foreign prisoner as thin, with a narrow face, balding, piercing eyes, narrow arms, hands and legs, which, of course, sounds like Wallenberg.

She remembered him because of his ceaseless complaints. If the food were cold, he called the guard, who got the doctor and then had to file a report, a daily annoyance. When feeding the prisoners, the staff took the heavy soup kettle and started serving on the first floor. That way the kettle was lighter, the soup colder and the foreign prisoner unhappier by the time the prison help reached the third floor. To avoid the complaints, the workers dragged the heavy kettle up to the third floor to let the prisoner in cell 49 have hot soup and Larina annoying memories of him.

This prisoner, whether he was Wallenberg or someone else, complained because he had given up hope and wanted to be remembered. "I went through that," Makinen explained. "At some point, you begin to feel that everything is lost, so you complain about everything."

Imagine living alone for 24 hours a day every day within an 8-foot by 12-foot cell. A bucket is your bathroom, and you dump that outside every morning, the only time you leave your cell, except for a weekly shower. For breakfast, you are given soup; for lunch, you get soup and mashed potatoes and for dinner a watery soup, mashed potatoes and a cabbage salad. Also, in the morning, you receive a 250-gram ration of harsh black bread, as big as a cup, which must last you throughout the day. If you're strong, you divide the bread into thirds and judiciously eat one-third for breakfast, one-third for lunch and one-third for dinner. But if you're human and starving, you devour the whole ration immediately. Then "You feel like you're an animal," Makinen said, the words choking in his mouth.

Makinen showed Larina pictures of several people, including Wallenberg, whom she identified as the complaining prisoner. When Makinen returned a year later in December 1994, Larina was still clear on the details about the complaining prisoner. He again brought several pictures, including Wallenberg's, for her to check. Larina immediately selected Wallenberg's picture in profile, which made sense to Makinen. A prisoner in complete isolation can only be viewed through the peephole. In the middle of the cell door is a trap door for food, which only opened from the outside. When Larina put the food in the trap door and looked through the peephole into the narrow cell, she would see the profile of the prisoner, who was either standing or sitting. To further help identification, Makinen used age progression pictures. Forensic artists can use the photo of a man in his youth and then age him, showing how he might look 50 years later. Larina identified Wallenberg at about age 40, but she couldn't identify his passport photo, which, of course, was taken during his younger, vibrant days. Instead, she recognized a somber picture, befitting a prisoner.

Another photographic technique is to use a picture of an aged parent to occupy half of a son or daughter's photo because the child looks like the parent as he ages. Since Wallenberg's father had died before he was born, Maj von Dardel's aged face occupied one half of a picture and the other half had her son's aged face. Larina identified this picture as that of the complaining prisoner.

In response to Makinen's inquiry, Larina said this prisoner was not German, but she knew by his accent that he was a foreigner. When asked to name him, she said, "Shinberg." To Makinen, "That's not necessarily a pointing finger." Vladimir housed a lot of German prisoners after World War II, and the name "Berg" was probably commonplace. Nevertheless, Larina's information helps—as do statements from Jan Loyda.

Loyda, a Sudeten German of military age who fought the Nazis and trained Russian soldiers, shared a cell with Wallenberg in 1945. Makinen traced Loyda's file, which strangely enough had the years 1943-1953 missing. His papers were sewn together at the binding. "The Soviets didn't have the type of society to invent the stapler," Makinen explained.

In the early 1990s, Makinen interviewed Loyda, who was in his 80s, but spry and alert, though guarded. He said Wallenberg had taught him some English, and he had taught his cellmate some Russian. Wallenberg also exercised every day in his cell and sang Swedish songs, which Loyda still heard on his radio. When Makinen walked into Loyda's home in Mittweida, Germany, which is about 200 kilometers southeast of Berlin, he was reading about the U.S. spy Alrich Ames in a German newspaper and said the cold warriors still employed the same methods. "A burnt child learns to avoid fire," Loyda said.

Loyda avoids fire and trouble. Anyone who sits with a foreign prisoner in a Soviet cell has a special assignment: informant. That meant links to and threats from the Russian authorities. Thus, Loyda is suspicious of everyone and will say little more about Wallenberg. The Russians even sent Loyda a letter, saying he could speak with Makinen about the Wallenberg affair, but he still refused to talk, Loyda—totally frightened—remained a victim of the Russian art of lifelong intimidation.

In 1994, Makinen traveled to Bonn to talk to another German, Theodor von Dufving, who was an aide to the commanding officer of Berlin. While in a Russian transit camp on his way to Vorkuta in February 1949, von Dufving noticed a commotion inside the mess hall. His fellow prisoners' excitement came from the appearance of a Swedish prisoner who was a diplomat, so Von Dufving pushed his way forward to talk to the Swede. He spoke in German, telling the diplomat the Russians wouldn't let him write home and, ironically, thought the Swede would get out before him. Von Dufving wanted the Swede to tell his wife in Wittenberg that he was alive. The clean-shaven diplomat had his own guard, wore civilian clothes and held a newspaper from which he read the news to the other prisoners. The diplomat told von Dufving in German, "I am here through a big error."

When Makinen isn't interviewing released prisoners, he spends his time at the commission meetings. The group meets for one to two days at a time usually in Moscow, but sometimes in Stockholm. All the meetings are formal affairs, done through translation, so everything is said twice—in Swedish and Russian. The groups meet all day, for eight hours, with a lunch break. The commission discusses information it has gathered and tells the Russians, hoping this will lead to more findings. "This is not done in an accusatory manner," Makinen said. "It's diplomatic." If the commission accused the Russians, they would "tell us to shut up." Politesse notwithstanding, the Russians usually say they know nothing about the new information.

In the early 1990s, "A few of the Russians wanted to crack the case. They would have been promoted." But the opportunity faded along with hopes of Russian liberalism. "Now it's as bad as the Brezhnev era," Makinen lamented.

With glasnost, everything in the Soviet Union opened, but Gorbachev couldn't contain the situation. The Russians wanted to improve the economy so they could survive, but they failed to understand the resulting groundswell, so they tightened everything, including access to the Wallenberg commission. "We have trouble getting documents," he complained. In every archive, there is someone who can control if anything is copied. When a foreigner goes to a building in Moscow, he must inform the director of security at least 24 hours in advance.

While the permanent Swedish-Russian commission keeps working, the earlier commission run by Canadian lawyer Irwin Cotler issued a stinging report in September 1990. First, the commission concluded Wallenberg lived long past 1947, and then the commission attacked the Soviets for their story about Wallenberg's "death" and their overall credibility in this affair.[18] The commission said Wallenberg lived into the 1950s and 1960s and probably into the 1970s and 1980s. Next, the commission rebuked the Soviets for lying about Wallenberg's whereabouts for 45 years while the multi-national group pledged to continue the investigation. "The evidence is incontrovertible that Raoul Wallenberg did not die in 1947 as the Soviets have claimed," the commission said.

Since the commission has evidence that Wallenberg was alive in the 1950s and 1960s and "credible evidence that he was alive in the 1970s and 1980s, the Commission has no other choice but to proceed on the assumption that he may still be alive unless there is evidence to the contrary."

During its fact finding, the commission discovered the Soviets failed to conduct an investigation on Wallenberg until 1990. That means the Soviets never examined prison archives, never talked to prison officials or witnesses. As Alexander Semyonov, chief of the Butyrka Prison, said, "Wallenberg was a nonperson for us until 1988—an unmentionable. We couldn't even talk about him before that, let alone investigate if he had been imprisoned here."

To the commission, this revelation was "particularly disturbing—and painful—as the Soviet Union continued to receive testimony from the Swedish government in the late 1940s and 1950s, based largely on witness testimony from imprisoned foreign nationals at Vladimir Prison who had left the Soviet Union, that Raoul Wallenberg was alive in the 1950s." But from 1945 to 1957, the Soviets said they knew nothing about Wallenberg.

When the Soviets issued the Gromyko Memorandum in 1957 saying Wallenberg had been in the Soviet Union but died of a heart attack in 1947, that, too, was not based on any investigation. "The Commission's finding not only discredits the Gromyko Memorandum and the Soviet position that Wallenberg died in 1947, but brings into question their moral standing to make any claim whatever."

Also, the commission learned, as was previously mentioned,

that "foreigners imprisoned at Vladimir—particularly those in the status of diplomats—were generally registered not under their own name but under a number or a false identity." This validated, said the commission, "legendary hearsay about 'The Man in the Iron Mask' in the Soviet Prison System. Tragically, most, if not all of these 'numbered prisoners' have disappeared into the dark spaces of Soviet history forever."

At Vladimir, the commission examined about 104,000 prison registration cards and chose 1,429 for more computer analysis and videotaping. Of these cards, about 30 were the "numbered" type and the commission found 10 of them. However, if Wallenberg's prison registration card is a numbered one, or registered under a false identity, the commission said, "it makes its discovery—and the discovery of his fate—well nigh impossible."

Under the prison system, all incarcerated foreigners as impor-tant as Wallenberg would usually have had personal, investigative and security-related dossiers attached to them and held by the KGB. Thus, as von Dardel said, it was no accident the KGB found some of his half-brother's items during the 1989 trip. For the commission, "the evidentiary trails converge with the KGB in Moscow, and that is where the 'smoking gun' is to be found."

In its report, the commission concluded [19] that Wallenberg lived after 1947; the Soviets have no evidence to support their position he died in 1947; the Soviets gave limited cooperation and the commission is "closer to the truth than ever before." However, the KGB has the evidence about Wallenberg but has not fully cooperated and the commission will "proceed on the assumption that (Wallenberg) may still be alive unless there is evidence to the contrary."

Makinen, who served on Cotler's commission and remains part of the existing body, had mixed feelings about both groups. He felt Cotler provided his own rendition of the commission's report, "but this is not the language in which it was given by the commis-sion." Makinen disagreed with Cotler on several points, but he agreed with all five of the conclusions except for use of the word "incontrovertible" to indicate Wallenberg did not die in 1947. "For me, there is no evidence about what happened."

As for the current commission, Makinen said, although the Russians have yielded some information, the "last couple of meetings have not been extremely productive." Makinen quickly added, "I'm giving you my personal feelings."

"This is such a case it should be laid bare," Makinen explained.

Makinen himself became a victim during his trips to Russia. At 6:30 p.m. on December 22, 1994, Makinen was leaving a Metro station in Moscow, and two men apparently followed the lone American. One assaulted him from the front, but Makinen forced the assailant to his knees. However, a confederate attacked Makinen from the rear while the first man put a knife to his throat and the university professor stopped resisting. The muggers, part of an almost lawless Russia, stole Makinen's money, but not his passport and cut him a few times in the face, but left no lasting scars.

"Since then, I've learned to become more vigilant. I'll take pepper spray and a stun gun, and I'll keep on going to Moscow," Makinen said.

Why does Makinen, teaching at one of the most prestigious universities in the nation, keep pursuing the Wallenberg matter?

His eyes filled with tears and his voice choking, Makinen told a visitor, "If you've been in those prison camps under those conditions, you want to help someone if you can."

But can Makinen or anyone help now? After all his effort, can Makinen answer The Question: Is Raoul Wallenberg still alive?

"There is a chance," Makinen said thoughtfully. "I say that in the sense that there is no real credible evidence that he has died."

Unless the commission can prove he has died, Wallenberg remains alive. Then Makinen declined to play cerebral detective. "On my own, I don't know how to evaluate that any further."

Perhaps Wallenberg is still alive. When the Soviets gave a prisoner a long sentence, they wanted to make sure he served it all. Maybe Wallenberg did know too much about something like Brezhnev and the diamonds. Maybe the Russians kept Wallenberg imprisoned—but always alive—because they too came under Wallenberg's intellectual power. Though imprisoned, Wallenberg still had a reputation. He faced down Eichmann; he saved 100,000 human beings; he survived the Soviet gulag. Such a courageous man deserves to live.

CHAPTER 19

While von Dardel and Makinen kept trying to locate Wallenberg via visits to Russia and working on the international commission, the CIA during the 1980s and 1990s kept expanding its Wallenberg file via reports from ex-prisoners, defectors and newspapers. Any observer reading the CIA file on Wallenberg feels twin irritations. First, the CIA maintains its aloofness toward Wallenberg, and then the agency exhibits fundamental ignorance about the case. While bashing the nation's main intelligence service often becomes an art form inside the Beltway, the CIA's many missteps make its own image stumble. If competence and accurate information are the American intelligence agencies' lifeblood, they need a transfusion.

For example, a July 18, 1988, memo to the "priority director" from someone whose name is blacked out said "a political colleague received a telephone call from Guy (von Dardel) who claims to be the half brother of Raoul (Wallenberg)."[1] Claims to be? Couldn't the agent rise from his chair and check Wallenberg's file, which mentions von Dardel numerous times? Perhaps ignorance is taxpayer money misspent.

Von Dardel said he had information he wanted sent through channels to Moscow, the memo said. Also, von Dardel "claimed to work at the European Laboratory for particle physics (CERN)."[2] Again, claimed? He did and that, too, was easy to check via the file. The memo said the colleague had "no additional info on von Dardel nor the type of info von Dardel wishes to relay to Moscow. Before looking further into this unusual case, [blacked out] requests . . . trace responses."

Cotler, the Canadian human rights activist, told the Toronto Globe and Mail in a March 8, 1988, article that he had evidence

Wallenberg was still alive and in prison near Myrna, which is located just off the main Moscow-Leningrad Highway.[3] But the CIA, in a March 16th memo from Montreal, could confirm neither the sighting nor the site. The U.S. intelligence agency said it knew nothing about Wallenberg being held in a prison facility in Myrna, and it couldn't locate Myrna in maps, atlases or gazetteers, but suggested that Myrna could be the name for a district or section of a city. A CIA memo dated October 27, 1992, contained this annoying passage, "We have also learned although we cannot confirm that Wallenberg was made an honorary U.S. citizen . . ."[4] That happened eleven years earlier in a widely-publicized ceremony at the White House.

More recently, one thinks of monumental CIA blunders like the fiasco involving the Soviet mole Aldrich Ames and the Guatemala scandal that encompassed charges the CIA intentionally covered up its ties to the murder of a Guatemala rebel leader married to an American woman, and the slaying of a U.S. innkeeper in Guatemala. Despite its incompetence and ignorance, the CIA in recent years still gathered more believable reports about Wallenberg sightings.

A Soviet witness, Janis Rozkalns, contended he had contact with a Soviet prisoner who said he met Wallenberg as late as 1979. Another partially blacked out memo to "Director" and dated December 29, 1987, discussed Rozkalns, who was arrested in Riga, Latvia, in April 1983 when the KGB searched his apartment and discovered bibles and religious writings.[5] The Soviets sentenced him to a penal camp with "strict discipline in Perm (Urals)," the memo said. "At that time he was about 35 and his wife Gunta had just given birth to Twins (13 January 1983)."

Thus, "the family's situation grew quite difficult, but during the legal proceedings Rozkalns stubbornly refused to name his associates or to agree to collaborate with the KGB," the memo continued. Rozkalns said that while imprisoned in the Perm camp, he met a Soviet prisoner who insisted that he had personally met Wallenberg in 1979 at another camp where the Soviet had been

interned before Perm. This prisoner contended that Wallenberg
had originally been arrested because the Soviet troops wanted his
beautiful car. Wallenberg refused and was then arrested. A Latvian
emigrant and his wife gave Rozkalns a photograph of Wallenberg
to show his prisonmate. This prisoner was sure that the man in the
picture and the person he met were the same, and he clung to his
story of meeting Wallenberg.

This Soviet prisoner said in 1984 he met another prisoner
who knew where Wallenberg was that year. Rozkalns described
the Soviet prisoner as "absolutely trustworthy." He refused to give
the other prisoner's name because he was either still in prison or in
the Soviet Union. After four years, the KGB released Rozkalns,
who resumed his previous activity. He campaigned for religious
freedom, human rights and similar issues. The American
government verified that the information Rozkalns gave was
accurate.

"He is a trusting man who campaigns for Christian morality
and values and who practices what he preaches," the memo said.
"The KGB did not take kindly to his activities and expelled him
from Latvia on October 16, 1987, to Vienna as a member of the
'Jewish Quota.'" To the U.S. government operatives, Rozkalns has
"never shown any lack of credibility. On the contrary, he has been
very careful in his statements and has always tried to double check
his facts."

When a POW/MIA (Prisoner of WAR/Missing in Action) team
went to Moscow in 1992, it met with a former Soviet political
prisoner, Valentina Grigor Pavlenko, who contended she had met
Wallenberg in a Soviet labor camp from April to June 1947.[6]
Furthermore, the ex-prisoner said Wallenberg and a "suspiciously
well dressed stranger" escaped from the camp in July 1947, the
American Embassy in Moscow reported to the Secretaries of
Defense, State, et al on July 13, 1992. After that, the prisoner
never saw Wallenberg again. The American Embassy gave this
information to the Swedish diplomats in Moscow, explaining that
the POW/MIA team interviewed Pavlenko. She had contacted the

team following recent publicity in the Russian press about the POW/MIA issue.

As a young girl living in Archangel, she visited the Seamen's Club and met many Americans from 1941-45. "In 1944, she became pregnant as a result of a relationship with an American seaman," the embassy said in its telex. She had a daughter in February 1945, but when the war ended she was sent to the gulag in 1946 as an American spy. Her crime, under Article 58, Part 2 of the Soviet Criminal Code, was espionage because of her obvious intimate relations with Americans.

The Soviets sent Pavlenko's daughter to an orphanage where she stayed until her mother could reclaim her after serving a six-year prison term. Pavlenko went to a camp in the Pechora area, called the Northern Pechora Railway Station Kozya. "In camp, she was known as 'The American' because of her background and because she could speak rudimentary English. There were many foreign prisoners at the camp, including Swedes, Finns, Englishmen and two Americans," but she never met the latter. Both male and female prisoners lived at the camp with most working at a brick factory, but the sexes were segregated, kept in different parts of the camp, divided by barbed wire fences. The hospital, though, treated male and female prisoners and that was where she said she met Wallenberg.

After Sweden made inquiries about him, Wallenberg was transferred to this prison, Pavlenko thought, "to erase traces of his existence. He was put in the dispensary as soon as he arrived at the camp because he was so ill with pellagra," Pavlenko said. She, in turn, went to the dispensary suffering from nausea and the inability to eat after a long time in solitary confinement, where she ate only bread and water. "It was there in 1947 that she met another prisoner who introduced himself as a Swedish diplomat named Raoul Wallenberg," the American embassy's telex said. "They soon were on a first name basis, with him calling her 'American' and she calling him Raoul. Because she spoke rudimentary English, and because his Russian was so bad, they communicated in English."

This odd couple only discussed the prosaic because of the language barrier. When Wallenberg met her, he supposedly said, "You're so young to be an American spy! What did you spy on?" While they were both imprisoned, Wallenberg told her he had come to the camp from Lubyanka after the Soviets released him from the hospital. During April through June 1947, Pavlenko and Wallenberg worked together at the brick factory.

"Toward the end of Wallenberg's stay in the camp, a suspiciously well-dressed Russian arrived in the camp and spent all his time with Wallenberg," the embassy telex reported. "This new prisoner apparently spoke fluent German and conversed with Wallenberg in that language. Sometime in July this stranger and Wallenberg escaped from the camp." Pavlenko said the escape created a hubbub and an ensuing search for three days. "Since neither Wallenberg nor his companion returned to the camp, the prisoners assumed the escape attempt might have been successful."

During 1951, Pavlenko was enrolled in drama school in the camp when the Soviets ordered that everyone in the camp had to work on construction. She tried to escape, but the Soviets captured and then beat her. Her jailers finally released Pavlenko in July 1952.

Wallenberg's name meant nothing to Pavlenko and it wasn't until 1991 when she saw a story about him in the newspaper Moskovskiye Novosti that she realized his identity. Sometime in 1991, Pavlenko said she visited the Swedish embassy in Moscow with a letter recounting her experiences and her meeting with Wallenberg. The embassy rebuffed her, but she gave the letter to a militiaman in front of the embassy to give to a Swedish official. Ten days later the newspaper Rabochoye Pravo printed her letter, accompanied by a detailed article about Wallenberg.

The newspaper concluded Pavlenko was a fraud because she had never been in camp in the 1940s. Instead, the newspaper said she had been in jail in the 1970s for embezzlement. To counteract that, Pavlenko provided the Americans with photo copies of her prison documents, which verified the dates and reason for her imprisonment. Also, Pavlenko said the camp where she and Wallenberg had been imprisoned was destroyed long ago. That was, in her opinion, "to eradicate traces of Wallenberg."

She doubted reports in the news media that prisoners had seen Wallenberg in Siberian camps. "She believes this was also part of a deception operation," the American embassy reported.

Technically, Pavlenko's story and the official Soviet version could match. Say Wallenberg did escape, the Soviets recaptured him, returned him to Lubyanka and liquidated him July 17, 1947.

Another, happier answer came from von Dardel. While on a trip to Moscow, he said, "Hypothetically, (Wallenberg) could have married a beautiful woman and may not even want to return to his former life," Izvestia reported on April 6, 1993.[7]

At the same time, the European press kept speculating about Wallenberg and occasionally reports again surfaced saying he was an American spy. In 1990, a former Hungarian official said Wallenberg had worked for both U.S. and German intelligence during World War II. The former aide, Laszlo Hertelendy, said in an interview on Radio Budapest that U.S. intelligence had enlisted Wallenberg to give information about the Germans. Furthermore, Hertelendy contended Wallenberg had given the Germans information on his American intelligence contacts. For this, the Nazis had not interfered with the diplomat's efforts to rescue Jews, according to Hertelendy. He said he knew nothing about what happened to Wallenberg after his arrest.

A spate of similar stories during 1990 in both the Western and Soviet press dictated another search through the CIA files about the Swedish diplomat's intelligence links to the United States, and that yielded two memos from William M. Henhoeffer, curator of the Historical Intelligence Collection. In the first memo, dated January 9, 1990, to the Chief of the European Division, directorate of operations, Henhoeffer mused about what approach to take with the Russians regarding Wallenberg. The memo went to the Chief of European Division, directorate of operations, and Henhoeffer confirmed to his less active colleagues Olsen's troika of operations.[8] "Strange as it may seem to our generation of intelligence officers, the documents affirm Olsen's belief that he was working simultaneously for *three* US government agencies—OSS, Treasury, and the War Refugee Board—while posted to Stockholm and in contact with Wallenberg . . ."

The press speculation about Wallenberg's alleged spy activities prompted Henhoeffer to list two options for the U.S. government—stonewall or tell a little.

1. "Say nothing; if pressed we can always claim we have released what we essentially know; to say more now might embarrass Wallenberg supporters and the Wallenberg family by suggesting, despite what Olsen said in 1955, that Wallenberg performed some intelligence-related assignments."

2. "Initiate a private official conversation with the Soviets; tell them we understand they have been doing their best to solve the Wallenberg mystery, but we want them to be certain of what we know about Wallenberg's connections with Iver Olsen so that they can pursue the 'Pattersson' ('Pettersson') lead." A recent story in Moscow News said that Wallenberg, under the name "Pattersson" or "Pettersson," was alive for at least four years after the Soviets said he had died.

Henhoeffer said the second approach would necessitate updating a 1979 State Department "non-paper" where the U.S. government told the Soviets that Wallenberg's money was American, "but omitted mention of Olsen and OSS. We would also be preempting criticism from US journalists—or Congressmen—that we were not doing our best to solve the mystery but were still trying to hide something."

Finally, Henhoeffer recommended wrapping the agency in a cloak of silence about Wallenberg. "Colleagues with whom I discussed this matter expressed doubts that anything worthwhile would be gained for the USG by pursuing the second option. As a historian I can see several gains, not the least of which would be finding out how the Soviets came to be suspicious of Wallenberg. As an intelligence officer, I share most of my colleagues' doubts."

Still, Henhoeffer thought the Soviets "might be more inclined to cooperate" with the American government "on other matters if they perceived we had shown *glasnost* on the Wallenberg case."

The second memo, filed February 21, 1990, to the head of the Central Intelligence Agency repeated the contents of the Olsen interview from 35 years earlier, emphasizing that Olsen insisted that Wallenberg only dealt with him in his War Refugee Board capacity.[9] "In 1979, the State Department told the Soviets that Wallenberg's humanitarian activities were funded by the U.S., but did not tell them about the fact that Wallenberg's contact—Olsen—worked for the OSS." Therefore, Henhoeffer concluded, "there are some loose ends to this story. In the coming months or years, there may be some criticism of (the) CIA because the OSS connection, though indirect, undoubtedly provided a pretext for the Soviet imprisonment of this heroic international figure." After admitting the CIA's culpability, Henhoeffer then finds salvation for the agency. "On the other hand, it should be deeply satisfying to every American intelligence officer that not only American funds but, at least indirectly, American intelligence expertise helped to save some Jews from the Holocaust."

An article in Studies in Intelligence, released in 1981 and dealing with Wallenberg's ties to Olsen, contained some key passages that were classified, deleted and not restored until 1993 when the CIA released the classified version, though some parts were still blacked out, like the author's name.[10] Nonetheless, the article said the State Department "failed to reveal, however, that Wallenberg's contact man at the US legation in Stockholm, Iver C. Olsen, was a member of the Office of Strategic Services (OSS), the parent organization of the Central Intelligence Agency." The article also declassified the portion saying Iver Olsen also was the War Refugee Board representative in Stockholm.

A third section, now declassified, said, "Although those of the Board's records dealing with Wallenberg fail to reveal any connection with any intelligence organization a still classified list of OSS employees identifies Iver C. Olsen . . . as a member of the Special

Intelligence Branch . . . If Olsen's identity was known to Soviet intelligence [blacked out portion] it is possible that Wallenberg's contacts with American intelligence may have aroused Soviet suspicion."

As the Soviet Union shattered into pieces, the CIA in 1992 read more clippings, these telling how the Soviets released documents from KGB archives detailing the names and circumstances involving the Wallenberg case. However, the documents failed to change the Russians' original explanation or provide any new information about what happened to Wallenberg, the CIA said in a memo dated October 27, 1992, the same memo that couldn't confirm Wallenberg's honorary citizenship. The Russians still insisted Wallenberg died of a heart attack in 1947.

Other press stories mentioned in the same memo said five Polish prisoners incarcerated with Wallenberg in Soviet labor camps came forward to say Wallenberg was alive three years after his supposed death at Lubyanka. These survivors were afraid to speak out about the experiences in the gulag, fearing Communist reprisals, but decided to come forward after the Soviet Union collapsed. Josef Kowalski told Reuters on April 28, 1992, he last saw Wallenberg in September 1950 at the port of Bukhta Vanina. "I traveled with Wallenberg for two weeks in the same wagon of a freight train.[11] He was taken away after we arrived in Bukhta Vanina and I never saw him again," said Kowalski in an interview with the news agency from his home in Karpacz in southern Poland. According to Kowalski, he initially met Wallenberg on Christmas Eve of 1949, or two years after the Soviets said he died. The Polish prisoners had arranged a party at the Bratsk labor camp on the Angara river, which was in south-central Siberia near the Mongolian border.

Boguslaw Baj, another ex-inmate from Bratsk, said an emaciated Wallenberg came to the camp in August or September 1947, right from Lubyanka, and told Baj he had been sentenced to 25 years for spying. Baj, now dead, was the most educated of the five

Poles. He spoke German and described the person kept in the Russian colony of the prison camp as Raoul Wallenberg. Seeing Wallenberg's feeble condition, Baj asked to have Wallenberg transferred to his compound, but the Russians refused. A third inmate, Jerzy Cichocki, who worked with Baj in the camp kitchen, said Wallenberg survived Bratsk because of aid from Poles who pilfered food for him after he supplied them with information about a Polish underground leader whom the Soviets had arrested. These three plus two other Polish prisoners, Alfred Frees and a man named Markushevsky, all independently told about Wallenberg and picked out his picture.

Now European interests wanted to know more about Wallenberg. Frans Andriessen, the European Community's external affairs commissioner, told Russian foreign minister Andrei Kozyrev, who visited Brussels in March 1992, that the EC wanted the Wallenberg case cleared up now that the Russians had evicted the Communists from power.[12]

Six months later Simone Lucki, the president of the Belgian Committee for Raoul Wallenberg, met with the American Embassy in Brussels, seeking President George Bush's support for Wallenberg's Nobel Peace Prize candidacy.[13] Lucki said Wallenberg had been nominated in absentia to recognize the Swedish diplomat for his "valiant efforts on behalf of Hungarian Jews and to force Russia to tell the truth concerning his incarceration and alleged death in 1947." Nothing ever came of this effort.

An October 16, 1992, CIA memo, heavily blacked out, said some man, who is not identified, had an old photo, which had been enlarged, and allegedly depicted a "scene in a Soviet concentration camp purporting to show Wallenberg.[14] He had found the photo inconclusive. He had also asked his KGB liaison last year for an information, a fruitless exercise."

The Raoul Wallenberg Committee of the United States used a few different pictorial techniques, which will be discussed shortly, to try to identify the Swedish diplomat.

Besides newspapers, the CIA also turned to defectors for

information. A counterintelligence report on September 14, 1993, specified the comments of a KGB officer, who had fled to the West, but whose name was (of course) blacked out. The defector told his CIA bosses, "according to KGB policy, archives can be destroyed under certain circumstances."[15] For instance, when a KGB agent dies, the agency could destroy his personnel file. Once destroyed, there were no traces of the file's contents in the KGB archives. "Even a record of the act of destruction is only kept for a few years," the CIA memo explained. "Therefore, it is understandable that documents about past dissidents or men like Raoul WALLENBERG [sic] cannot be found in the KGB archives."

To further compound any search, the KGB often can't find the files of those executed, the defector told the CIA. "The KGB has no real reason to conceal archival material on the fate of Raoul WALLENBERG since his death in Stalinist jails is openly admitted." Then the defector discussed the KGB's stupidity. "The Soviets did not have Western-style archives in the 1930s and many officers in the NKVD were not literate so records were primitive and incomplete. In some cases, 'records' were only one torn piece of paper with the words (date), executed XXX number of people." Within the KGB's second chief directorate (internal security and counterintelligence), it was common knowledge by late 1989 that "the Swedish diplomat, Raoul WALLENBERG, was shot after three or four years of captivity" in Lubyanka prison in 1948 or 1949, according to the defector.

"Several years ago a KGB representative met with a relative of WALLENBERG to inform the family that the diplomat had died in a camp in 1948 or 1949. In the KGB mindset, however, WALLENBERG was too famous a figure to put in a prison camp where he might have been recognized and his treatment later reported to the world. Therefore, the rumor that WALLENBERG was seen in a prison camp in the 1950s and 1960s was untrue," the CIA reported after talking to the KGB defector. The NKVD kidnapped Wallenberg in 1945 and accused him of being an agent for Western intelligence. "WALLENBERG was taken directly to

(Lubyanka) where he was interrogated for several years and then shot," the CIA reported via the defector.

Dropping from the narrative to the subjective, the CIA permitted the defector to give an opinion. [Source Comment: WALLENBERG's death was typical for this cruel period in Soviet history.]

Like the CIA, the KGB had little interest in Wallenberg's file. As of late 1989, the defector reported, no one in "Department 2" was holding Wallenberg's file. If it existed, the file was probably in the Central KGB Archives in the city of Tomsk, where many of the files from 1917 to the late 1940s were sent. The archival building in Tomsk was located on a hill in the center of the city, and the brick was a "rosemary [sic] color, in the late nineteenth century tradition," the defector reported. A combination of brick walls and fences surrounded the building, which had bars on the windows.

As the entire Soviet Union changed, the CIA established more linkage with the KGB, which led to discussions with Svyacheslav Nikonov, a grandson of former Soviet foreign minister Vyacheslav M. Molotov.[16] A CIA agent, whose name was also blacked out, had several discussions with Nikonov. A November 20, 1991, CIA memo, probably from Moscow, to the information director said Nikonov was "regarded as extremely intelligent and capable but gave the impression he was an ideological hardliner . . . He was likely to be a rising star in the Soviet system."

Nikonov worked at the KGB because he was a close friend of Bakatin. During the August 1991 coup attempt, Nikonov said he refused to follow his leader's orders to act in accord with the declared state of emergency. For that, he was dismissed and called Bakatin for advice. The latter told him he also was opposing the coup and would watch out for Nikonov once order was restored. After the coup failed, Bakatin called Nikonov to ask if he would help restructuring the KGB. He agreed and joined the agency as Bakatin's deputy, but in a civilian, not military, capacity.

The CIA then throws out this tantalizing tidbit. "Nikonov

personally reviewed KGB files to determine if Lee Harvey (Oswald) had been a KGB agent.[17] He viewed the five thick volumes of files on Oswald. Nikonov is now confident that Oswald was at no time an agent controlled by the KGB. From the description of Oswald in the files he doubted anyone could control Oswald, but noted that the KBG [sic] watched him closely and constantly while he was in the USSR." Furthermore, Nikonov said the file showed Oswald had a "stormy relationship with his Soviet wife, who rode him incessantly. The file also reflected that Oswald was a poor shot when he tried target firing in the USSR."[18]

After reporting those comments about President John F. Kennedy's assassin from Nikonov, the CIA said the KGB deputy then checked on Wallenberg's fate. "Nikonov was amazed to find out that the KGB had not been able to previously establish whether Wallenberg had died and under what circumstances." Nikonov could find partial evidence from 14 sources.

"Nikonov now believes, but found no conclusive proof, that Wallenberg was executed in late 1947." The files indicate the Soviets suspected Wallenberg of having contacts with others who were accused of providing false diplomatic identity documents to others beyond Jews saved from the Holocaust. "Among these were Nazi criminals who were allowed to escape. There was no proof of Wallenberg's guilt in any of these charges," Nikonov told the CIA.[19]

CHAPTER 20

Inside the office of the Raoul Wallenberg Committee of the United States, one image jumps out at the visitor: A bronze bust of Wallenberg crowned with a Michigan hat. This makes Wallenberg— a Michigan graduate—a vital, living human being, instead of an historical hero, said Diane Blake, a vice president of the organization, based in midtown Manhattan.

Blake adamantly believes Wallenberg lives. "If I didn't believe there was a chance he was alive, I wouldn't be here."

Others disagree, creating a divisive issue for this and other Wallenberg Committees around the world. Is Wallenberg still alive? If so, one faction says, the U.S. committee and every Wallenberg committee should funnel its funds into research to try to save him from imprisonment. If he is dead, another faction says, let's spend the money on statues, something to honor his memory.

That necessitates a Solonic-like solution on funding. "We split our money into two areas—direct help for Wallenberg and an educational program that's in the public school system now in New York, the study of the hero," Blake said. "There isn't much you can do sitting in New York City other than fund raising, which is mundane, but crucial." Without funding, "nothing is going to happen." About 70 percent of the U.S. committee's funding comes from Jewish organizations and a big part of that is from Swedes. "Our basic membership is Jewish, and they're the ones who want the money to go to help Wallenberg."

Therefore, the U.S. committee funds Makinen's trips to work on the international commission, something he couldn't afford himself. The commission, which began after the von Dardels were invited to Russia in 1989, meets constantly, but Makinen can only go periodically due to his other obligations. Since he is the only U.S. citizen on the panel, "They call him 'Marvin the American,'" Blake related.

While researching in Russia, the commission found the cremation papers for Wallenberg, the printed log for Lubyanka prison and the daily diary that was kept by the head of the prison. "On the day Raoul supposedly died in his sleep in that prison, there are notations such as 'This prisoner wouldn't eat his lunch.' Nothing about this healthy young man who just died," Blake said.

In any event, "Nobody can convince us he died before the early '80s." If alive, Wallenberg could be in bad condition, but Blake believes the Russians know what happened to Wallenberg. "I don't believe they can't find out. I certainly believe there is a handful of people at least that know the truth."

But, a visitor asked, if Wallenberg died under Gorbachev's rule, why wouldn't the Russians want to release the information? "They would make glasnost explode," Blake replied

Like many others, Blake has concluded if the United States had made Wallenberg "any kind of priority, we could get him out, one way or another. All through these years there have been so many deals made. Other people have come out. I think until the last 10 years there was not much public pressure put on the government of the United States simply because people never heard of this person."

For a while, the U.S. Wallenberg Committee tried getting information from the federal government. "What we request under the Freedom of Information Act comes out all scratched out and blackened continuously," Blake complained. "You can't make sense of it. We had a few pages that came back; there were three words on them." So, the committee abandoned that effort. "We don't even ask anymore because it's a waste of time," Blake said.

Instead, the U.S. Wallenberg Committee tried to use the techniques popularized on milk cartons. For years, the pictures of missing children have appeared on the sides of these cartons. Though not a child, Raoul Wallenberg has been missing for more than 50 years, so why not try this method?

The committee asked the National Center for Missing & Exploited Children in Arlington, Virginia, to provide a comparison between a 1944 standard photo of Wallenberg with a 1955 Russian prison photo that supposedly shows Wallenberg as part of a group of prisoners in the Soviet Union. This newer photo shows three rows of a total of twenty-eight men, apparently a band and chorus. All are dressed in uniforms with white shirts, a ribbon-like decoration down the front and matching dark slacks.[1] Five of the men in the front row, all sitting, hold musical instruments—two clarinets, an accordion, a guitar and a violin—while a suited man with a tie, apparently the leader, sits in the middle of the first row. Over his right shoulder, in the middle of the second row, stands the man thought to be Wallenberg.

His hair is almost gone, his arms are behind his back, and his clean-cut features stand out among the Slavic tones of his companions. His gaze, serene, falls upon something to the right of the camera while most of his comrades look straight ahead. When comparing Wallenberg's standard photo, showing him at age 31 in the prime of life, one could conclude this was an aging version of the same man. While exercising the necessary precautions, Horace J. Heafner, an age progression specialist at the National Center for Missing Children, said in a letter dated May 10, 1994, he found some correlations between the two pictures.[2]

The Wallenberg photo taken when he was 31 years old reflected a "sizeable loss of hair for that age. The prison photograph also shows a similar shape in the cranium and the hair loss appears consistent with the period of aging for this individual," said Heafner. Also, the ears matched in both pictures, but the expert saw some discrepancy in the brow line. The first picture showed heavy brows that were straight and hanging over deep-set eyes while the prison photograph showed, indistinctly, a curved ridge. Changes due to aging were possible, "but the lack of clarity leaves in question the two faces' similarity," Heafner said. He found dissimilarities in the mouth and chin, but the jaw and neck were consistent in both pictures. In conclusion, Heafner remained dubious about a perfect photographic match.

"As you can see, I feel there are some crucial areas that could leave the observer in doubt as to the comparison and identity of the person in the prison photograph and Wallenberg's face," the expert explained, ending with the ultimate hedge. "It is possible that the subject could be Wallenberg, but it is at the same time also possible that it is not him."[3]

Using another technique, the Federal Bureau of Investigation aged Wallenberg photographically for the U.S. Wallenberg Committee, showing him as he might appear in his 80s. Makinen used the same method via a forensic artist to show a Russian prison worker a picture of an aged Wallenberg. With the FBI's aid, all of Wallenberg's hair is gone, his face lined and weathered and, as appropriate for a man who spent 50 years in the gulag, Wallenberg wears a sorrowful look.

Besides the photographic research and other work in the United States and Russia, research is continuing in Germany, where the files of the Stasi, or secret police, were recently opened. Blake said Helmut Kohl, former chancellor of Germany, had been "wonderful." He felt it would be the "most wonderful thing in the world if Germany could play a part in finding a living Wallenberg," she said. That would be a "blessing" for Germany. Gerhard Schröder defeated Kohl in 1998, and the new chancellor's feelings about the Wallenberg matter are unknown.

Besides rescue and education, the U.S. committee also tries to get Wallenberg a Nobel Peace Prize, an effort first begun by some prominent Swedish citizens in 1948. Then members of the Swedish Parliament, an author, a professor and former postmaster general, who were already nominating Wallenberg for the Nobel Prize, wrote to Harry Truman in a letter dated January 9, 1948, asking the President for his support.[4] In a reply dated January 21, 1948, the State Department acknowledged the letter, but said, "For your information, the President does not make recommendations for the Nobel Peace Prize."[5]

After the Wallenberg Committee tried to nominate Wallenberg, the Nobel Committee, which does not discuss its selections, told the committee it had no address for Wallenberg and couldn't send him the check for the money. "We don't want the money," countered Blake, so the U.S. committee received permission from the legal guardian to forfeit any money tied to the prize.

Next, the committee persuaded former Nobel winners to write letters on Wallenberg's behalf, which prompted a response that the prize only goes to living people. "We sent a harsh letter, saying, according to our government and Sweden, this man is alive," said Blake, her ire rising. "How dare they make a decision like that. Do they know something no one else knows?"

Wallenberg will probably never win a Nobel Prize. Thus, others want to honor him in different ways. Many people on the Wallenberg committees are certain Wallenberg has died, and they must look to the future. "How could he still be alive?" they ask. "You are wasting your money," says the opposite side. "Do something to honor his name," like erecting statues.

Blake would rather "see the money go into Marvin (Makinen) and Guy (von Dardel's) hands while there is a chance (Wallenberg is) still alive. I hate statues." Statues would be "nice . . . if I knew for sure that Wallenberg was no longer alive."

In Hungary, two statues exist—the first next to a pharmaceutical factory in Debrecen and the second in a park in Budapest. How they got there is an interesting tale.

Nicolas M. Salgo, a former American Ambassador, commissioned Hungarian sculptor Imre Varga to design a statue of Wallenberg, which was erected in 1987 and stands in a grassy park in Buda. Salgo, a Jew who fled Hungary before the Nazi takeover, paid for the monument as a private citizen. He returned to the United States in November 1986.[6] By coincidence, the statue was put at a spot related to Wallenberg's last days in Budapest. At that site, Wallenberg's Studebaker was found abandoned in February 1945 shortly after he left for Debrecen.

In an interview with the New York Times, Varga said the statue had twin purposes. First, this was a tribute to Wallenberg. "He did his best with an audacity rare at the time. He showed the way of honesty, the way of real heroes. There were very few at that time."

Second, the monument provided personal satisfaction. "My professor, later my friend, Pal Patzay, made the first Wallenberg monument," Varga explained. "I made the next one."

After money was collected in 1948, Patzay crafted a sculpture that showed a man dominating a snake. The statue was raised in a square in central Budapest, but the monument disappeared overnight even before it could be dedicated, for the Communists had by then taken over Hungary. Within a few years, the statue appeared in front of a pharmaceutical factory in Debrecen. The Times thought the man-snake symbolism at the new site was supposed to represent Asclepius, the Greek god of medicine.

Varga, in tribute to his late mentor, etched into the granite slabs beside the bronze sculpture of Wallenberg a gold-lined drawing of Patzay's statue. To provide unmistakable meaning, Varga carved swastikas into the snake's body. The sculpture itself shows Wallenberg with his left hand in his raincoat pocket and the right gesturing ahead as he walks toward an opening in a wall created by the two slabs. The Latin inscription says when the weather is good, you have many friends, but when skies get cloudy, you will be alone. Varga also designed a metal weeping willow tree sculpture near the Budapest Synagogue with a leaf naming every Hungarian victim of the Holocaust.

Besides statues, people associated with Wallenberg committees want to educate the public about him. To these people, the search for truth is important, but they would rather put their money toward educating the young about the future. When someone asks a child of the 1990s who is a hero, "They'll say Michael Jordan," Blake explained. The Wallenberg program tries to teach children about heroes other than basketball superstars and to find the hero within the individual.

This program is targeted for schools nationwide as well as community and interfaith programs. It will be "generic, adaptable to environments as varied as inner city schools and small rural communities," the U.S. Wallenberg Committee said. The Hero's kit will contain videos, a curriculum guide and a range for suggested programs that encourage "interaction between students, teachers, parents and community."

Since Wallenberg risked his life "for a people not his own, the Heroes Curriculum will lend itself to diffusing religious and racial differences," the U.S. Wallenberg Committee said. To this group, "Wallenberg's heroism offers a striking example for today's children," who can learn one is not born a hero, but becomes one in response to "challenging situations." The committee first tested the curriculum in New York City Public Schools as well as in the Oak Hill School District in High Point, North Carolina, and wants to expand it around the country. At the end of 1995, the curriculum was in use in about 100 schools in New York, Pennsylvania, Massachusetts and North Carolina.

CHAPTER 21

Eleven steps diagonally across from the bust of Lajos Kossuth, a 19th Century Hungarian freedom fighter, stands the bust of the 20th Century freedom fighter for Hungary, Raoul Wallenberg. After the November 2, 1995, dedication ceremony, the Wallenberg bust was taken to the level below the Rotunda and placed there on the sandstone masonry floor.[1] Like Kossuth, Wallenberg's brief reign ended with a Russian invasion. Kossuth battled Austria; Wallenberg fought Germany. Both men defeated the first adversary but lost to the second. Kossuth fled into exile and died in Turin, Italy, in 1894 at the age of 91. However, a cloak of mystery encircled the fate of Wallenberg.

The Lantoses, believing Wallenberg is probably dead, have just about abandoned hope of freeing him from the gulag. Instead, "We are involved in trying to keep his story alive," Annette Lantos said. That meant establishing the bust in the Capitol, which Mrs. Lantos thinks "will become the site of a pilgrimage."

Fittingly, an Israeli artist, Miri Margolin, created this bronze bust, which is 20 inches high, 17 inches broad and 11 inches deep and sits atop a four and a half-foot-high granite pedestal donated by the Swedish government. One of Margolin's nephews, Benjamin Netanyahu, was elected Israel's prime minister in 1996, narrowly winning the leadership for his right-wing Likud party. Three years later Benjamin Netanyahu was voted out of office. The articulate, good-looking Israeli first became familiar to American television audiences when he served as delegate to the United Nations and became a frequent guest on talk shows. During the Persian Gulf War, every international network eagerly sought sound bites from Netanyahu, then deputy foreign minister and Israel's spokesman. One of Benjamin's brothers and another of the artist's nephews, Yonatan Netanyahu, died while leading an Israeli rescue unit during the daring raid at Uganda's Entebbe Airport in 1976 that freed 91 passengers and 12 crew members of a hijacked Air France plane. Yonatan's death transformed him into an Israeli legend.

Margolin, the Israeli sculptress, and Lillian Hoffman, an octogenarian widow of a Denver liquor store king, combined art and commerce to bring the Wallenberg bust to the Capitol. After her nephew died during the Entebbe raid, Margolin became interested in sculpture as an art form. "That's what got me started," said Margolin, a short, gray-haired woman who wears her hair softly coiffed. "My first bust was of Yonnie in 1976," she added, the memory evoking fresh sadness nineteen years after his death.

Netanyahu's bust remains in Margolin's house in Givat Savyon, a small town near Tel Aviv, but other busts of famous Israeli leaders are scattered all over the country. The one of David Ben-Gurion is at his gravesite in the Negev while the busts of Shimon Peres and Yitzhak Shamir are in their homes in Israel.

In the mid-1980s, Margolin met Guy von Dardel at a memorial service in Israel for Wallenberg and told him, "I want to make a bust of Wallenberg."

Why? "Each Jew is interested in Wallenberg," Margolin explained. "Every Jew has heard the story of Wallenberg."

Nina Lagergren sent Margolin a picture of her half-brother, enabling Margolin to start working on the bust, a more difficult task than "having people standing next to you" as models, Margolin said. Nevertheless, she sent a sketch to von Dardel and Lagergren, who were impressed, and in 1987 the artist finished the Wallenberg bust, which had special meaning for her. "Wallenberg saved so many Jews," Margolin told a listener during a long distance telephone call to Israel months before the bust unveiling. "He was such a tremendous fellow, gave his life to save Jews. Jews still tell stories about Wallenberg, all the survivors."

Her task completed, Margolin had nowhere to place the bust, so it stayed in her home. Then enter Lillian Hoffman. For 38 years, her husband, Harry Hoffman, ran a Denver liquor store bearing his name. At one time, it was the biggest store of spirits in Denver and the preferred stop for Denverites. Harry Hoffman sold the business in 1988 and then died shortly thereafter, leaving his money and memories to his widow, Lillian. She had her own causes, like a 20-year involvement with the Colorado Committee of Concern for Soviet Jewry, where she serves as chairman. During her work there, she learned about Raoul Wallenberg's imprisonment, a cause that seized her interest.

"I like to keep up on his case. It's been a major thing in my life," related Hoffman, who doesn't believe Russia's story of Wallenberg's death in 1947 but doubts he is still alive.

As part of her work for Judaism, Hoffman—whose father came from Russia—went to the Soviet Union twice and Israel several times. On her trips to Israel, Hoffman met Margolin. "We talked about many things and discussed Wallenberg," Hoffman said. "It was like friends talking to each other." Hoffman told Margolin the Lantoses were interested in having something commemorating Wallenberg in the United States. Margolin told Hoffman about the Wallenberg bust, which Hoffman decided to buy—"I won't say [for] how much"—and send it to the Capitol.

Politics—Swedish, Russian and American—have condemned Wallenberg to imprisonment and probably death while simple ceremonies to honor him also tumbled before similar pressures. For instance, Congressman Lantos, a Democrat, had planned to unveil the Wallenberg bust January 17, 1995, on the 50th anniversary of his capture. However, the Republican electoral sweep in November 1994 created seismic changes throughout the nation. Now in charge of Congress for the first time in 40 years, the Republicans wanted to push their own agenda and forced postponement of the Wallenberg ceremony until November 2, 1995. Meanwhile, the pedestal arrived from Sweden and the bust from Israel, long before the November ceremony. Both were kept "in the basement of the Capitol, under lock and key," said John Zucker, a Congressional aide to Lantos.

After the ten-month delay, Newt Gingrich, then Speaker of the House, did permit the ceremony to take place in the Rotunda, a hallowed part of America. Presidents like Lincoln, Garfield, McKinley and Kennedy and Senator Hubert Humphrey have lain in state in the Rotunda to let people pay their final respects. The Rotunda, which links the wings of the House and Senate, is thought of as neutral territory, so during the ceremony for Wallenberg, harmony replaced political partisanship. Gingrich, a bitter foe of Democrats, spoke favorably about Democrat Lantos and eloquently about Wallenberg.

After praising the Lantoses' efforts on behalf of Wallenberg, Gingrich said, "Ignorance is the breeding ground of barbarism and brutality." Without learning, memory and understanding, "It is impossible to build and create and sustain a civilization," said the Speaker of the House. "What Wallenberg did was not some abstract, noble gesture. But that day by day he woke up each morning and in an act of enormous courage, he voluntarily risked his life to save people he had never met, people of a religion he didn't belong to . . .

"If by placing this bust in the Capitol, in future years thousands of visitors will come through the Capitol and as some young people come through and as the guide explains why we honor the man from Sweden who worked in Central Europe . . . if only a handful of those people go back and read the life of Raoul Wallenberg and . . . take some risks for others, then, in fact, we will have made a contribution for the future," Gingrich said.

After his talk, Gingrich left to handle the Republican agenda while Lantos periodically slipped away for votes in the House, but then returned to resume his role as master of ceremonies. With the television lights focused on the podium during the two-hour ceremony, every other speaker addressing the audience—sitting on black plastic chairs, an unusual sight in the Capitol, where normally everyone must stand—spoke in superlatives about Wallenberg. Zoltan Gál, Speaker of the Hungarian Parliament, Shevach Weiss, Speaker of the Israeli Knesset and himself a

Holocaust survivor from Poland, as well as Birgitta Dahl, Speaker of the Swedish Parliament, sincerely spoke about their personal and natural gratitude and admiration for Wallenberg, whom Dahl described as "a sparkling torch in the darkness."

Thomas Daschle, the Democratic Minority Leader in the Senate, talked about the "indomitable Swedish diplomat" and said, "We pay tribute to what he represented."

Miles Lerman, then chairman of the U.S. Holocaust Memorial Council, said Wallenberg "transcends geography" while Ruth Bader Ginsburg, an associate justice of the Supreme Court, called Wallenberg the "saving angel of Budapest" and then said, "We honor him best, however, not by a ceremony, but by taking his deeds as an example of what we must try to do individually and as a people."

Lillian Hoffman—a tiny woman, broken by age—needed Tom Lantos' assistance to reach the podium, where she said Wallenberg's "remarkable feat will remain in the heart of every Jew as a lasting memory."

After that, four women—Nina Lagergren, Annette Lantos, Miri Margolin and Lillian Hoffman—slowly removed the bust's covering cloth. Everyone stood as the still cameras flashed and the television cameras got a 30-second shot for the local Washington TV news. Uncovered, the bust depicted an older Wallenberg, somber and plaintive as befitting a man in captivity, but still aristocratic with perfect bearing.

Nina Lagergren—in her 70s, but still looking regal—moved to the podium amid a standing ovation. A gray-haired woman who used bifocals, Lagergren wore a red jacket with dark trim on the lapels, set against gold necklaces and a matching black blouse and skirt. She thanked everyone in her Swedish-accented English for the honor on behalf of her "beloved brother," who has become world famous, but then she lamented, "We have not been able to get Raoul back."

This monument to Wallenberg's life, standing in the Capitol, commemorates his achievement but fails to act as a salve on a few raw questions:

Why did Russia imprison Raoul Wallenberg, possibly for as long as 50 years? "You're asking for a rational answer from an irrational system," Makinen said.

Nina Lagergren, a Swede who has lived with Russia as her neighbor, agreed. "The Russians are unpredictable and illogical."

For some answers about Russia, one can look to foreign observations and a few historical facts. Astolphe Louis Léonor, the Marquis de Custine, a 19th Century traveler to Russia, described the despotism of that country while his compatriot, Alexis de Tocqueville, at almost the same time, wrote about America's new culture of democracy. In 1839, Custine wrote, "Men have adored the light, the Russians worship the eclipse: when will their eyes be opened?"

From 1917 to 1985, the KGB killed 40 million of its own people through slave labor, starvation, execution and exposure, according to a book, The New KGB.[2] Another three million more Russians were never born because of the Stalin-induced famine. Besides that, three million children were abandoned and died in the same period. During World War II, Russia had twenty million Soviet military and civilian casualties and two million to four million of those died because of "Stalin's policy decisions enforced by NKVD, and are not ascribable to enemy combat operations."

After 70 years of Bolshevik rule, census estimates called for Soviet population of almost 400 million, not 262.4 million as recorded in 1979. The KGB enforcers, say the authors of The New KGB, "more than Stalin alone, are to be credited with this disparity."

The Soviet secret police killed "at least four times as many Russians, Poles, Jews, Latvians, Lithuanians, Estonians, Japanese, Koreans, Chinese, Gypsies and Romanians as Hitler did in his eleven years as head of the '1,000 year Reich.'"[3]

With such wholesale loss of life, the Russians couldn't understand why some Swedes cared so much about one individual: Raoul Wallenberg.

Westerners understandably ask why Stalin or any Russian would engage in such mass murder? The answer probably deserves a book by a Russian expert, but a few facts are indisputable. After the October 1917 coup d'etat thrusting Lenin and his Bolsheviks into power, Lenin formed a secret police to maintain the new order. On December 20, 1917, Lenin signed the documents establishing the Extraordinary Commission to Combat Counterrevolution, Speculation and Sabotage. The title quickly evolved into "Cheka." The Cheka's name changed to the GPU, OGPU, NKVD and KGB. To run the Cheka, Lenin chose Felix Edmundovich Dzerzhinsky, a 40-year-old Polish revolutionary. A week after his appointment, Dzerzhinsky said, "To save the revolution, we must first destroy the counterrevolutionaries."[4]

That meant killing up to forty million people, according to the authors of The New KGB. Others put the death count much lower. Robert Conquest, who wrote, "The Great Terror," puts the number at twenty million. In a collection of essays by revisionists, "Stalinist Terror: New Perspectives," two essayists put the total at four million to eleven million. Whatever the number, it remains unconscionably high. The Bolsheviks' sinister logic was that they would make a preemptive strike on people who could oppose them in the future, for the revolution creates the "seeds of counterrevolution." Like most Russians, the Bolsheviks felt insecure and thought the Cheka was the only way of preserving the power they had seized and that this new organization had become a "permanent, enabling instrument of Bolshevik rule."

With his campaign of death, Dzerzhinsky controlled the Russian populace, guaranteeing Lenin's supremacy over the new Soviet state. To achieve his aims, Dzerzhinsky successfully eliminated trust among all Russians and destroyed their ability to resist. The Cheka employed terror to control the Russian populace, including indiscriminate mass terror to consolidate the Bolshevik's authority. This way the Cheka eliminated entire classes like the bourgeoisie, landowners and capitalists. Jews were also favorite targets for the Cheka, making its agents suspicious of Wallenberg, for he had different priorities than his diplomatic associates, mainly saving Jews. That made him equally unpopular with the Swedes and the

Russians. The anti-Semitic Russians, "couldn't understand why a Swede would be there to save Jewish lives," Lars Berg, a fellow diplomat with Wallenberg, said during a documentary film. "Why should a Swede do that, and why should he have to have money at his disposal?"

Fellow diplomat Per Anger added, "From the Soviet viewpoint, it was very difficult to understand how a neutral country could have an embassy on the battlefield just for saving Jewish people. There must be something else behind this."[5]

When Wallenberg became an honorary American citizen, Congressman Tom Lantos offered, "There is no doubt in my mind that . . . his imprisonment in the gulag is related to the false Soviet assumption that he had been an American spy."[6]

Even if Wallenberg survived beyond 1947 to die a peaceful death in the 1980s, one can understand—but not forgive—the Russian paranoia that forced the imprisonment and possible execution of Wallenberg.

Paranoid Russia and neutral Sweden remained antagonists throughout the Wallenberg imprisonment, but one must ask another irritating question: Why didn't the Swedish government try to free its own diplomat? Makinen's research yields the answer that diligent, diplomatic Swedish underlings tried, but their superiors lacked interest.

All three Socialist premiers who ran Sweden for much of the last 60 years and could explain their lack of interest in Wallenberg are now dead. Per Albin Hansson died in 1946; Tage Erlander died in 1985, both of natural causes, while Olof Palme, the man who advocated peace and disarmament, was shot to death in 1986 on a street in downtown Stockholm.[7]

After almost 60 years of nearly uninterrupted rule, the Social Democratic Party of Sweden was swept from power in 1991, but that only lasted until the next election. On September 18, 1994, the voters reinstated the Social Democrats, giving that party control of Sweden from 1932 through 1995, a reign of 63 years with only two brief interruptions in 1976-82 and 1991-94. The same party that continuously ignored Wallenberg again ruled.

In an apparent—and unsuccessful attempt—to sway voters to
the opposition conservative coalition, the top executives of Sweden's
four largest exporting companies on September 12 threatened to
pull their planned domestic investments if taxes rose and the bud-
get was not stabilized after the election. The executives of Volvo
AB, Telefon AB L.M. Ericsson, Stora Kopparbergs Bergslags AB
and Asea Brown Boveri AB, in a jointly written newspaper article
six days before the election, said they would reconsider investing
fifty billion Swedish kronor, or about $7 billion, annually in their
country.

Political analysts thought Swedish voters longed for the good
old days of the welfare state that had virtually no unemployment.
But three days later Peter Wallenberg, ruler of the Wallenberg clan
and Sweden's richest industrialist, said during an interview with
Sweden's Expressen newspaper that reductions were necessary in
the welfare state, long sanctioned by the Social Democrats.[8]

Thus, the Social Democrats and Wallenberg family remained
adversaries into the late 20th Century. As mentioned previously,
Dahl, speaker of the Swedish Parliament, disagreed. When asked if
the Social Democrats and Wallenberg family were perpetual opponents, she replied, "Nothing of the kind. There are many contacts between the government and the Wallenberg family. Peter
Wallenberg (and government officials) all know each other."

Though many disagree with Dahl on the camaraderie between
the Social Democrats and the Wallenbergs, one fact remains
indisputable: Peter Wallenberg controlled a fortune as vast as
American entrepreneurs Warren E. Buffett and Bill Gates. In the
late 1990s, Investor A.B., the holding company for the Wallenbergs,
controlled at least 40% of the Swedish stock market and had a
market value of $6.4 billion.[9] Under Peter Wallenberg's leadership,
his family has advanced its dominance in Swedish industry and
solidified the family as Europe's strongest industrial dynasty. As
chairman of Investor, Peter Wallenberg, in his early '70s, held many
titles carrying vast wealth.

He was first vice chairman of Skandinaviska Enskilda Banken

in Stockholm, one of the 120 largest banks in the world with more than $55 billion in assets; chairman of ASEA AB, Sweden, and co-chairman of Asea Brown Boveri, a global electrical engineering group. ASEA owned half of Asea Brown Boveri (ABB). ABB, which has 20,000 U.S. employees, has annual U.S. sales of $4 billion. Peter Wallenberg was also vice chairman of Ericsson Inc., a world-wide telecommunications company whose U.S. sales alone exceed $1.2 billion annually. The Investor Group's holdings also included Saab, the automobile company owned 50-50 with General Motors Corp. In 1990, GM paid $600 million for its 50 percent interest in Saab, which has more than 30,000 employees. Ten years later Investor sold its 50 percent interest in Saab to GM. To move into global markets, Investor sold half of Scania, a truck manufacturer, in 1996 and raised $2.7 billion and three years later sold the balance. Other holdings include Electrolux AB, a giant general equipment firm that handles machinery, boilers, cleaning equipment, commercial refrigeration and nuclear reactors and their parts; and SE Banken, a holding company that owned three-sevenths of Scandinavian Airlines System; the Grand Hotel and TV 4 in Stockholm.[10]

In 1997, Peter Wallenberg, 71, said he was leaving as chairman of Investor and termed this a "shift of generations." Though he appointed, a nonWallenberg, Percy Barnevik, as chairman, Peter Wallenberg didn't think this would dilute the family influence. "I will still be chairman of the family foundation, and they are the largest shareholder in Investor," he said. Investor has controlling interest or is the largest shareholder in companies reporting a market capitalization of $98.1 billion.[11]

In early 1999, Investor appointed 42-year-old Marcus Wallenberg as its new chief executive officer. This was a symbolic move that marked the continuity of the Wallenberg dynasty. With such family wealth available, one understands why a live Raoul Wallenberg would have no financial worries. Sven Hagstromer, a cousin and investment banker who manages Wallenberg's estate, said if the missing diplomat ever returned to Sweden, "He will be well off."

While the Social Democrats were running Sweden, they cared little for capitalists and less about Raoul Wallenberg. Documents show the Swedes wanted information about Wallenberg, but the Soviets usually refused. "The Swedes were genuinely asking about Wallenberg," Makinen said. But at a "higher level, the Swedes didn't try."

In 1949, a spy swap was possible for Wallenberg, but the Swedes never followed through. "There was a different level about that," Makinen said. "Always puzzled me."

At the higher levels, the Swedes practiced "Rysskräck," the fear of Russia, a powerful force in Sweden after the Second World War. Sweden knew it couldn't fight the Soviet Union and retreated to Rysskräck. In another Scandinavian country, fear of Russia created a subservient attitude and a new verb, "Finlandized." The Finns feared Russia so much they did nothing to antagonize their neighbor, acquiescing even before asked.

To make certain the Swedes didn't offend the powerful, snarling Russians, Stockholm avoided contentious issues, like trying to free Raoul Wallenberg. Even when a conservative government took over Sweden, from 1976-1982, the new government declined to trade for Wallenberg. In 1981, Sweden had the Russian submarine trapped inside its territorial waters and the Swedes still did nothing.

When the Russians said they didn't know anything about Wallenberg, "They just accepted their denial in Sweden," complained Nina Lagergren.[12]

Sjöquist, the journalist, said, "You can see a line from 1945 . . . when Russia told the U.S. we have him. The Swedes didn't do anything. It's the same thing today. They don't do anything. Why shouldn't they have tried to push the Russians during the submarine incident to at least discover what had happened to Raoul Wallenberg? If he's dead, let us get the facts—why, when, how he died."[13]

Also, many in the Swedish government probably resented Wallenberg, who had been extraordinarily successful. Bureaucrats running a desk in Stockholm could never even reach a base camp on the mountain Wallenberg had climbed, but they could help keep him from ever returning to Sweden. The longer the Swedes waited to try to free Wallenberg the easier it became to justify their reticence.

As Berg said in a documentary film, "Raoul Wallenberg was not a career diplomat and had his own way of doing things. Really, Raoul was the one who did everything."[14]

Soon, only an old woman was bothering the Swedish mandarins and after her death, her elderly children. Nina Lagergren said her mother tried constantly to force the Swedish government into action, but everyone ignored her. Lagergren quoted the top Swedish officials, as saying, "with very cold eyes, 'How can you believe your son is alive?'"[15]

Since 1945, the Swedish government maintained it has done everything possible to free Wallenberg. That includes numerous demarches, visits to Russia by the Swedish prime minister and persistent requests of visiting Russian leaders.

The Wallenberg committees of the world brush this aside as a flimsy excuse. Instead, they and Wallenberg supporters ask these questions: Why didn't the Swedes immediately offer a spy swap? Why didn't Staffan Soderblom, the Swedish ambassador to Moscow, when talking to Stalin in 1946, press for Wallenberg's release instead of saying he thought the diplomat had died, giving Stalin a reason to keep Wallenberg imprisoned? Why didn't the Swedish government release all documents as soon as possible, creating a publicity campaign to free Wallenberg? Why didn't the government make freeing Wallenberg, one of Sweden's greatest heroes, a top priority?

If the Swedish government failed to help Wallenberg, why didn't the wealthy Wallenberg family? The undercapitalized Russians knew Wallenberg was born into a famous capitalist family, said Sjöquist, speaking during a documentary film. "Why didn't this rich, powerful family do anything to save Raoul Wallenberg? They could have very early brought him out."[16]

Jacob and Marcus Wallenberg, Raoul's cousins, are dead, and their descendants don't discuss the matter.

To Wallenberg supporters, the obvious answer is that the Wallenberg family carried out a lucrative business with the Nazis during World War II and recovering Raoul Wallenberg would re-awaken those unpleasant memories. During the war, the Swedes had warring nations on both sides and below them. The Nazis occupied Norway to the west and Denmark to the southwest while Russia lay to the east and Germany directly south.

The conflict failed to stop the Wallenbergs' press of commerce. Jacob Wallenberg had served as head of the Swedish trade delega-tion to Nazi German and had arranged for material to be supplied to Germany. Marcus and Jacob had trade agreements with Ger-many and Britain and had trade links with both covering iron ore, something Germany needed badly. Besides, to the family elite, Raoul really wasn't a Wallenberg. His father had died before Raoul's birth, and he was raised in the von Dardel household, making him, at best, a cultured half-breed. If the Soviets could have un-derstood the subtle Swedish discrimination, they probably would never have incarcerated Wallenberg for so long. Or, if Raoul's last name had been von Dardel, not Wallenberg, he also would have never wasted the balance of his life in the Soviet gulag.

Instead, Wallenberg became the Soviet Union's most famous prisoner, making it impossible to release him. Thus, the Russians instituted a monumental coverup, first denying Wallenberg's ex-istence and then inventing a clumsy story that he had died in prison. Wallenberg's release would become too embarrassing for too many top Soviet officials. They probably reasoned neither the Swedes nor the Americans really tried to free Wallenberg.

Anger, the Swedish diplomat, provided a verbal reflection of the Russian diplomatic goals. "The only language the Soviets understand is they don't give anything without getting anything instead."[17]

Therefore, the Russians imprisoned Wallenberg while the Swedes abandoned him, leaving only the Americans to save him.

The United States had recruited and sent Wallenberg into danger, but this country failed to try to retrieve him. After the Russians abducted Wallenberg in January 1945, the U.S. government, aware of Russian duplicity in this matter, had many options to free Wallenberg. First, the Americans could have vigorously and officially protested the disappearance and abduction. Second, the U.S. government could have asked the Soviets why they were holding Wallenberg. Only the Swedes did this, but tepidly.

Or, the United States before World War II ended could have told the Soviet Union, its ally, "We want Wallenberg." After the war, the United States could have halted some aid to the rebuilding of the Soviet Union in exchange for Wallenberg. Or, the Americans could have exchanged a Soviet spy, like Valentin Gubitchev, for Wallenberg during the 1940s. Or, America could have swapped other spies during the 1950s, 1960s, 1970s, 1980s or 1990s. This country exchanged spies to free many Americans—like Francis Gary Powers, Marvin Makinen and Nicholas Daniloff—as well as for prominent Soviets like Anatoly Shcharansky and Yuri Orlov. Why not a spy swap for a hero of the Twentieth Century?

Freeing Wallenberg did not mean nuclear war. Freeing Wallenberg did not mean any armed conflict, the tiniest skirmish or the loss or commitment of one soldier. The United States didn't have to risk one life even for a man who saved 100,000 lives. Instead, America could have arranged a spy swap or used its economic leverage, like better terms on a grain deal, to free Wallenberg.

Henry Morgenthau, FDR's Treasury Secretary, was interested in freeing Wallenberg, and at first the Americans tried, but after an initial rebuff from both Sweden and Russia, the United States dropped its efforts and became observers. Coldly, dispassionately, the American intelligence service and the State Department gathered information and did nothing to try to free Wallenberg.

After reading the CIA documents, the State Department documents and doing other research, one formulates an inescapable conclusion: The U.S. government just did not care about Wallenberg. Once imprisoned by Russia, he had lost his value,

and the U.S. government simply abandoned him. It was intellec-
tually dishonest to say Wallenberg, whom the United States had
recruited and sent into peril, was a Swedish citizen and thus the
United States had no responsibility to save him. When Wallenberg
became a U.S. citizen in 1981, that ripped away this excuse.

Jimmy Carter, pushed into action by Annette Lantos, tried to
help Wallenberg. Alexander Haig and George Shultz, when secretary of state, also tried. Abraham Sofaer, the State Department's
legal adviser, when meeting with the Soviets said he always asked
about Wallenberg because he considered it an important issue.
Most other current or former State Department employees avoided
even discussing Wallenberg.

"Surprise, surprise," said Mark Zaid, a Washington lawyer dealing with the issue of human rights. "They never talk. The State
Department is very protective; often it makes rulings that are
not favorable. They don't like to talk about it. They have that
nature."

The few American moves were feeble efforts that ended in failure. Perhaps it was easier to do nothing and every day of doing
nothing made it easier to keep doing nothing about Wallenberg.
Better to utter platitudes about Wallenberg than try to save him.
Maybe the virulent anti-Semitism that infected this country before and during World War II influenced the do-nothing decision.
In the end—and this should be identified as author's supposition—some influential people thought, "Wallenberg only saved
Jews."

Whether he saved Jews or Gypsies, Elena Bonner, an old woman
with thick glasses and a perpetual cigarette, who was married to
the late Andrei Sakharov, put Wallenberg's accomplishments in
perspective.

"We do not have anything like it in history," she said. "No one
of the Europeans has done as much to save peoples' lives and not
one, hundreds of thousands of lives."[18]

Despite a half century of setbacks, von Dardel—now frail and
weakened from Parkinson's disease—is still investigating information

about his half-brother's whereabouts, but he remains secretive. "It is too early to say anything about new efforts."

He did say he has "very good relations with the human rights arm of the Russian government." With the breakup of the Soviet Union, the tectonic plates of politics have shifted. When president, Boris N. Yeltsin had a commission on human rights, something as alien to Russia as the invisible hand of Adam Smith. It's unknown how Vladimir Putin, who took over for Yeltsin after his sudden resignation in 1999, will handle the Wallenberg matter.

In January 2000, Wallenberg was honored in a ceremony in Stockholm's main synagogue just before the start of the Stockholm International Forum on the Holocaust, a 44-nation conference dealing with the question of education about the Holocaust. In the last years of the 20th Century, the Holocaust has veered into financial questions about how Nazis and their sympathizers looted bank accounts, insurance policies and art works from Jews and other Non-Arayans. A U.S. triumvirate of lawyers, state insurance commissioners and federal government officials forced the start of restitution in all these areas. As the Holocaust issue again became fresh in the worldwide psyche, Wallenberg's name reappeared, or perhaps it never disappeared.

Nina Lagergren accepted the tribute to her half-brother at the Stockholm ceremony, but Guy von Dardel, her brother, who was ill, was unable to attend. Edgar Bronfman, the World Jewish Congress president, gave Lagergren the award, but her remarks were equally divided between gratitude and bitterness. While she praised the Jewish community for all the honors, awards, monuments, street names and other memorabilia that keep Raoul Wallenberg's name alive, she still asked the cutting question: "Where were you 55 years ago?"

Why did the Jewish community not save her beloved brother? A few weeks later back in New York, Evelyn Sommer, chairwoman of the American sector of the World Jewish Congress, responded: "Where were we? In concentration camps, in DP (Displaced Person) Camps. That's where we were. Of course, I didn't say anything (to

Lagergren). That would have been rude." Instead, to her audience back in New York, she talked about how the top U.S. and Swedish government officials, unfettered by prison camps, could have worked to save Wallenberg. In the end, no matter how many nice awards go to him, how many schools or streets they name after him, Raoul Wallenberg still had most of his life stolen from him. The U.S. government could have saved him but chose to ignore him. It participated in the conspiracy of indifference that cheated a 20th Century hero out of his life.

In July 2000, Russian officials said the KGB destroyed documents about the fate of Raoul Wallenberg. The officials talked about Wallenberg with former Israeli Ambassador Yohanan Bein, who visited Moscow. The Russians did drop their position that Wallenberg died a natural death while under Soviet control. Jan Lundvik, a Swedish diplomat, said the Russians long ago gave up the official line that Wallenberg died of a heart attack. Expressen, a Swedish tabloid, said the Russians acknowledged Wallenberg had probably been killed. Again, no time, no place, no specifics.

In November 2000, Russia indicated it might confirm the theory that Wallenberg was killed in a Moscow prison. Alexander Yakovlev, chairman of the presidential commission on rehabilitation of victims of political repression, said, "we do not doubt that he was shot at Lubyanka," according to the news agency Interfax. "We must put an end to this story, which has acquired an acute international significance and has been poisoning the atmosphere for a long time." This was one of the strongest statements from Russia, but still there is no definitive proof.

In December 2000, the Russians acknowledged for the first time that they had wrongfully imprisoned Wallenberg and killed him in a Soviet prison in 1947, but, as earlier mentioned, the Russians supplied no details about the circumstances of his death. Lagergren told the Associated Press she was not satisfied and wanted specifics and evidence about what happened.

"The rehabilitation means that they have confessed that Raoul was the victim of their repression. But it is no concrete evidence of what happened to Raoul," Lagergren said.

In their statement, the Russian prosecutors said that the investigation, "has failed to reveal the true reasons for the arrest and imprisonment of Wallenberg and Langfelder and the factual circumstances of their death, or locate materials of the criminal case or their personal dossiers." As means of a coverup, the Russians—the meticulous record keepers—destroyed the Wallenberg files, so we may never know what happened to the Swedish diplomat and his driver.

Vladimir Ustinov, the Russian Prosecutor General, signed a verdict posthumously rehabilitating Wallenberg and Langfelder as "victims of political repression." They had been arrested illegally, though they were diplomats, as "socially dangerous" individuals and deprived of their freedom.

In January 2001, an investigating panel released its findings in Moscow. Framed by 71 blue binders of newly declassified information on a shelf behind them, panel members issued their final report, which criticized Sweden for failing to make trades to free Wallenberg. The reports indicated the Soviets wanted to exchange Wallenberg for defectors and other Soviet citizens in Sweden, but Sweden rejected the offers. Goeran Persson, Sweden's prime minister, apologized—after the report was released—to the Wallenberg family for "mistakes" that were made. "We must continue with our efforts to obtain new facts which would throw light on Wallenberg's fate," Persson said in news service dispatches. "These efforts must be based on the assumption that Raoul Wallenberg may have lived after 1947."

The Russians were succinct. On page 34, the report said, "All the circumstantial evidence confirms, that Raoul Wallenberg died, or most likely was killed on 17th July 1947." The preferred Soviet method of execution was a bullet to the back of the head without warning.

Then the report explained, "Practically, all the direct evidence was destroyed at the time."

Wallenberg was famous and the assailants wanted to cover their tracks, avoid leaving a paper trail. If the joint commission couldn't unearth any crucial documents in more than nine years, their successors will have the same misfortune. The Russian government may still be holding some documents somewhere, but the changes in government have yet to produce any definitive pieces of paper telling what happened to Wallenberg

Either Wallenberg's time on this planet ended abruptly in 1947 or it oozed from him, day after day, month after month, year after year in the Soviet Gulag Archipelago. Diplomats and former prisoners both spoke of Wallenberg's possible longevity. Lars Berg: "Knowing his very strong character, his way of getting out of any difficult situation, I believe there is a very fair chance, he is still alive."[19] Kalinski, a prisoner in the gulag who died after his release, had explained, "You can live a long time in prison if you behave like Wallenberg. He never gave up any walks. He exercised every day; he was a man of sport and the way he behaved he could live a long time."[20]

Both Guy von Dardel and his sister, Nina Lagergren, believe their half-brother is alive until the Russians prove otherwise. "That keeps us all the time working and absolutely engaged in our efforts," he said.

Alive or dead, Wallenberg "was my hero," Lantos said. "He has remained my hero because he exemplifies the best in human beings. He was his brother's and sister's keeper."[21]

Whether Raoul Wallenberg died in 1947 (possible) or 1983 (also possible) or if he is still alive today (highly doubtful), his amazing accomplishment was a thunderbolt—swift and powerful and leaving an eternal imprint. His ultimate fate may remain a mystery, but perhaps that became his unique destiny. Moses never made it to the Promised Land.

In any event, the people he saved and the descendants of the people he saved and those that later learned of his heroics at that focal point in history will always keep Raoul Wallenberg alive.

Ironically, a Russian proverb may put it best: "The earth is kept warm by people who believe."

FOOTNOTES

CHAPTER 1

1. Auschwitz, By Dr. Miklós Nyiszli, Fawcett Crest Books, 1962, Page 46.
2. Righteous Gentile: The Story of Raoul Wallenberg, Missing Hero of the Holocaust. By John Bierman. the Viking Press, 1981. Page 20.
3. Ibid.
4. Justice in Jerusalem, By Gideon Hausner, Harper & Row. 1966. Page 32.
5. Lindfors was the most famous actress in Sweden when she left in 1946 for the United States. Lindfors, who starred in films, on Broadway and in television, married and divorced four times. She died October 25, 1995, at the age of 74 of complications from rheumatoid arthritis. The New York Times printed a full obituary about her on October 26, 1995, Page B8.
6. Raoul Wallenberg: Buried Alive, Documentary Film, Direct Cinema Ltd., 1983.
7. The Chairman: John J. McCloy. The Making of the American Establishment. By Kai Bird, Simon & Schuster, 1992, Page 203.
8. The Chairman, Page 201.
9. The Chairman, Page 204.
10. The Chairman. Page 205.
11. The Chairman, Pages 206-207.
12. Auschwitz, Page 88.
13. Box 111, War Refugee Board Records, Franklin D. Roosevelt Library, Hyde Park, New York.

Chapter 2

1. Box 111, WRB Records, FDR Library, excerpts from letter of August 10, 1944, from Iver C. Olsen.
2. Ibid.
3. Folder 14, Page 22, CIA Documents on Raoul Wallenberg, National Archives, Washington, D.C.
4. Folder 14, Page 23, CIA Documents, National Archives.
5. Folder 14, Page 21, CIA Documents, National Archives.
6. Folder 14, Pages 26-27, CIA Documents, National Archives.
7. Folder 14, Page 30, CIA Documents, National Archives.
8. Raoul Wallenberg by Jan Larsson, Page 6. This is a pamphlet published by the Swedish Institute, a government-backed foundation to promote Swedish interests.
9. Ibid.
10. Box 111, WRB Records, FDR Library.
11. Ibid.
12. Ibid.
13. Folder 2, Pages 36-37, CIA Documents, National Archives.
14. Ibid.
15. Box 111, WRB Records, Excerpts from Iver C. Olsen's letter of August 14, 1944, FDR Library.
16. Buried Alive, Documentary Film.
17. Ibid.
18. The State Department files on Wallenberg are a researcher's nightmare. They are grouped in seven boxes, but in no order within each box. Inside are hundreds of documents about maids at the Swedish Embassy being hired and fired and other such trivia. After wading through a few hundred of these documents, a relevant one about Wallenberg appears. Thus, I will footnote the appropriate items per this example: Box 4, State Department Files, National Archives.
19. Ibid.
20. Box 111, WRB Records, FDR Library.

21. Ibid.
22. Buried Alive, Documentary Film.
23. Ibid.
24. Box 111, WRB Records, FDR Library.
25. Box 4, State Department Files, National Archives.
26. Buried Alive, Documentary Film.
27. Ibid.
28. Ibid.
29. Ibid.
30. Ibid.
31. Ibid.
32. Lost Hero: The Mystery of Raoul Wallenberg, By Frederick E. Werbell and Thurston Clarke, McGraw-Hill Book Company, 1982, Pages 104-105.
33. Buried Alive, Documentary Film.
34. Folder 3, Page 5, CIA Documents, National Archives.
35. Buried Alive, Documentary Film.
36. Raoul Wallenberg's Children, Special Issue for Raoul Wallenberg: A Study of Heroes, a pamphlet produced by The Raoul Wallenberg Committee of the United States, New York, Page 4.
37. Buried Alive, Documentary Film.
38. Ibid.
39. Ibid.
40. Ibid.
41. Ibid.
42. Justice in Jerusalem, Pages 28-29.
43. Buried Alive, Documentary Film.

Chapter 3

1. Folder 17, Page 11, CIA Documents, National Archives.
2. Folder 4, Page 2-42, CIA Documents, National Archives.
3. Ibid.

4. Ibid.
5. Ibid.
6. Ibid.
7. Ibid.
8. Ibid.
9. Ibid.
10. Ibid.
11. Ibid.
12. Ibid.
13. Ibid.
14. Ibid.
15. Folder 12, Page 49, CIA Documents, National Archives.
16. Ibid.
17. Folder 12, Page 50, CIA Documents, National Archives.
18. Folder 1, Page 43, CIA Documents, National Archives.
19. New York Times, December 12, 1995. Page 1.
20. Folder 9, Page 7, CIA Documents, National Archives.
21. Folder 9, Page 51, CIA Documents, National Archives.
22. Folder 9, Page 52, CIA Documents, National Archives.

Chapter 4

1. Box 111, WRB Records, FDR Library.
2. Ibid.
3. Ibid.
4. Ibid.
5. Ibid.
6. Box 111, WRB Records, Box 111, State Department Letter of May 8, 1945, FDR Library.
7. Box 3, State Department Files, National Archives.
8. Box 111, WRB Records, FDR Library.
9. Ibid.
10. Ibid.
11. Folder 17, Page 12. CIA Documents, National Archives.

12. Ibid.
13. Box 3, State Department Files, National Archives.
14. Associated Press, transmitted from New York at 8:46 a.m. May 22, 1996.
15. Reuter, transmitted from New York at 8:44 p.m., May 20, 1996.
16. Ibid.
17. Folder 10, Pages 15-19, CIA Documents, National Archives.
18. Box 111, WRB Records, Eleanor Roosevelt Papers, General Correspondence, 1945-1948, FDR Library.
19. Box 3, State Department Documents, National Archives.
20. Box 111, Eleanor Roosevelt Papers, FDR Library.
21. Ibid.
22. Ibid.
23. In 1948, Wallace ran for president but finished fourth in a field of five. Truman won, followed by Thomas E. Dewey, the Republican candidate, and J. Strom Thurmond, the States' Rights Democratic Candidate. Norman Thomas, the Socialist Party Candidate, finished behind Wallace, who received 1,157,326 popular votes, but no electoral votes.
24. Box 111, Eleanor Roosevelt Papers, FDR Library.
25. Ibid.
26. Ibid.
27. Ibid.
28. Box 3, State Department Documents, National Archives.
29. Ibid.
30. Ibid.
31. Ibid.
32. Ibid.
33. Ibid.
34. Ibid.
35. Ibid.
36. Box 34, Internal Security File, Harry S. Truman Library, Independence, Missouri.
37. Box 3, State Department Documents, National Archives.

38. Ibid.

39. Box 34, Internal Security File, Truman Library.

40. Folder 1, Pages 54-57, CIA Documents, National Archives.

41. Ibid.

42. Folder 1, Page 23, CIA Documents, National Archives.

43. Folder 1, Page 29, CIA Documents, National Archives.

Chapter 5

1. Folder 17, Page 24, CIA Documents, National Archives.

2. Folder 17, Pages 25-26, CIA Documents, National Archives.

3. Ibid.

4. Ibid.

5. Folder 17, Page 27, CIA Documents, National Archives.

6. Folder 17, Pages 29-32, CIA Documents, National Archives.

7. Ibid.

8. Folder 5, Page 11, CIA Documents, National Archives.

9. Box 3, State Department Documents, National Archives.

10. Box 1, State Department Documents, National Archives.

11. Folder 2, Pages 2-3, CIA Documents, National Archives.

12. Folder 5, Page 22, CIA Documents, National Archives.

13. Folder 6, Page 28, CIA Documents, National Archives.

14. Folder 16, Page 27, CIA Documents, National Archives.

15. Folder 6, Page 29, CIA Documents, National Archives.

16. Folder 2, Page 14, CIA Documents, National Archives.

17. Box 1, State Department Documents, National Archives.

18. Ibid.

19. Ibid.

20. Ibid.

21. Ibid.

22. Ibid.

23. Folder 6, Page 31, CIA Documents, National Archives.

24. Folder 6, Pages 41-48, CIA Documents, National Archives.

Chapter 6

1. Folder 10, Page 25, CIA Documents, National Archives.
2. Folder 10, Page 26, CIA Documents, National Archives.
3. Ibid.
4. Ibid.
5. Box 1, State Department Documents, National Archives.
6. Folder 6, Page 17, CIA Documents, National Archives.
7. Folder 16, Pages 32-33, CIA Documents, National Archives.
8. Ibid.
9. Ibid.
10. Folder 6, Page 19, CIA Documents, National Archives.
11. Ibid.
12. Folder 6, Pages 22-25, CIA Documents, National Archives.
13. Folder 6, Pages 2-4, CIA Documents, National Archives.
14. Ibid.
15. Ibid.
16. Folder 10, Page 9, CIA Documents, National Archives.
17. Folder 10, Pages 7-12, CIA Documents, National Archives.
18. Ibid.
19. Folder 10, Page 16, CIA Documents, National Archives.
20. Folder 10, Pages 7-12, CIA Documents, National Archives.

Chapter 7

1. Folder 8, Pages 18-19, CIA Documents, National Archives.
2. Folder 8, Page 15, CIA Documents, National Archives.
3. Folder 8, Page 16, CIA Documents, National Archives.
4. Folder 8, Page 37, CIA Documents, National Archives.
5. Folder 20, Page 1, CIA Documents, National Archives.
6. Folder 8, Page 34, CIA Documents, National Archives.
7. Folder 8, Page 20, CIA Documents, National Archives.
8. Folder 8, Page 22, CIA Documents, National Archives.

9. Ibid.

10. The Mission of Raoul Wallenberg, Documentary Film.

11. Ibid.

12. Ibid.

13. New York Times, February 27, 1982, Page 3.

14. New York Times, July 7, 1990, Page 6.

15. Ibid.

16. Raoul Wallenberg: Angel of Rescue. By Harvey Rosenfeld, Prometheus Books, Buffalo, New York, 1982. Page 167.

17. Folder 8, Page 12, CIA Documents, National Archives.

18. The Mission of Raoul Wallenberg, Soviet-made documentary film, 1990, Russian with English subtitles.

19. Folder 8, Page 40, CIA Documents, National Archives.

20. Folder 8, Page 45, CIA Documents, National Archives.

21. Folder 8, Page 40.

22. Folder 11, Pages 15-16, CIA Documents, National Archives.

23. Folder 14, Pages 6-7, CIA Documents, National Archives.

24. Folder 9, Page 7, CIA Documents, National Archives.

25. Folder 14, Page 16, CIA Documents, National Archives.

26. The Mission of Raoul Wallenberg, Russian Documentary Film.

27. Folder 14, Page 17, CIA Documents, National Archives.

28. Folder 17, Page 14, CIA Documents, National Archives.

29. Folder 14, Pages 17-19, CIA Documents, National Archives.

30. Folder 14, Page 19, CIA Documents, National Archives.

31. Folder 14, Page 36, CIA Documents, National Archives.

32. Ibid.

33. Folder 14, Page 37, CIA Documents, National Archives.

Chapter 8

1. Folder 11, Page 10, CIA Documents, National Archives.

2. Folder 10, Page 54, CIA Documents, National Archives.

3. Folder 11, Page 39, CIA Documents, National Archives.

4. Folder 10, Page 44, CIA Documents, National Archives.

5. Folder 12, Pages 19-20, CIA Documents, National Archives.
6. Folder 10, Page 25, CIA Documents, National Archives.
7. Buried Alive, Documentary Film.
8. Angel of Rescue, Page 191.
9. Buried Alive, Documentary Film.
10. Washington Post, January 6, 1983, Page A23.
11. Washington Post, January 7, 1983, Page A18.
12. Washington Post, January 16, 1983, Page B7.
13. Washington Post, January 18, 1983, Page A16.
14. Folder 15, Page 2, CIA Documents, National Archives.
15. Folder 15, Page 3, CIA Documents, National Archives.
16. Folder 15, Page 5, CIA Documents, National Archives.
17. Folder 15, Page 6, CIA Documents, National Archives.
18. Folder 15, Page 7, CIA Documents, National Archives.
19. Turmoil and Triumph: My Years As Secretary of State. By George P. Shultz. Charles Scribner's Sons, New York, 1993. Page 467.
20. Folder 16, Pages 22-24, CIA Documents, National Archives.

Chapter 9.

1. Statement by Marvin W. Makinen at the Raoul Wallenberg Hearing, Stockholm, January 15, 1981.
2. Ibid.
3. Chicago Tribune, October 1, 1991, Section 5, Page 1.
4. Ibid.
5. New York Times, March 4, 1993, Page B9.
6. Ibid.
7. The Swiss research facility is now called the European Laboratory for Particle Physics, but it is still known by the acronym, CERN. New York Times January 5, 1996, Page A9.
8. Contemporary Issues in International Law, The Frolova Case By Anthony D'Amato. N.P. Engel, Publisher, Arlington, Virginia, 1984, Page 89.
9. Contemporary Issues in International Law, Page 92.

10. Contemporary Issues in International Law, Page 94.
11. Chicago Tribune, Page 1, June 19, 1982.

Chapter 10

1. Court of Oyer and Terminer &c. at Philadelphia, October Sessions, 1784, Respublica v. De Longchamps, Brooklyn, New York, Law Library, Page 109.
2. Federal Supplement, Cited as 567 F. Supplement 1,490, (1983), Brooklyn Law Library.
3. Hearing Before the Subcommittee on Human Rights and International Organizations of the Committee on Foreign Affairs, House of Representatives, August 3, 1983.
4. Page 9, Human Rights Hearing.
5. Page 13, Human Rights Hearing.
6. Page 9, Human Rights Hearing.
7. Page 35, Human Rights Hearing.
8. Page 45, Human Rights Hearing.
9. On April 24, 1997, the United States Postal Service issued a commemorative 32 cent stamp of Raoul Wallenberg.
10. Page 58, Human Rights Hearing.
11. Page 59, Human Rights Hearing.

Chapter 11

None.

Chapter 12

1. Transcript of NBC's Today show, February 2, 1984, page 35.
2. Ibid.
3. Today Transcript, Page 36.

4. Today Transcript, Page 37.

5. Ibid.

6. The Wallenberg law case, officially called Guy von Dardel v. the Union of Soviet Socialist Republics, is a voluminous document with filings that stretched for more than six years. To examine the entire case, someone must go to the Washington National Record Center in nearby Suitland, Maryland. The federal government runs free shuttle buses there from the National Archives. To schedule a review, you must call at least 24 hours in advance to the record center and provide the case file number, 84-0353, the accession number, 21-90-38, the box number, 10, and the location number 20-75-31-1.4. Then call at least a day later to make sure the file is available.

Chapter 13

1. New York Times, June 5, 1993, Page 28.

2. Washington Post, June 8, 1993, Page A21.

3. Barrington D. Parker Jr. had his own high profile case in April 1995 when he presided in White Plains, New York, over the trial of baseball luminary Darryl Strawberry. Judge Parker sentenced Strawberry to six months' house arrest and three years' probation on charges of conspiracy and federal tax evasion since Strawberry failed to report about $350,000 in income from card and memorabilia shows. But that did not prevent Strawberry from later playing the same season for the New York Yankees.

4. National Record Center, Oral Argument, August 10, 1984, Page 3.

5. National Record Center, Oral Argument, Page 8.

6. National Record Center, Oral Argument, Page 17.

7. After serving eight years, Stig Bergling escaped from prison in 1987 during an unsupervised conjugal visit. He spent seven years hiding until surrendering to Swedish police in 1994,

saying he was homesick. In 1997, Bergling, who was afflicted with Parkinson's disease, was freed after serving 11 years.

8. Angel of Rescue, Page 181.

9. National Record Center, Notice of Withdrawal of Counsel, filed September 20, 1985.

Chapter 14

1. National Record Center, Judge Parker's Decision, October 15, 1985.

2. National Record Center, Judge Parker's Decision, Page 7.

3. National Record Center, Judge Parker's Decision, Page 8.

4. National Record Center, Judge Parker's Decision, Page 9.

Chapter 15

1. National Record Center, Statement of points and authorities in support of plaintiff's motion for an order holding the defendant Union of Soviet Socialist Republics in Civil Contempt. Page 15. April 28, 1986.

2. Lois Frolova v. Union of Soviet Social Republics, No. 83-1451. United States Court of Appeals, Seventh Circuit, Decided May 1, 1985.

3. Miami Herald, September 4, 1986, Page 20A.

4. National Record Center, Statement of Points, Page 4.

5. National Record Center, Statement of Points, Page 20.

6. National Record Center, Letter from Judge Parker dated October 29, 1986, to Royce C. Lamberth, Esq., Chief, Civil Division, U.S. Attorney's Office for the District of Columbia.

Chapter 16

1. Wall Street Journal, March 23, 1987, Page 54.
2. Ibid.
3. Ibid.
4. Ibid.
5. While in private practice, Sofaer became entangled in another controversial case, defending Libya in the lawsuits resulting from the destruction of the Pan Am Flight 103 over Lockerbie, Scotland, in December 1988. In July 1993, Libya retained Sofaer even though the country was not involved in any of the civil or criminal litigation. Since 1991, however, Libya had sanctions placed against it because two Libyan nationals were indicted in the United States on charges that the pair was responsible for the bombing that caused 270 deaths. Sofaer, a partner at the law firm of Hughes, Hubbard & Reed, said in a statement then, the firm "will advise the government of Libya with a view to developing solutions for the differences which exist in these litigations, and which are acceptable to all parties; we will not litigate actively in defense of Libya or the individual [criminal] defendants." A good source for this is the Wall Street Journal of July 13, 1993, Page B3. A few days later a tidal wave of negative reaction forced Sofaer to drop the case. Both the public and U.S. officials criticized the former State Department legal adviser for representing Libya. His Washington law firm issued a statement, saying, "Regrettably, the public perception of this undertaking and the reaction of government authorities has [sic] been so negative as to lead us to conclude that we could not effectively carry out this representation." The Wall Street Journal of July 19, 1993, had a five paragraph story about this on Page B8.
6. Stanford University Campus Report, November 2, 1994, Page 2.
7. National Record Center, Statement of Interest of the United States, December 8, 1986, Page 5.
8. National Record Center, Copy of Proceedings before Judge Parker, December 22, 1986. Page 4.

9. National Record Center, Copy of December 22, 1986, Proceedings, Page 8.

10. National Record Center, Copy of December 22, 1986, Proceedings, Page 43.

11. National Record Center, Declaration of Abraham Sofaer, July 28, 1989, Page 1.

12. National Record Center, Sofaer Declaration, Page 4.

13. National Record Center, Sofaer Declaration, Page 11.

14. National Record Center, Reply of Union of Soviet Socialist Republics to opposition of plaintiffs to motion for relief from judgment by default and for dismissal, July 31, 1989, Page 2.

Chapter 17

1. Robert Ho, individually and as personal representative of the estate of Yuk Yee Ho, deceased, on behalf of himself, of Lam Ho, of Kwan Ho, of Park On Ho and of Pak Chuen Ho v. Korean Air Lines Inc. and the United States of America, Docket No. 83-2794, U.S. District Court for the District of Columbia.

2. Ho v. Korean Air Lines, U.S. District Court, District of Columbia, Page 16.

3. The American Bench, 1993-94, Page 526.

4. National Record Center, Judge Robinson's dismissal motion, March 9, 1990.

5. Certiorari to the United States Court of Appeals for the Second Circuit, No. 87-1372. Argued before the Supreme Court December 6, 1988, and decided January 23, 1989.

6. Ibid.

7. Ibid.

Chapter 18

1. The Mission of Raoul Wallenberg, Russian Documentary Film.

2. Ibid.
3. Ibid.
4. Ibid.
5. Ibid.
6. Ibid.
7. Ibid.
8. Facts on File Yearbook 1990, Volume L, Page 505.
9. The Mission of Raoul Wallenberg, Russian Documentary Film.
10. Ibid.
11. Ibid.
12. Los Angeles Times, October 26, 1989, Page A9.
13. MacLean's October 30, 1989, Page 47.
14. Andrei Sakharov, "The Fate of Raoul Wallenberg," Moscow News, No. 37, 1989.
15. U.S. News & World Report, June 26, 1989, Page 36.
16. New York Times, August 28, 1990, Page A2.
17. New York Times, December 28, 1991, Page 6.
18. Summary of Findings of Soviet-International Joint Commission on the Fate and Whereabouts of Raoul Wallenberg.
19. Ibid.

Chapter 19

1. Folder 16, Page 55, CIA Documents, National Archives.
2. Ibid.
3. Folder 16, Page 59, CIA Documents, National Archives.
4. Folder 16, Page 63, CIA Documents, National Archives.
5. Folder 16, Page 64, CIA Documents, National Archives.
6. Folder 16, Page 13, CIA Documents, National Archives.
7. Folder 16, Page 18, CIA Documents, National Archives.
8. Folder 17, Page 3, CIA Documents, National Archives.
9. Folder 17, Page 1, CIA Documents, National Archives.
10. Folder 17, Pages 3-7, CIA Documents, National Archives.
11. Boston Globe, April 29, 1992, Page 2.

12. Folder 16, Page 63, CIA Documents, National Archives.
13. Ibid.
14. Folder 16, Page 66, CIA Documents, National Archives.
15. Folder 16, Page 2, CIA Documents, National Archives.
16. Folder 16, Page 67, CIA Documents, National Archives.
17. Folder 16, Page 68, CIA Documents, National Archives.
18. Ibid.
19. Ibid.

Chapter 20

1. The Raoul Wallenberg Committee of the United States, Photo copy.
2. Letter from National Center for Missing & Exploited Children, Arlington, Virginia, dated May 10, 1994.
3. Ibid.
4. Box 5, State Department Documents, National Archives.
5. Ibid.
6. New York Times, April 15, 1987, Page A9.

Chapter 21

1. This level is called the crypt, a room designed as the tomb for George Washington, who died in 1799, but his will said he wanted to be buried at his home in Mount Vernon, so the crypt now contains various exhibits. The Washington Times had an excellent story on the Rotunda in the Weekend Section, Pages M4-M6, in the November 2, 1995, edition.
2. The New KGB: Engine of Soviet Power. By William R. Corson and Robert T. Crowley, William Morrow and Company Inc., 1985, Page 22.
3. The New KGB, Page 24.
4. The New KGB, Page 32.

5. Buried Alive, Documentary Film.

6. Ibid.

7. Palme was fatally shot on the night of February 28, 1986, as he and his wife, Lisbeth, walked from a movie theater in central Stockholm. A taxi driver told police via his office that he had seen a gunman escape in a waiting automobile. Eventually, Swedish police arrested Carl Gustaf Christer Pettersson, an alcoholic and drug abuser with a long criminal record. In July 1989, a Swedish court convicted Pettersson, who insisted he was innocent. But three months later a Swedish Appeals Court overturned the conviction and on the same day, October 12, Pettersson was set free. Palme's assassination remains unsolved.

8. Facts on File Yearbook 1994, Page 688.

9. The New York Times May 12, 1996, Section 3, Page 1.

10. Europe Magazine, September 1995, Pages 16-19.

11. Wall Street Journal, April 4, 1997, Page B8.

12. Buried Alive, Documentary Film.

13. Ibid.

14. Ibid.

15. Ibid.

16. Ibid.

17. The Mission of Raoul Wallenberg, Documentary Film.

18. Buried Alive, Documentary Film.

19. Ibid.

20. Ibid.

21. Ibid.

BIBLIOGRAPHY

Anger, Per, With Raoul Wallenberg in Budapest, Holocaust Library, 1981.

Andrew, Christopher and Gordievsky, Oleg, KGB. The Inside Story Of Its Foreign Operations From Lenin to Gorbachev.

Bierman, John, Righteous Gentile: The Story of Raoul Wallenberg, Missing Hero of the Holocaust, The Viking Press, 1981.

Bird, Kai, The Chairman: John J. McCloy, The Making of the American Establishment. Simon & Schuster, 1992.

Corson, William R. and Crowley, Robert T., The New KGB: Engine of Soviet Power, William Morrow and Company Inc., 1985.

Hausner, Gideon, Justice in Jerusalem, Harper & Row, 1966.

Letters and Dispatches: 1924-44, Arcade Publishing Inc., 1995.

Marton, Kati, Wallenberg, Random House, 1982.

Nyiszli, Dr. Miklós, Auschwitz, Fawcett Crest Books, 1962.

Rosenfeld, Harvey, Raoul Wallenberg, Angel of Rescue, Prometheus Books, 1982.

Sakharov, Andrei D., Memoirs, Alfred A. Knopf, New York, 1990; Moscow and Beyond, 1986 to 1989, Alfred A. Knopf, New York, 1991.

Shultz, George P., Turmoil and Triumph: My Years As Secretary of State, Charles Scribner's Sons, New York, 1993.

Smith, Danny, Wallenberg: Lost Hero, Templegate Publishers, 1986.

Werbell, Frederick E. and Clarke, Thurston, Lost Hero: The Mystery of Raoul Wallenberg, McGraw-Hill Book Company, 1982.

Printed in the United States
125994LV00004B/110/A